When Borne Across

When Borne Across

Literary Cosmopolitics in the
Contemporary Indian Novel

Bishnupriya Ghosh

Rutgers University Press

New Brunswick, New Jersey, and London

Library of Congress Cataloging-in-Publication Data
Ghosh, Bishnupriya.
When borne across : literary cosmopolitics in the contemporary
Indian novel / Bishnupriya Ghosh.
p. cm.
Includes bibliographical references and index.
ISBN 0-8135-3344-9 (hardcover : alk. paper) — ISBN 0-8135-3345-7
(pbk. : alk. paper)
1. Indic fiction (English)—History and criticism.   2. Politics and
literature—India.   3. Cosmopolitanism—India.   I. Title.
PR9492.5.G47 2004
823'.9109358—dc21

                                                      2003009685

A British Cataloging-in-Publication record for this book is available from the
British Library.

The publication program of Rutgers University Press is supported by the Board
of Governors of Rutgers, The State University of New Jersey.

Manufactured in the United States of America

To my mother,
and the memory of my father

Contents

List of Illustrations

Acknowledgments

While they can be simply put, thanks are rarely a simple matter, and especially so with first books, where the trail of debts is formidable. But at least to simulate simplicity, I align my thanks along two vectors. Without the first kind of support—inspiration, guidance, and assistance—this book would not be; without the second—everyday care—I would not be here to write it.

Thanks to those, then, who made *When Borne Across* possible, substantially and in spirit: my professors at Presidency College, Kolkata (notably, Kajal Sengupta, Sukanta Chaudhuri, and Supriya Chaudhuri), and my lively cohort in those formative years (Brinda Bose, Ishanti Ghosh, Srimati Basu, Mrittika Datta, Subhobrata Bhattacharya, and Tufan Ghosh, among others); my equally stimulating feminist and queer cohort at Wellesley College; my professors, dissertation committee, and friends at Northwestern University (especially Jules Law, Françoise Lionnet, Michal Ginsburg, John Brenkman, and Colin Bailey); my colleagues at Utah State University who read initial drafts (Anne Shifrer, Jane Catlin, and Helen Cannon) and my chair (Jeffrey Smitten), who made sure I had the necessary means to conduct research; my colleagues and mentors at University of California, Davis (specifically, Elizabeth Freeman, Linda Morris, Margaret Ferguson, David Simpson, Catherine Robson, and Lynn Freed); others in the field who have energized my intellectual trajectory, such as Parama Roy, Esther Yau, Gautam Kundu, Reed Dasenbrock, Feroza Jussawalla, John Hawley, Hema Chari, and Sumita Charavarty; and my students and research assistants—Jana Kay Lunstad, Melissa Bender, and Steven Blevins—who have taught me to approach old matters in fresh ways. Steven Blevins deserves special mention for the many hours he has contributed to pulling the manuscript together in its final stages and preparing the index. In fact the present shape of the project owes much to his perspicacious insights. Finally, thanks to the National Endowment for the Humanities, the Utah State University Faculty Grant, the University of California New Faculty Grant, and Dean Elizabeth Langland at UC Davis for funding; and to Melanie Halkais at Rutgers University Press for her gentle but incisive editorial guidance.

A different modality of thanks to those who enable me to write with their steady love, stories, arguments, and demands: my mother and grandmother, whose strength and fortitude I rely on; my many families in Kolkata and Salt Lake, New Jersey, Boston, Bahrain, Bangalore, Freemont, and Boston—and especially Debjani Banerjee and Mahua Sarkar—who still constitute my most challenging "public sphere"; Sushoma, for her unerring sustenance in my early years; Rohini Chowdhury, for continuing to keep up with me; my extended family (Jennifer Burwell, Mrittika Datta, and Cesare Casarino); my community in Los Angeles (especially Afzal Shah, Alex Rabrenovich, and Connerly Casey); friends and colleagues in New York; and friends and mentors in Santa Barbara (Janet Walker, Charles Wolfe, and Constance Penley, among others). To my three grandparents who have passed, I owe the sense of history that renews my present; and to my father, whom I have known posthumously through his books, I owe my formative political inflections. Most of all, thanks to Bhaskar Sarkar—critic, editor, playmate, and love of these last twenty years—without whom I would be shorn of those pleasures that make this writing possible.

When Borne Across

Prologue

Under darkened skies, an event "the likes of which has never been held on Indian shores" finally unfolded: the dazzling International Festival of Indian literature, hosted by the Indian Council for Cultural Relations in Delhi and Neemrana, 18–26 February 2002.[1] Originally slotted for 8 December 2001, the meet was postponed because of the Twin Tower terrorist attacks and subsequent intimations of war. Absent from this gathering of sixty-two Indian authors and literary critics, Salman Rushdie wrote as the "newest of New Yorkers" as official body counts rose to 2,825: "To this bright capital of the visible, the forces of invisibility have dealt a blow. No need to say how dreadful; we all saw it, are all changed by it, and now must ensure the wound is not mortal" ("A Nation Challenged" 2002, 234; Rushdie 2002e, 336).

The day after the festival closed, the Godhra carnage—the longest bout of violence in recent South Asian history—became the Indian ground zero. A Muslim mob attacked the bogeys of the Sabarmati Express in Gujarat (chillingly reminiscent of the historic train carnage of 1947 and 1984), claiming fifty-eight lives.[2] In the seventy-five-day clash between Hindus and Muslims to follow, the official body count rose to three thousand, though most other sources put it at three times that figure ("A Cannibal Time," 2002, 35). Amitav Ghosh, who had attended the ICCR meeting, wrote with anguish: "The recent carnage in Gujarat is not just a fresh chapter in the sub-continent's annals of horror: it may well prove to be the prologue to horrors yet-undreamt-of" (2002d).

The dismembered bodies of these two cataclysmic events haunt this critical narration, as do the heightened fluctuations of global, national, and local borders that these events commandeered. For the moment, let us focus on the

1

strange porthole in time that was the ICCR festival, an opening of frontiers just before other barriers were so viciously reerected. Aimed at consolidating literary community, the ICCR festival was in many respects a "conciliatory handshake" between "English and Indian languages," after Rushdie's infamous denigration of Indian regional vernacular literatures in the *New Yorker.*[3] I will return to this remark more substantially later in the book; but suffice to say it became a recurrent trace in all the national coverage of the festival, as it has indeed become in this book. As the ICCR fêted the new Nobel laureate for 2001, V. S. Naipaul, it was not surprising that the meeting bore the banner "At Home in the World"—an allusion to Rabindranath Tagore's novel on early-twentieth-century cosmopolitanism and nationalism, *Ghare Baire*, written in 1915, just after Tagore had received the 1913 Nobel Prize for his translation of the *Gitanjali.*[4]

These international signatures, the Booker and Nobel Prizes among them, will be another iterable trace in my cultural analysis, for they clearly underwrite the global and national visibility of South Asian writing in English. So ubiquitous is this writing that it has warranted its own acronym in the national press, as is common practice in the postliberalized technophile vocabularies. Indian writing in English, or IWE (a traditional literary-critical category that hegemonically references all South Asian writing in English), occupied pride of place at the festival with international stalwarts like V. S. Naipaul, Amitav Ghosh, Rohinton Mistry, Amit Chauduri, and Vikram Seth rubbing shoulders with regional giants like U. R. Anathamurthy and Sunil Gangopadhyay. Many of the regional writers were awardees of the nationally prestigious (but globally unknown) Jnanpith Prize. In fact, as if to drive home the currency of IWE, Naipaul was poised to hand the Jnanpith to the Assamese writer Indira Goswami, compelling some commentators to wonder with apprehension, "What happens when a freshly minted Nobel laureate presides over some acclaimed Indian writers?" (Khosla 2003).

Despite the festival organizers' obvious intention to close a historical literary divide, regional writers in the eighteen officially recognized Indian vernaculars remained critical of IWE currencies. Said the illustrious Kannada writer, U. R. Ananthamurthy, who is one of the few regional writers translated into English: "There are any number of top quality regional writers who don't get international recognition only because their language is not the global language of America." And Marathi writer Dilip Chitre quipped: "Why should nimbu pani [Indian lemonade] compete with Coca-Cola? Regional writing doesn't have to consult an English language mirror to know its own face" (Reddy 2002). Cognizant of this divide, Sheela Reddy, covering the story for the Indian English-language weekly *Outlook*, chose to tag the IWE writers "Midnight's Orphans," displaced by their postcoloniality and increasingly visible after the publication of *Midnight's Children* in 1981. Fifty years after the birth of the "midnight's children" of Rushdie's novel, in 1997 a Renaissance in IWE had appeared on the horizon.

What first appeared as a bringing together of the home and the world, a meeting of imaginations "irrespective of passports," soon brought to the fore a yawning chasm.[5] Nowhere was this rift more evident than in the two keynote addresses, one by the fêted Naipaul and the other by the prime minister, Atal Bihari Vajpayee. Asked about the fortunes of South Asian literary production in the vernaculars, Naipaul intimated that these literatures suffered in comparison to Indian writing in English because of their lack of circulation (Khosla 2003). Yet, unlike the regional writers who underscored the postcolony's dependence on international recognition fueled by the current economic muscle of English, Naipaul remained vague about global cultural hegemonies: "They [novels] are an industrial good, which needs publishers, readers, critics and newspapers. A society on the move gives rise to the kind of writing [in English] we see today" (Khosla 2003). On the opposite end, Vajpayee appeared disgruntled at the very procedures of the festival: "It may seem somewhat ironic that the literary heritage of India is celebrated in the medium of English" (Reddy 2002).

This surfacing divide, albeit bewailed by many at the conference, is central to my look at how contemporary global flows and public cultures have substantially altered the constitution of literary value, and indeed of print circulation. Surfing global terrain without attention to the new anxieties over borders can be dangerous, as recent calamities have brought home to us. Hence I propose discrimination in exploring the very category of Indian writers in English, where all writers, regardless of modality of their literary practice or their political and ethical imperatives, are herded together and become indistinguishable from each other. Throughout the ensuing discussion, the reader may notice fluctuations in my deployment of the received literary-critical categories "Indian writing in English" and "South Asian writing in English." While the latter best fits the literary cosmopolitics I describe in this book, I use "Indian writing in English" to reference extant discourse; "Indian," then, attaches to the literary-critical object and not to the geopolitical entity (that the cosmopolitical writers interrogate).

Amitav Ghosh and Salman Rushdie, both internationally known public intellectuals and writers with substantial literary production, are avowedly not cut from the same literary cloth as Naipaul. This is eminently clear in the rather guarded response to Naipaul on their part. While respectful of Naipaul's writing, which moves him like "aching wisdom teeth," Amitav Ghosh remains critical of Naipaul's racism and the anti-Islamic pronouncements in Naipaul's nonfiction (in *Area of Darkness*, 1964, and *India: A Million Mutinies Now*, 1990).

Ghosh decries the increasingly "faded out" worlds of the Caribbean and Africa, so "richly textured" in Naipaul's early fiction, that are now "half-made" in comparison with Europe (2002b). Noting that Naipaul chose to dedicate his Nobel Prize to England, his adopted home, Ghosh remarks that the reactionary turn in Naipaul's work heralded by *An Area of Darkness* (1964) has "proved immensely popular in the West and he was quickly canonized for his indictment of the 'Third World.' It is a measure of his influence that in the West today, travel writers are taken seriously only to the degree to which they replicate the familiar Naipaulean tone of derision" (2).

As if to mark his difference from some South Asian writers in English, and Rushdie in particular, V. S. Naipaul did not agree to Rushdie's inclusion of his work in an anthology commemorating India's fifty years of independence, *Mirrorwork: Fifty Years of Indian Writing, 1947–1997*, edited by Rushdie and Elizabeth West in 1997. In his introduction to the volume, Rushdie notes that "one of the important voices in the story of modern literature, V. S. Naipaul, is regrettably absent from this book, not by our own choice, but his own" (xvii). Later in the piece, Rushdie "part[s] company altogether" from Naipaul's dim view of the creative potentials in India (expressed in *An Area of Darkness*) (xviii). Rushdie's and Ghosh's reservations about Naipaul are also mine, as they are those, I suspect, of many South Asian progressive writers and critics. So in this book, I depart from Naipaul, engaging in some critical border drawing to demarcate a different province of the imagination within the exploding sphere of contemporary South Asian writing in English. The closing of some literary borders quixotically enables the opening of disciplinary borders, as I begin to define a distinctive South Asian cosmopolitical discursive formation.

A Tale of Two Worlds

I am after a certain discernible strand of writing within the larger cultural phenomenon cited as a "Renaissance." This is a cosmopolitical South Asian writing that shares not just distinctive literary features but, more crucially, fundamental political and ethical commitments. Rather than range these cosmopolitical writers alongside their post–*Midnight's Children* South Asian counterparts, I will argue that they should be considered in the context of a new South Asian Left emergent in the post-Emergency years. The Emergency, Indira Gandhi's politically violent experiment of 1975–1977, galvanized response from the Indian Left—no doubt stimulated by the vociferous criticism of the Emergency from the Hindu Right. The response ended the co-optation of the Indian Left within a nation-building process under the aegis of the Congress Party, with the party's lip service to socialism and its pro-Soviet geopolitical affiliation. New positions that sought to rethink Marxist orthodoxy and Indian socialism in an internationalist frame heralded the "innovative epistemic break" most visible globally in the work of the subaltern studies scholars (Young 2001, 339). If these new positions seemed gradually to coagulate into an observable discursive formation in the next decade, two other jolts made this critical activism urgent. India's trade liberalization and media privatization through the 1980s made globalism troubling in fresh ways; and the viciousness of the Hindu Right (known as the Sangh Parivar coalition) manifest in the riots following the Babri Masjid destruction in 1992 imparted an ethical charge to political dilemmas.[6] While the violence of capitalism and the nation-state could be politically analyzed, the corrosive violence at the heart of communities pointed to something else. The 1992 riots became a lesson in "how humans create absolute others out of other human beings," as Dipesh Chakrabarty explains, compelling discussion of the "inhuman" capacities lodged in the self (2002, 141). Chakrabarty, whose political staging of epistemological différance is seminally constitutive of South Asian cosmopolitical thinking, characterized this communal violence more broadly as the fundamental problem of social violence—"the difficulty of recognizing that violence belongs to the self that speaks" (141–142).

Those writers to whom I attach the moniker "cosmopolitical" are part of this South Asian progressive discursive formation, challenging both the forms of nationalism reinforced by global flows and the pernicious globalism surfacing in dispersed local contexts. It is a formation that shares, I will argue, a social imaginary of sorts: of democratic self-rule, and of contingent cosmopolitics. Its political articulation is dispersed, defined by the dispersed nature of the common enemy, globalism. And it is constituted by the local struggles of artists, writers, historians, activists, ethnographers, and filmmakers, among others, who move toward imagining new modes of collective life and agency. Capital flows, hegemonic political and military flanks, and the increasing violence of nation-states against subaltern groups (indigenous peoples, the migrant poor, refugees) come under fire from these cosmopolitical thinkers.

I focus on a group of writers who exemplify the cosmopolitical writing that is the subject of this book, both in their direct political overtures (in interviews, manifestos, nonfiction) and in their indirect literary expressions. Salman Rushdie, Vikram Chandra, Amitav Ghosh, Upamanyu Chatterjee, and Arundhati Roy are the writers under scrutiny, all fourth-generation South Asian writers in English. These writers are the chosen representatives for both historical and heuristic reasons. Historically or generationally speaking, they are either some of the earliest practitioners of this cosmopolitical writing or its luminaries. Rushdie needs little introduction as the father of the new Renaissance in Indian writing, a matter to which I shall turn shortly; Arundhati Roy was the stimulant for the euphoria over the Renaissance in 1997, its glamorous pinnacle; and Amitav Ghosh has emerged lately as a focal point after his abrogation of the Commonwealth Prize for Literature in 2001 (Ghosh 2001a). Upamanyu Chatterjee and Vikram Chandra are perhaps less known, but I consider them to be noteworthy progenitors of this cosmopolitical writing. Moreover, their fiction has consistently exemplified, sometimes to a radical degree, some of the distinctive literary features and the politics of localism that I catalog here. In such a selection, the quantity of these writers' literary production takes a backseat to the modality of their cosmopolitical writing.

Indicative of how young this literary tradition is, criticism on "Indian writing in English" almost always adopts a generational rhetoric, the periodizing gesture imparting sought-after literary credentials. Wherever feasible, I avoid such literary stipulation because I see my investigation differently—as a cultural analysis cognizant of its own situatedness in the present (from where I construe this recent past). The Renaissance as event marks that present. Yet, as we shall see, it is a moment that is overwritten by other historical occasions formative of these cosmopolitics, such as the *Satanic Verses* affair, the Emergency, and the riots of 1992. These flash points propel my critical narration into disjunctive but contemporaneous temporalities.

I pause on one of these historical flash points now, because it is the one that underwrites extant criticism of the literary practice at hand. We know this as the publishing event that entrenched the rhetoric of birth (and rebirth) so deeply in the critical and popular discourses on South Asian novels in English: the appearance of *Midnight's Children* in 1981. Rushdie has consistently privileged this event as memorable not only because it propelled him to international celebrity, but also because he had clearly touched a nerve in the postindependence South Asian generation: "I've always thought it was the most important moment in my life as a writer—the Indian response to *Midnight's Children*," reiterates Rushdie in a 2002 interview. "That moves me far more than Booker Prizes," he continues, sensitive to allegations of his legendary self-promotion. "It's been a book that seems to speak to people wherever it showed up. It's been translated into 40 languages and seems to have managed to find wide readerships in bizarre places: Korea, Ukraine, Serbia. What would any of these places have to do with India?" (2002d, 11, 6). While Rushdie is quick to emphasize the cosmopolitan resonance of the book, he highlights *Midnight's Children*'s salience to post-Emergency India. Rushdie's vitalist ontology of the postcolonial nation surging with a promise now eclipsed under capital's death drive caught on.[7] It soon was received opinion that this novel had birthed a new literary phenomenon, hailed by critics as a perceptible rupture in Indian literary production. Other valences of this birth of more significance to my project circle in critical discourse on this event: the new treatment of the novel as political treatise in the national media; the stimulus to Indian writing that came with Rushdie's Booker triumph of 1981 (later reinforced by the "Booker of Bookers," an award that marked the twenty-fifth anniversary of the prize); and the sighting of an alternative social imagination that could ameliorate the possible collapse of the postcolonial imagined community. In these ways, *Midnight's Children* as event remains crucial to this book. Yet to consolidate all contemporary writers as "post–*Midnight's Children* writers," signaling the centrality of a *literary* rupture above all else, loses the political and ethical resonance of South Asian cosmopolitical writing. Consequently I depart from grouping all new South Asian writers under one rubric, a metonymic slide apparent in the jubilee discourses explored throughout the book. By the same token, there are notable absences in my narration. Writers like Amit Chaudhuri, Mukul Kesavan, Rohinton Mistry, and Michael Ondaatje, among others, who fit the cosmopolitical profile both in their politics and literary practice, circulate in the book as actors in concert. This faded visibility is not a measure of their stature. Rather, I hope that the lightness of their tread leads us to future considerations of writerly cosmopolitics in contemporary South Asian writing in English.

Amit Chaudhuri commands special mention as the editor of a volume on "modern Indian writing" (*The Picador Book of Modern Indian Literature*) that incorporates the linguistic divisions in Indian writing as its conceptual rubric. While emphasizing that the anthology was "not a riposte to any other"—possibly alluding to the globally visible *Mirrorwork*—Chaudhuri draws our attention to the work of Indian publishers such as Katha, Seagull, and Manas who have diligently increased the circulation of vernacular Indian literatures by publishing translations for a number of years (2001, xxxiii). Such work, Chaudhuri insists, goes a long way in closing the perceived gap between IWE and vernacular literatures. Remarking that the two canons share a common idiom of modernity and should indeed be read *together*, Chaudhuri remains critical of the "glare of publicity" accorded to a "handful of writers" (xvii). Hence his collection begins with the evolution of modern Indian literatures from the mid–nineteenth century, and includes eighteen selections from IWE and twenty from Indian vernacular writers who have been translated into English. Chaudhuri's discriminating look at the question of global markets as they impact literary value is a self-reflexivity that many of the cosmopolitical writers share, albeit to varying degree (with Rushdie at the other end of the spectrum).

But this critical maneuver is not the driving force of my argument. Most of the writers pursued here are public intellectuals of some stature; others are activists. Their cosmopolitical writing offers critical resources for living in our contemporary globality, refocusing attention on our mutuality in speaking of many and contingent translocal solidarities. A pithy rubric like "the Renaissance" that sounds the alarm on popularity and commercialism serves to undercut these writers' literary and personal activism. Indeed, to sweep their literary production under the rug in the name of commercial success is a significant loss for left thinkers critical of globalism and resurgent nationalisms. On the other hand, it would be equally naïve not to recognize the power of the market. So one of the main agendas of the book is to retain a bifocality in our approach to the literary practice of cosmopolitical writing: to see it as both a canny play to emergent global and local markets for world literatures by the effective production of linguistic localism, and a cosmopolitical intervention into stable national-global cultural dialectics through privileging provisional and contingent local contexts. I argue for the efficacy of this bifocal look in evaluating immensely marketable and popular literary texts with explicit political agendas. Such a gaze recognizes the complicity of the cultural translator in facilitating global literary flows, while also acknowledging the limits of "specialized" postcolonial knowledge in unpacking local and vernacular subtexts.

The Customary Map

From scenes and tales, we turn to a (customary) map for the reader to navigate this critical narration as it loops through the varying production and reception contexts constitutive of this writing and our evaluation of it. Perhaps the reader will notice a circular motion within this narration on circulations: For instance, I start here with *Midnight's Children* and return to it in chapter 3 while discussing the embattled heritage of "Indian writing in English"; terrorism and dismembered bodies return in my discussion of history, violence, and subalterneity in chapter 4; and writers like Rohinton Mistry or critics like Meenakshi Mukherjee enter and leave the text at various points as characters and interlocutors. This circling is in part deliberate, dramatizing the multiple refractions of the writers circulating at high velocities in global mediascapes. The writers' textuality habitually dwarfs their literary production, the refractions impacting that production in numerous ways that I track throughout the book. In the increasing velocities and dispersions in global flows, it is no longer possible to speak of literary value as constituted only by the literary cultures of print circulation. The post-1989 *SatanicVerses* controversy forever split that seam of print circulation, as literary value came to be transacted—even defined—in electronic and audiovisual media. It is inconceivable that we treat these different media only at the level of content. So one of the translations that *When Borne Across* undertakes is between media: following the flows of the cosmopolitical writers and their texts across radio, television, print, magazine covers, and sometimes, the pulpit.

Chapter 1 tracks this flow of writers and texts across media in comparative frame. I attempt to consolidate the very different values that accrue to these writers in varying reception contexts, as the divergences that speak to struggles over the literary production are key to my argument. I contend that like other public cultures, postcolonial literary practices in global circulation are substantially engaged in the contested productions of locality, given the uneven multiple modernities of our historical moment. Attending to a literary cosmopolitics enables me to foreground such an engagement, so subsequently I explore the nature of those cosmopolitics in context of the lively conversations on cosmopolitanisms today.

Chapter 2 moves to the specific contexts of literary production for the cosmopolitical writers analyzed here. I examine the intellectual backdrop for the writers' linguistic localism, earmarking those debates that shape their self-reflexive experiments. I argue that the cosmopolitical writers emphatically target cultural globalism in their construction of English vernaculars, since English has never been just another language in the postcolony but always a concept-metaphor for global linguistic hegemony. Chapter 3 delves into the particulars of linguistic localisms, closely analyzing the English vernaculars in Arundhati Roy's *The God of Small Things* (1997), Upamanyu Chatterjee's *English, August* (1988) and *The Last Burden* (1993), and Salman Rushdie's *The Moor's Last Sigh* (1995). The representational worlds of metropolitan, small-town, and village India—Rushdie's Bombay, Chatterjee's Madna, and Roy's Ayemenem—are layered linguistic topoi, with multiple spoken and written languages existing in politically hierarchical relation to each other. These are highly "constructed" linguistic contexts where the situated English vernaculars, tailored to each postcolonial locale, come to fruition.

While these localizing strategies are, to some extent, canny plays to emergent heterogeneous reading constituencies, the remarkable self-reflexivity of linguistic innovation points beyond the market. All the cosmopolitical writers foreground the process of constructing an English vernacular: For instance, the mixture of languages that enable Roy's subjects to inhabit the contemporary postcolonial world of Ayemenem is relevant *only* to this self-consciously artificial locale; it is a deliberately crafted idiom of choice, rather than a literary version of an existing stable English-Malayalam vernacular. Such provisionality undermines any fetishistic reproduction and circulation of this localized vernacular. Further, the writers are considerably self-reflexive about the nature of print culture and circulation in the information age. Hence we encounter numerous and memorable readers, publishers, editors, critics, writers, painters, and storytellers in the pages of the cosmopolitical novels. While in chapter 3, I focus primarily on language, I turn to the various critical exegeses on media more substantially in chapter 5.

In this latter half of the book, I turn to the cosmopolitical writers' commitment to minoritarian nationalist politics. Chapter 4 focuses on the intellectual contexts for the cosmopolitical production of the subaltern subjects and lives, by way of an epistemological restoration of recessive knowledges. The translation of the subaltern and of "lost" narratives of community, with all its attendant difficulties, carries particular ethical charge in the cosmopolitical writers' rigorous critiques of rising national chauvinism. But what imagination, ask the writers, can capture the violent erasures by humans of their "others," dehumanized beyond recognition? Where political rhetoric balks, an ethical spectrology comes into play in these novels as recompense for those human costs that exceed norms of political accountability. These shared South Asian cosmopolitical concerns with violence, history, and subalterneity compel the narratological innovations that are the subject of chapter 5. There I explore the disjunctive temporal schemes, intrusive spatial memories, and posthuman subjects in Amitav Ghosh's *The Calcutta Chromosome* (1996), Vikram Chandra's *Red Earth and Pouring Rain* (1995), and Salman Rushdie's *Moor's Last Sigh* (1995). The disjunctures in narration, in turn, tune us to the labors of rendering the local communicable, foreclosing any easeful fetishistic consumption of subaltern subjects and their pasts. The writers stage epistemological différance through the exercise of textual grafting, in the embedding of vernacular epistemologies in their novels. For instance, in *The Moor's Last Sigh*, Rushdie grafts the visual idioms of Bollywood and of contemporary Indian painting onto his novel in English, while Phanishwar Nath Renu's and Tagore's ghost fiction turns out to be the vernacular literary blueprint that "explains" the mystery of Amitav Ghosh's *Calcutta Chromosome*.

The literary cosmopolitics of these novels, then, share discernible features: a linguistic localism that shores up the irreducible supplementarity of the postcolonial English literary text; vernacularity; self-reflexivity in staging communicability and self-conscious notations of IWE circulation; a political commitment to subalterneity, engendering an ethical spectrology; and finally, the acts of cultural translation that attempt to mediate the globalization of knowledge. To highlight these elements, I have chosen texts by the five authors that showcase these features. Not all of the features expounded here, however, have the same valence: ethical spectrology, for instance, does not carry through all the cosmopolitical novels. In this regard, it is a more emergent attribute, but clearly relevant to the recent renewed anguish over social violence that runs against the grain of the decolonized nation's vitalist ontologies. All the novels discussed here were written after the riots of 1992, with the exception of Upamanyu Chatterjee's *English, August*, published in 1988.

Upamanyu Chatterjee, in fact, sits at a slight angle to the other writers discussed here. Yet he remains most courageous in his linguistic and narrative experiments, as one finds out in attempting to read the excruciating (and deliberately) slow *Mammaries of the Welfare State* (2000). (One reviewer wittily titles her review of the novel "August in Winter," since Agastya or August of Chatterjee's *English, August* returns in this sequel [Saran 2002]). But signs of the radical experiment overtaking readability were already present, I will argue, in Chatterjee's *Last Burden,* where he relexifies English to the syntax of spoken Bengali. Almost all the texts I select here are experimental novels that privilege a politics of the local while self-reflexively negotiating their own privileges as writers in English. Hence I focus on Rushdie's *Moor* because it is his book about different kinds of media (along with *The Ground Beneath Her Feet*), and not on *The Satanic Verses*—although the latter is usually considered the obvious text on globalism, public culture, and language. And hence my choice of *The Calcutta Chromosome,* with its staging of epistemological loss, over the thematically relevant *Shadow Lines* (1988), where Ghosh engages directly with social violence and historical trauma. Given the experimental quality of the novels chosen here, these texts are also, arguably, the least popular in the writers' respective oeuvres. Salman Rushdie's *Moor's Last Sigh* is not his most acclaimed novel, despite its winning the Whitbread Prize and making the Booker shortlist; Vikram Chandra's *Red Earth and Pouring Rain* is often regarded as overly ambitious; Amitav Ghosh's *Calcutta Chromosome* was mostly reviewed as failed science fiction; and Upamanyu Chatterjee's *The Last Burden* was reviled for its labored and clumsy prose style. The distinctive experimental features of these novels extend more gracefully into celebrated texts like *The God of Small Things* or *English, August*, with the latter now a feature film.

Finally, throughout the book I distinguish between the "direct" and "indirect" localizing praxes only to veer away from intentionalist fallacy. That is, the explicit self-fashioning of these cosmopolitical writers cannot be the *reason* for considering their literary cosmopolitics as progressive interventions. Indeed there are some palpable disjunctures between their explicit political agendas and literary articulations. We see this most dramatically in Arundhati Roy's passionate immersion in everyday local struggles while she reifies the "subaltern" of *The God of Small Things* in the godlike Velutha. The notion of the "cosmopolitan activist" seeks to relate the direct *and* indirect (literary) politics of the local, but not necessarily as continuous projects. This might not sit well with the writers who habitually attempt to arrest their refracted image in the press. Roy, for instance, cautions us not to pose the writer in opposition to the activist: "Why am I called a "writer activist" and why . . . does that term make me flinch?

I'm called a writer-activist because after writing *The God of Small Things* I wrote three political essays. . . . Now, I'm wondering why it should be that the person who wrote *The God of Small Things* is called a writer, and the person who wrote the political essays is called an activist? *The God of Small Things* is a work of fiction, but it is no less political than any of my essays" (2001, 11).

But the arbitration of images, politics, and ethics is equally a province of reading. In our tracking of these writers, their texts, and the Renaissance, the reader is "borne across" media and reception contexts. The activist reader who takes up the challenge of everyday cultural translations can further be "borne across" to the local and vernacular contexts harnessed in these novels. Fully swollen with the valences of birth and rebirth that "being borne across" implies, the "when" of the title insists on the *performativity* of readerly and writerly acts of migration. As we prepare to enter this bustling global scene of the Renaissance, I underscore this provisionality by "unfinishing" one particular summation of Indian writing in English: Bill Buford's verbal photograph of the IWE in his introductory remarks to the *New Yorker* double issue on contemporary Indian writers in English.

The Unfinished Photograph

Photographs are prone to lying, as we have learned in the digital age. Things get rather complicated when print—that dinosaur medium—can convert a glossy pic into time-lapse photography. But this is what I will attempt in *When Borne Across*, shading that distinctive province of writing that I have endeavored to carve so far. When the *New Yorker* double issue on Indian fiction appeared in June 1997, it sold like hotcakes. Upon calling the magazine's office for back issues recently, I learned that there are no back issues to be found. The issue carried a historic photograph of Indian writers in English who had assembled in London for the photo shoot. With Anita Desai and daughter Kiran Desai, who had finished *A Hullabaloo in the Guava Orchard* (a 1998 novel excerpted in the *New Yorker* jubilee issue), the generational legacy was obvious. What seemed most striking, however, was Bill Buford's highlighting of the photograph in his introductory remarks to the issue.

This is not a quarrel with Buford's vibrant commentary on South Asian writing in English. As fiction editors often do, Buford was simply bringing to global attention a fairly substantial literary output that demanded some literary-historical outlining for a Western audience. But it is his curious focus on the photograph as an event, an occasion where many of the writers from around the world met for the first time, that is of interest here. Buford begins his address with the photograph: "Just over halfway through this issue," he says, guiding the reader, "you're going to find a photograph of eleven people—men and women, all dressed informally, and all conveying an impression of what might be described as uneasy intimacy" (Buford 1997, 6). He then continues to emphasize the historic nature of this meeting, which could have taken place anywhere (New York had been the initial venue) "except India." Despite the presence of many who live in India (Anita Desai, Kiran Desai, Upamanyu Chatterjee, and Arundhati Roy, among others), Buford's remarks foreground the Indian writer in English as migrant. In perusing the photograph this way all through his introduction, Buford unmistakably visually assembles a literary community for his audience, bearing out my contention that things literary are now increasingly translated through other media.

This translation, after all, guides our own perceptions in consolidating IWE as an identifiable group. Bill Buford's allusion to "uneasy intimacy" does suggest differences within the group, but in my view not all of these can be put down to the personal unfamiliarity suggested by Buford's rhetoric. Generational or locational differences are, in my construction of critical boundaries, facile in defining particular intellectual traditions within the IWE assemblage; they rarely reveal sharp political divergences among these writers. In articulating a notion of literary cosmopolitics, then, I separate certain writers from others in this visually close-knit group. The edges of the visual fray: The photograph disintegrates on exposure to this critical narration.

One

Sighting Circulation

A Renaissance at the Golden Jubilee

> *"To be born again," sang Gibreel Farishta tumbling from the heavens, "first you have to die. Ho ji! Ho ji! To land upon the bosomy earth, first one needs to fly. Ta-taa! Taka-thun! How to ever smile again, if you first won't cry? How to win the darling's love, mister, without a sigh? Baba, if you want to get born again . . ." Just before dawn one winter's morning, New Years's Day or thereabouts, two real, full-grown men fell from a great height, twenty-nine thousand and two feet, toward the English Channel, without benefit of parachutes or wings, out of a clear sky.*
> —Salman Rushdie, Satanic Verses

Salman Rushdie's *Satanic Verses* famously commences with the delusional Indian megastar Gibreel Farishta, and his sidekick, Chamcha, transformed into magical beings as they sail down to earth after terrorists blow up their plane. The scene is jolting. Inhabiting his screen persona, Farishta survives the treacherous passage (the plane crash) to the West as Rushdie tropes the many life-threatening journeys of the Indian diaspora to Canada and the United Kingdom. His language moves fluidly between realism ("parachutes") and fabulism ("wings"), effectively rendering communicable to global audiences the felt dislocations of the migrant "when borne across." My book takes its name from this culture-specific notation of the migrant, one who is "translated" when borne across *kala pani* (black water). The incident dramatizes the book's primary argument on the capacities of the literary to translate local struggles, a cosmopolitan literary activism within the political limits that are evident even in this initial scene.

Farishta's descent conjoins a Bollywood screen memory with a real terror-ist attack: the actor Shammi Kapoor's descent to the water-skiing Sharmila Tagore in *Paris Ki Ek Shyam* (*An Evening in Paris*, directed by Shakti Samanta, 1967), and the tragic crash of Air India Flight 182 off the coast of Ireland on 23 June 1985, believed to be the work of Sikh separatists. The Bollywood film is an early depiction of the Indian cosmopolitan whose corporate counterpart, the "global Indian" and his cultural dilemmas, is now a staple in nineties Indian mass culture. Bollywood vernacular has ever been Rushdie's transcription of a national lingua franca within his novels in English, and his citations often insist that the reader migrate textually to the vernacular context of Bombay. Hence our encounter with the *ghazal*-singing Farishta necessarily becomes an act of cultural translation, one of the many demands for textual migrations that com-prise a distinctive feature of the literary practice I investigate here.

The figure of the Angel Gibreel/Gabriel reminds us of Rushdie's sustained condemnation of religious cultural affiliation as a fortified and dangerous local-ism; and the presence of the separatists obliquely references the violence of the Indian nation-state (Indira Gandhi's infamous storming of the holy Sikh Golden Temple in 1984) against subnational dreams, a violence that implodes else-where. Both memories are of political salience to our literary practice under scrutiny. While Rushdie eloquently records the psychic violence of migration and ethnic marginality, the tragic costs of the Air India crash become an abstract trope in this literary inscription. Thus we confront the limits of our elite practice—the post-eighties much-touted "Renaissance" in Indian writing in English.

The image of the dismembered Flight 182 with which *The Satanic Verses* commences has strange resonance in the aftermath of the controversy. That epic battle between Western and Islamic public spheres quite radically dismembered the "literary," splitting the seams of literary circulation. In this modality the affair is the ur-text for my inquiry into the cosmopolitics of the contemporary (post–*Midnight's Children*) South Asian novel. Ayatollah Khomeni's fatwa against Salman Rushdie on grounds of blasphemy in *The Satanic Verses*, ironically, cat-apulted the writer into celebrity between 1989 and 1993. As we shall see, it was in these years that Rushdie's *Midnight's Children* achieved its current stature as a singular publishing event. In 1989 Rushdie seemed ubiquitously present in print and on television and radio. No longer circulating only among print-based publics, *The Satanic Verses* became better known as electronic sound bite, its pedagogic translations radically reshaping the book's cultural value. The novel became best known for its Jahalia sections, in which Rushdie recounts the birth of Islam as an idea that is borne across into other times and places. By con-trast, the London sections on black British immigrant mobilization in the

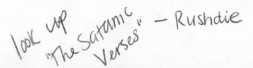
look up "The Satanic Verses" — Rushdie

Thatcher years receded in significance. Rushdie's many refracted images, as sound bites from the offending text, entered mass circulation. Rushdie became at once the "father" of a new kind of writing, political icon, westernized betrayer of Islam, prototypical beleaguered and muzzled writer, and fêted celebrity. The postcolonial writer was now irrevocably enmeshed in a larger public culture, imbricated in the uneven battles over producing a localized modernity.

Renaissance Sightings at the Golden Jubilee

The impetus for this book derives from a historical event: India's commemoration of her golden jubilee, celebrating fifty years of independence from British rule. That Friday morning, 15 August 1997, the headlines of the *Statesman*, a venerable daily in Calcutta, read: "Midnight's Children Greet New Dawn: President Addresses Parliament, Asks People to Fight Corruption." And Arvind N. Das, writing for *Outlook Magazine,* chose to title his piece on the postcolonial polity "Journey into Twilight: Midnight's Child Came of Age in India in a Strange Age." Quite unobtrusively, it seemed as if Salman Rushdie's writing of the postindependent nation had become a signifier for an evaluation of the postcolony, its defeats and successes. In the *Business India* issue that week, columnist Malavika Singh further refined the epithet to connote post-Emergency India: "In 1977 we started again. The passion and commitment that came in the wake of freedom had dissipated into words in contemporary history books. Midnight's children had grown up" (1997, 33).

These fleeting allusions to the narration of the nation found flamboyant avowal in the transnational and local commentaries on a Renaissance in Indian writing, no doubt glamorized by the hue and cry over Arundhati Roy's Booker Prize triumph.[1] Several national and local commentators rather cynically noted the fortuitous conjunction between the independence celebrations and the symbolic sanction of the prize; but others gloated unselfconsciously about the "first Indian" who "lives in India" to win this prestigious trophy (covertly cordoning off Roy from Rushdie), an Indian who had opened up the "global market" to Indian writing in English.[2] The irony of celebrating the global consumer on the eve of the golden jubilee was not missed by the national press. A sardonic report in *India Today* on the fifty-year commemoration as a "corporate theme," titled "Patriotism Inc.," listed products such as watches, cassettes, hotel discounts, and alcoholic beverages marketed to celebrate the "golden jubilee." Strikingly present in this list of consumer fetishes marking India at fifty was a "host of *books*," such as *Beach Boy, Love and Longing in Bombay*, and *The Idea of India* (Bhandare 1997, 46–47; my emphasis).

Across media, the Renaissance was big news. On the eve of the anniversary, PBS Los Angeles aired a program on India that featured writers as national rep-

Salman Rushdie → magical realism

resentatives in which Salman Rushdie and Arundhati Roy expounded their respective visions of the nation (Roy 1997a). And in June of the same year, the *New Yorker* woke up to a Renaissance in Indian writing introduced by the man who was named the father of this new Indian literary movement—Salman Rushdie.[3] In his preface to the magazine's 23 and 30 June 1997 double issue, Bill Buford (1997) remarked on the hyperbolic tenor of the historic meeting of Indian novelists gathered for the group photo shoot. Everyone was "infected with the excitement," observes Buford, not just for the golden jubilee but with the collective sense that maybe "the hype was true after all"—that they *were* a part of a cultural rebirth now in the global eye.[4] Finally, in an NPR show aired 10 August 1997, Jim Fleming chose to highlight two aspects of the subcontinent that would be of significance to a Western audience: India as a "democracy that works for all the apparent chaos," and "a new literary movement . . . happening now in India" (Fleming 1997). Among the three interviewees on this show, two were South Asian writers in English, Rohinton Mistry and Gita Mehta; the third was a journalist, Palagummi Sainath, whose acclaimed *Everybody Loves a Good Drought* (1997) had just won the Amnesty International Human Rights Prize for Journalism. Across public spheres it was a moment of dual celebration: of political self-determination and of a cultural phenomenon.

There is a curious inversion in the *India Today* caption that applauded *Roy* for opening up the global market to Indian writing in English. In fact the high purchase of this writing is a product of global demand, the markets for "non-Western," "postcolonial," "multicultural," and "Anglophone" literature. Such commodification of intellectual labor—the subject of vociferous debate in post-colonial cultural studies since the early nineties—remains a salient feature of our contemporary "empire," that deterritorialized global landscape recently described by Antonio Negri and Michael Hardt (2000). In such frame, the rapid subsuming of all social activity into a global exchange system necessarily means that the global purchase of the Renaissance is indicative of its abstraction into global commodity. Yet the questions that many critics of cultural globalism now pose are: Given the new capital-generating global economic and communication networks, what can literary production accomplish in struggles for political and social justice? Can a glamorized practice such as this recent explosion in South Asian writing effect cultural intervention into globalism?

Since the eighties, progressive South Asian historians, sociologists, ethnographers, artists, filmmakers, writers, and public intellectuals suspicious of the consensus to globalize have substantially reconsidered new evocations of the national-global dialectic. They have dismantled fetishes like the "global Indian" subject and its attendant biographies from the perspective of the migrant, both the cosmopolitan activist and the displaced subaltern of the Indian interior. As we will see, the "global Indian" is the middle-class subject wooed by cars, laptops, cosmetics, televisions, and washing machines in India's rapid transition to a consumer economy. How this subject is articulated along gender lines (in the beauty business, for example) has been amply explored elsewhere in the feminist analyses of Rajeswari Sunder Rajan, Mary John, and Arvind Rajagopal, among others (see John 1998; Sunder Rajan 1993; Rajagopal 2001b). In his perusal of a Hindu identity sold as a "brand" through televisual address, Arvind Rajagopal has amply demonstrated how "national" essences are crystallized and internalized within the ideal "global Indian citizen-consumer" (2001a). I will return to the finer lines of his arguments later in the book, but my point here is this: Since the eighties, cultural constructs like "the global Indian" have been the sites for forging consensus on globalization, and in these sites the national is reterritorialized as one aspect of a larger cultural identity. This dissolves painful oppositions. One can be nationalist in the most reactionary of ways while cheerfully participating in economic and cultural globalism. It is precisely against such a fetish that I pose the progressive "cosmopolitan activist," one who is concerned with the impact of these nationalizing and globalizing agendas for local and subaltern communities threatened by economic violence and cultural erasure.

In the jubilee discourses we see a popular valorized version of the cosmopolitan migrant in the figure of the writer. For example, in an advertisement for Gita Mehta's *Snakes and Ladders* in the *New Yorker* golden-jubilee issue, 23 and 30 June 1997, a smiling Mehta is framed as a native informant "uniquely qualified to interpret her homeland" and "formidably informed," but also a "passionately returned emigrée" (58). The blurb stages the salience of the migrant perspective on the "homeland" but commodifies Mehta as the "intelligent voice of India." While I develop the political efficacy of this specifically modulated migrant perspective in this book, much of my analysis takes issue with the unguarded treatment of privileged cosmopolitan writers as *the* spokespeople for India.

Toward this end I provide a critical framework and vocabulary for a discriminating look at postcolonial South Asian writing in English. The conception of a situated literary cosmopolitics—one that mobilizes the imagination for newly urgent ethical and political tasks of worlding—is especially relevant to our literary example. Post-eighties South Asian writing in English has always been tagged "cosmopolitan" writing, ever since Timothy Brennan's evocation of Rushdie's literary politics as the "boastful cosmopolitanism" of "third world metropolitan elites" (Brennan 1989). Brennan's early study of Rushdie was the first monographic exploration of the writer and thus stands as a historic critical marker of sorts (P. Joshi 2002, 232). But a decade has passed since then, and globalism has come to stay. New global linkages in our moment of empire have refocused progressive efforts on engendering popular global consciousness. My inquiry here will direct this gaze to the function of literature. Past the collapse of the Soviet bloc and the consequent call to a new world order, what are the capacities of the literary imagination to fashion new forms of collective life and agency?

Positing Cosmopolitics

Cosmopolitanism has historically signified a sense of belonging to the world. This implied act of worlding alone can serve to make postcolonial scholars suspicious of such belonging. The universalism in modern variants of cosmopolitanism (epitomized in the modern traveler, exile, and avant-garde nomad) with its proximity to Western geopolitical epistemology has fallen into disrepute, making way for a very different privileging of migrancy. Homi Bhabha and Arjun Appadurai's decade-long work on nomadism represents such celebration. Bhabha has received lengthy treatment elsewhere, so I will only tangentially reference his oeuvre here.[5] I see Appadurai's placing of migrancy in the context of manifold struggles over producing modernity as more significant for my project. In exploring the "current crisis in nation," Appadurai (1993, 411) provides a "part of the apparatus of recognition for postnational social forms," posing "ethnic collectivisms" in opposition to the "cosmopolitanisms" of our current historical juncture. He criticizes ethnic collectivists who lack the global imagination of the cosmopolitan who, by contrast, relishes nonnational nomadism and celebrates migrancy, hybridity, and mobility.

Yet such an opposition of reactionary collectivism versus nomadism is strongly attacked by many cultural theorists, who point a finger at the *luxury* of cosmopolitanism. Revathi Krishnaswamy, whose essay appears in one of the early collections on this "explosion" in Indian writing in English, argues that Rushdie's self-conscious parody and irony are marks of his privilege—those "momentary indulgences in self-pleasuring destabilizations" not accessible to laboring or nonconsensual nomads (1995, 126). In other words, given their political and cultural visibility, for elite cosmopolitans migrancy assumes mythological status. But migrancy remains a physically and socially painful experience for other (underprivileged) diaspora cultures and migrant peoples. Others, such as Aihwa Ong, insist that the global belonging of elite transnationals has nothing to do with a progressive vision of globality. Rather, we should think of elite cultural productions like John Woo movies as constitutive of a "flexible citizenship" pitched at ameliorating the cultural dislocation of transnational elites who participate enthusiastically in capital-generating processes.[6] In such critiques new cosmopolitans appear to fetishize their marginality as migrants, while synchronizing the global flows that underpin the new world order.

Clearly readers of these South Asian novels are, as Brennan reminds us, deeply implicated in the very neoliberal global networks that the cosmopolitical writers often scorn as corporate conglomerates. Elaborating on his earlier work, in *At Home in the World: Cosmopolitanism Now* (1997) Brennan examines new forms of cosmopolitanism in the features of third-world elites posing as postcolonial subalterns. Third-world metropolitan fiction writers are new cosmopolitans whose politics must be regarded with suspicion: They trope democracy in the face of poverty, disease, dictatorship, and revolution. For Brennan, the language of the humanities, and particularly of postcolonial theory that takes a privileged U.S. experience as the point of departure, further facilitates the functioning of global capital-generating networks. The endless troping of mobility, hybridity, travel, nomadism, and flexibility in postcolonial critical theory, despite all claims of resistance to oppressive political and economic regimes, finally serves to flatten structural antagonisms and make light of abiding cultural differences.

Brennan's work is critical for locating celebrity writers within larger transnational flows (both immigration and media), which I further scrutinize in chapter 2. Brennan's attention to the material underpinnings of new (metropolitan) cosmopolitanism explains why these literary stars can easily assume idioms of perennial wandering while appropriating their native cultures (a fetishistic localism) for global consumption. Such privileging of postnational forms of belonging overlook, asserts Brennan, the great revolutionary nationalist narratives of the "third world." Despite his rigorous critique, Brennan does underline the heterogeneity of the field of cosmopolitan literary production, one that may include both flashy multiculturalism and a radical critique of geopolitical power distributions. My project attempts to carve a space within this field of "third-world" cosmopolitan writing where, despite the glare of international visibility, certain writers engage in a literary politics that interrupts their own global circulation and rejects an overt fetishistic localism.

Such revision of cosmopolitanism has emerged on many fronts. Acknowledging both the historical and contemporary problems of cosmopolitanism, several postcolonial and cultural critics in recent years have reconceptualized the rubric in ways that enable us to confront cosmopolitan privilege without dismissing cosmopolitanism as politically bankrupt. Some of the accounts cited later in this chapter provide a selective vocabulary for the literary practice at hand. The idea of a situated cosmopolitics underscores the world's particularisms; it makes cosmopolitanism more mobile. Thus even critics of elite nomadism have returned to the idea of cosmopolitanism with renewed interest. For instance, Anthony Appiah, famous for his trenchant critique of a "comprador elite," global voyeurs who cynically sell their home cultures on a global

market, now writes enthusiastically of local attachment: a "cosmopolitan patriotism" in which one remains "rooted" to a home culture while still belonging to
the world (1991). Cosmopolitics further involves direct political engagement, as
opposed to the "detachment" of older cosmopolitanisms exemplified in V. S.
Naipaul's disengagement from local political struggles.

The return to cosmopolitanism as a critical resource finds manifold treatment in an issue of *Public Culture* (a journal that has systematically tracked
effects of globalization for more than a decade), now available as an anthology,
Cosmopolitanism (Breckenbridge et al. 2002). In their joint introduction, the editors present their case: "Cosmopolitanism, in its wide and wavering nets,
catches something of our need to ground our sense of *mutuality* in conditions
of mutability, and to live tenaciously in terrains of historical and cultural transition" (4; my emphasis). Their sense of a mutable historical time on the one hand
(given the increasing velocity of structural changes that we name globalization),
and of the closing nets of neoliberalism on the other, imparts urgency to the
mobilization of those who fall through the cracks of new global equations. As
wide and as wavering a net as it might be, cosmopolitanism remains one option.
Not cosmopolitanism as a positive mode of being (a liberal individualism), but
rather cosmopolitanism as contingent acts aimed at producing a "minoritarian
modernity" (6). This description, variously modulated by the writers in the volume, answers the current need for a backdrop of mutuality against which we
may forge new global solidarities. The editors underline their distance from the
fetishized cosmopolitanism of liberal individualism often found in rhetorics that
valorize features of a Mother Teresa or a Lady Diana. Hence the editors arrest
the slide between the different valences of cosmopolitanism—the minoritarian
and the neoliberal—in insisting on minoritarian cosmopolitanism as contingent
action.

The modality of cosmopolitanism as a series of acts has a predecessor in
Bruce Robbins's (1999) and Pheng Cheah's (1999) account of "cosmopolitics."
Robbins and Cheah quite self-reflexively hone discussions of cosmopolitanism
to contemporary progressive agendas, be it the struggles over multiculturalism
in the North (for Robbins) or the embedded cosmopolitanisms of the South (for
Cheah). Early in his introduction, Cheah cautions us: "An existing global condition ought not to be mistaken for an existing mass-based feeling of belonging
to a world community (cosmopolitanism) because the globality of the everyday
does not necessarily engender an existing popular global political consciousness" (31). The distinction between everyday globality that constitutes, say, the
practices of flexible citizenship and the strategic "belonging to a world community" is an important one for the postcolonial literary cosmopolitics that I
attempt to posit here. "Strategic belonging" means the galvanizing of global

resources (like the resources of language) for local struggles. For Robbins and Cheah, popular cosmopolitanisms need to be distinguished from elite varieties because of their potential for global progressive ethicopolitical transformations. Far from the comforts of privilege, these cosmopolitanisms are often produced in local contexts under considerable duress. We see this in the case of Arundhati Roy, for instance, brought to trial for her trenchant affidavit against the Supreme Court's "false charges" against her 'Medha Patkar' and Prashant Bushan (all anti-dam-building activists). Roy was jailed for a day and fined a nominal Rs.2000 (approximately forty-two dollars) in a deliberate performance of the nation-state's power over this globally known activist. In fact the meager jail time was commuted because Roy was a woman. I will return to the specifics of such cosmopolitical engagement more substantially later in the book.

Roy's direct cosmopolitics can be further understood as a performance pitched at forging collective agency. In many respects, she typifies the political and ethical drives of cosmopolitical writing: the unflinching political commitment to the local struggles, and the subsequent ethical stance. The five cosmopolitical writers I examine variously dismantle any stable emplacing national-global dialectic in favor of local heterogeneity. Highlighting the struggles of "minority" communities, disenfranchised urban migrant labor, *adivasis* (tribal and indigenous peoples) and *dalits* (low-caste subjects), the rural poor, and other politically and culturally "displaced" subjects of nationalizing and globalizing "development," they invoke a social imaginary where the cosmopolitical writer acts in solidarity with these subaltern populations.

New Globality and Literary Circulation

In arguing for the emergence of the imagination as a perceptible sovereign entity in a world of mass-media flows and increased migrations, in many respects it is Appadurai's work that makes possible my present conception of social imaginaries; his etching of globalscapes might be commonplace by now, but its legacy is formidable. As collective matrices, social imaginaries in general enable subjects to inhabit contemporaneous modernities. In his introduction to the *Public Culture* issue on *new* social imaginaries, Dilip Gaonkar describes these collective matrices as "ways of understanding the social that become social entities themselves, mediating collective life" (Gaonkar 2002, 4). At our contemporary moment, with the dizzying speed and dispersion of current media flows, new social imaginaries are markedly self-reflexive. The individual's participation in the global market, for instance, now constitutes a register of belonging, where the "market"—objectified in third person—emerges as a social entity. Yet the market, I have argued, is one among many other matrices of collective identification, such as the nation or the public sphere. To insist on the preeminence of the market in quotidian modern life is to be rather reductive. Indeed, social imaginaries enable many valences of collective life. When they assume collective agency, they become social movements. In this regard, the popular cosmopolitanisms theorized by Cheah can be understood as translocal social movements.

For our purposes, conceptualizing social imaginaries becomes vital for the analysis of a cosmopolitics aimed at producing minoritarian modernity. To retain its particular modality, however, the cosmopolitical struggles to produce minoritarian modernity must be differentiated from others of different political inflection. In the national culture wars that I peruse in chapter 4, for instance, not to mention the spectacular conflict over *The Satanic Verses* with which we began, we witness some of these other political inflections. As Gaonkar notes, the Rushdie affair made visible the presence of very different social imaginaries: the Islamic public in objectified opposition to "civil" (rational) Western publics. The full drift of uneven global modernities shored up the existence of alternative imaginaries as the matrices that underpinned local arbitrations of the offending text.

The South Asian cosmopolitics I have described earlier draws substantially from Western alternative progressive imaginaries. Yet nested within these is a distinctive South Asian social imaginary of democratic self-rule. Just after his comments on *The Satanic Verses*, Gaonkar in fact underlines this South Asian imaginary of democratic self-rule alongside the example of another national imaginary—Singapore's entrepreneurial culture. The South Asian cosmopolitical thinkers we have perused adhere to a minoritarian agenda on *both* fronts, attempting to forge global and national (democratic) mutuality. The peculiar persistence of a national imaginary—the reason for my underscoring of "South Asian" in describing the cosmopolitics under scrutiny—speaks of a postcoloniality in which the "nation" is still the domain of unrealized political potential. I will return later to the persistence of nation for the global South, but for now identifying the social imaginary of democratic self-rule as definitive of our brand of cosmopolitics will suffice.

We see the social imaginary of democratic self-rule vibrant in the South Asian cosmopolitical writers' political commitment to subaltern struggles, and in their ethical censure of violence. Too much has been said on the political franchise of the subaltern, so here I will only briefly address those for whom any invocation of the subaltern raises a red flag. Quite differently modulated in Ranajit Guha and Gayatri Spivak's formulation, in South Asian contexts, the subaltern as figure of disenfranchisement first emerged in the subaltern studies critiques of colonialism and nationalism.[7] In subsequent conversations, however, the pitfalls of cursorily evoking the subaltern became eminently clear. Spivak (1996) herself rigorously insisted on retaining the specificity of the analytic category, applying it to those people cut off from all lines of mobility and "sighted" at points of their insurgency. Yet the subaltern has survived as critical shorthand for registering insurgencies outside the purview of mass mobilizations like freedom movements or revolutions.

More importantly, the subaltern is an absence that haunts all hegemonic discourse, as the editors of *Subaltern Studies* surmised in volume 10 of their series. Disagreeing with views of "silent" subaltern speech as a critical failure, the editors emphasized the value of the subaltern as essentially deconstructive. While it may not be possible to identify an autonomous field for the subaltern, they explained, there is also no field autonomous from the subaltern: hence the pervasive "subaltern-effect" on dominant discourses (Bhadra, Prakash, and Tharu 1999, 1). My book traces the subaltern effect in dominant literary discourses exemplified in globally circulating South Asian writing in English, particularly in the texts of writers interested in foregrounding localized forms of collective agency. With varying degrees of success, these cosmopolitical writers struggle against turning the subaltern into abstract trope, taking on all the baggage of incommunicability, translation, and textual disjuncture that the subaltern effect commands.

While the inclusion of subaltern struggles marks the political drive of the cosmopolitical writers, their preoccupation with ongoing violence in South Asian communities—a violence that fundamentally transforms a politicized other into a nonhuman thing—signals the ethical vector of these literary projects. Here the vitalist ontologies of postcolonial nations, so thoroughly explored by Pheng Cheah, come into play in the cosmopolitical writers' varying negotiations of what Derrida (1994) names an "ethical spectrology." Some of these writers traffic in the "in-human" (or that which appears as monstrous within rational discourse); they speak in Derridean mode to "those certain others" invisible in our "living present."[8] Others follow Dipesh Chakrabarty's lead in staging the incommunicablity in "speaking of" others: those travails of translating subaltern "life-worlds" that register as the "shock of the uncanny" in forms of modern discourse (2000). In this overt display of their difficulties as translators, the cosmopolitical writers convey their deepest conundrum: how to render local struggles globally communicable without emptying out the specificity of the local? Appositely put: how to be attentive to the radical polysemy of the other without recourse to silence?

Cosmopolitics, after all, implies a commitment to communicability in the service of a "global popular consciousness" of the sort we witnessed at the Seattle anti-WTO insurrection of 2000 (Cheah 1999, 31). Given that contemporary global flows largely originate in the North, Cheah asks how the popular cosmopolitanisms of the global South can articulate their struggle in world media? Where and to whom are these local struggles communicated? These key questions of circulation and translation haunt all literature written in English from the postcolonies. South Asian cosmopolitical writers pick up the gauntlet in their self-reflexive acts of cultural translation.

Self-reflexivity of circulation, then, emerges as a central attribute of cosmopolitical writing. Here the *Satanic Verses* affair is once more instructive. The controversy precisely dramatized the self-reflexivity of the reading public who saw themselves *as* a public: the implicit third-person-subject "we" who do not condone treating literature as blasphemy as "they" do, and vice versa. In their discussion of the increasing self-reflexivity about circulation among contemporary readers, writers, critics, editors, and distributors, Benjamin Lee and Edward LiPuma theorize the emergent "cultures of circulation" of today. These are *constituted by* and *constitutive of* the cultural forms, like the "literary work," circulating through them (2002). In their circulation, these cultural forms are abstracted, evaluated, and constrained. We see this everywhere in the cultures in which the cosmopolitical writers circulate. Often the writers quite emphatically contest, arbitrate, or buttress their own refractions through public announcements, essays, and interviews, a phenomenon we shall pursue in some detail throughout the book.

Self-reflexivity becomes literary praxis in cosmopolitical novels. It is manifest in the cosmopolitical writers' long arguments about media and circulation framed through a variety of narrative situations. Readers, writers, painters, critics, academics, listeners, storytellers, and even publishers proliferate in these novels: Saira (the listener), Zeeny Vakil (the critic), Markline (the English book publisher), and Comrade Pillai (the institutional cultural arbiter) are some of the more memorable presences to whom we shall return in chapter 5. More importantly, the writers affect a linguistic localism in self-conscious response to the globalism of English, always cognizant of that embattled sign—Indian writing in English—under which they write the South Asian postcolony. A look at these self-reflexive praxes that address the vicissitudes of global literary circulation will remain a major line of inquiry in the book. If Arundhati Roy embeds untranslated Malayalam in *The God of Small Things*, what "public" can she assume? Whom does she "privilege" and whom does she "constrain" in such inclusion?

Finally, the *Satanic Verses* affair also exploded the boundaries of print circulation. Literary values, credentials, and reputations were bartered at incredible velocity across electronic media. Referring to these refractions of literary texts and authors across print and electronic media, Aamir Mufti argued for a "reconceptualization" of literary reception in the wake of the Rushdie affair: "Extracts published in the print media, in English and in translation; commentary in print, on the airwaves, and from the pulpit; fantasticated representation in popular cinema; rumors and hearsay—such are the means by which the novel [*The Satanic Verses*] has achieved circulation in the Islamic world" (1999, 52). The literary had become public culture in unforeseen ways.[9] The translations of the writers that arbitrate their "value" in oral, visual, and print circulation will be another line of investigation in this book. We shall see how, on many occasions, the writers adopt politically contradictory postures in response to a deluge of refractions in the print and electronic media—postures more accentuated in the case of the famous of this ilk (Salman Rushdie, Amitav Ghosh, and Arundhati Roy).

The task at hand is first to bring these refractions into sharper focus, and I attempt just this by tracking the Renaissance—the commodity fetish of cosmopolitical writing—across several reception contexts. When borne across reception contexts, one inevitably becomes aware of the disjunctures between the values that accrue to these literary practices in local, national, and transnational circulations. In turn, the refractions enable us to consider the cosmopolitical writers' direct and literary mediation of them. The discussion that follows stages a bifocal look at the circulation of cosmopolitical writing, starting with the Renaissance as a commercial success and proceeding to record those evaluations that challenge the easy equation of marketability with political dysfunction.

In Global Flow

One dominant strain of thinking on globalism posits the market as the fundamental shaping force at our contemporary historical moment. My elaboration of the political and ethical potentials of the social imagination, of course, suggests that this is only a part of the story. Nonetheless, it is imperative to pause on the accounts of ubiquitous global commercial flows because of the obvious popularity of the Renaissance. Michael Hardt and Antonio Negri's notion of "empire," their shorthand for the "new economic-industrial-communicative complex," typifies an extreme instance of this strain of theorizing globalism, by now a decade-long conversation on that "untotalizable totality" called "globalization" (Jameson 1998, xvi).[10] In these discussions, globalization was understood both in the historical sense (our contemporary phase of capitalist expansion) and in the structural sense (a terrain marked by flows of information, goods, and people). The centrality of capital to global cultural production posed the primary problem for most progressive theorists of cultural globalism. For instance, Fredric Jameson demonstrated how economic relationships such as the GATT and NAFTA agreements define national subsidies and quotas on cultural practices; by the same token, symbolic transmissions in their marketability become economic products. Jameson records this "becoming cultural of the economic, and the becoming economic of the cultural," as a feature of postmodernity (1998, 3). Other theorists add military power to defining the postmodern: George Yúdice (1996), for instance, argues for the continuing financial and military dominance of the heavily industrialized global North, an observation that tragically resonates with the post–September 11 bombing of Afghanistan.[11]

In their long exegesis on "postmodernization," whose primary feature is informatization, Hardt and Negri argue that this biopolitical "machine" subsumes all affective relations within it. For instance, social relations such as physical and mental healthcare become abstracted into forms of labor, now sold as commodities. Their narrative marked a shift in emphasis from Jameson's, Miyoshi's, and Appadurai's accounts that privileged *de*territorializing flows. Hardt and Negri are at pains to elaborate on the common modes of *re*territorialization, a reading of some salience to the cosmopolitical localisms examined in this book. In the contemporary expansions of capital, the "local" (often cited as a point of resistance to the global) is now a perspective produced by the logic of capital, Hardt and Negri surmise, as "social machines that create and recreate identities and differences that are understood as local" (2000, 45).

Other cultural critics of globalism also see the penetration of the local by the global, but to very different ends. Nestor García Canclini has been the most vocal proponent of the liberatory local rejuvenated by global flows. In this sense, like Hardt and Negri, Canclini sees local difference as generated by global capital. Yet for Hardt and Negri, this very fact evacuates the local as a place "outside" that might challenge "empire." Canclini, on the other hand, claims political ground for the local. In his most recent work, he illustrates how global consumer options enable performances of localized antistate cultural citizenships (2001).[12] These opposing views represent a larger theoretical debate on the "problem" of the local in critiques of globalism.

Simon During (2000) brings the discussion on global consumerism and local revitalization to a case congruent with our practice—the "Maori Renaissance" of the eighties. For During, it is critical postcolonialism, with its North-based academic links, that stands ever in danger of recycling local products for new audiences on a global market. This critical discourse insists on the "recovery" of colonized and subaltern voices and positions itself as an intervention into globalism. Taking critical postcolonialism to task for its "weakly dialectical" relation to globalization, During proceeds to examine how Maori access to global capital actually transformed Maori-Pakeha (white settler) relations in the eighties.[13] He offers proof in the political outcomes of the Maori Renaissance: the reassertion of Maori rights, land marches, the extension of the Waitangi tribunal for Maori grievances, and the rewriting of Maori history.

This conversation on the local has considerable resonance for the literary cosmopolitics whose localisms I will read bifocally in the forthcoming analyses. While I argue that the localizing strategies of the cosmopolitical writers in part produce fetishistic locales for commercial consumption, they also privilege a "performative local" that cannot be stabilized, reproduced, or circulated on a global market. Readers who acknowledge the irreducible supplementarity of local idiom, citation, and reference in the cosmopolitical texts perform constant textual migrations to local contexts; there are no native informants here. These constant textual migrations foreclose any constituent synthesis of a perspective, narrative, or linguistic place. Yet it is these privileged writers and their equally privileged English-speaking readers who perform these migrations. This requires a look at the reading publics of this literary phenomenon: Who are the target audiences of the touted Renaissance? And within those parameters, who are the addressees of the cosmopolitical writers?

While the economic and communicational vectors of globalization in postliberalized India (like the establishing of global North-based publishing houses in the Indian metropolises) have much to do with the circulation of the Renaissance, so does the increased desire for Indian artifacts among diasporic and transnational networks of the 1980s and 1990s. The global North-based diaspora in Britain and the United States, where there has been large-scale immigration from the professional middle and upper classes, is distinct in social, cultural, and political configuration from the working-class Indian diaspora (indentured laborers and the urban migrant poor in Britain and the United States), and from the Indian diaspora in Africa, the Caribbean, Southeast Asia, and Hong Kong. These latter diaspora cultures and new migrant laborers remain largely invisible in most allusions to the Indian diaspora in literary-critical circuits. No surprise, since it is the elite Indian diaspora who have gained global visibility in the last decades, and Indian writing in English as an exalted literary object has done much to glamorize this diaspora in Britain and the United States. Further, in this last decade, we have witnessed a growth in mobile elite transnationals (employed by multinationals) who nevertheless play a significant role in defining national interests and systems—subjects best described as a "third culture" inhabiting a "borderless world" (Miyoshi 1993, 726–727).[14] Privileged bourgeois Indians and mobile transnational Indian elites in part constitute the growing reading constituencies hungry for a Renaissance.

To some extent the localism of the cosmopolitical writers plays to these newly articulated desires for Indianness, especially on the part of these English-speaking migrant populations with access to global communications networks. It is a desire that fuels the rapid expansion in venues through which India is consumed. For instance, we see a growth in North American editions of major Indian magazines (some of whose production designs resemble *Time*'s and *Newsweek*'s; see figure 3 for an *India Today* cover). A 1997 advertisement for the "India Today newsgroup" ethnicizes India for elite Indian transnational and national consumers, the *mehendi*-covered hand signaling a hot Indian item in global North-based circuits of consumption (see figure 1). The essentialized (and disembodied) Indian artifact is placed against the backdrop of outer space, alluding to the new frontiers of global markets. To be Indian now—"to tap your fingers to the finest in Indian music"—is to be globally connected, to "have India at your fingertips." In their analysis of the North American edition of *India Today*, Jerry McGuire and Lalitha Pandit (1995) precisely interrogate such exoticization of India for transnational Indian consumers by excavating the packaging of local Indian festivals for readers who crave the authenticity of a "home" culture. More recently, *India Today* has begun to feature a whole section titled "The Global Indian." In the International Advertising section of the 6 May 2002 issue, which features a cover story on a new crop of Indian writers in English, there is much exultation over an emergent Indian chic: "With ethnic clothing becoming a veritable leitmotif for most Indians at public gatherings and native Americans too taking the cue, Indian fashion across America has come into its own."

By the same token, the global gaze moving across media frames local sightings of the Renaissance in 1997. Arundhati Roy's interviews on PBS and her comments in the Anglo-American press were dutifully reported in all the major local Indian newspapers. As we shall see in all the gloating over Roy's Booker Prize, national readers placed great value on the global North-based celebration of South Asian writing in English. This cultural practice above any other seemed to catch the Indian moment, for in globalizing India, English as the language of trade and of technocracy had gained even more economic muscle than it had in the postindependence years.

As we shall see throughout the book, the cosmopolitical writers ride these globalizing drives despite their progressive politics. This is quite overt in Salman Rushdie's pitch to English-speaking readers that sells the Renaissance as the premier contemporary literary object. In his introduction to the *New Yorker* issue on the Renaissance, Rushdie became notorious for his remark:

> This is it: The prose writing—both fiction and non-fiction—created in this period by Indian writers working in English is proving to be a stronger and more important body of work than most of what has been produced in the six-

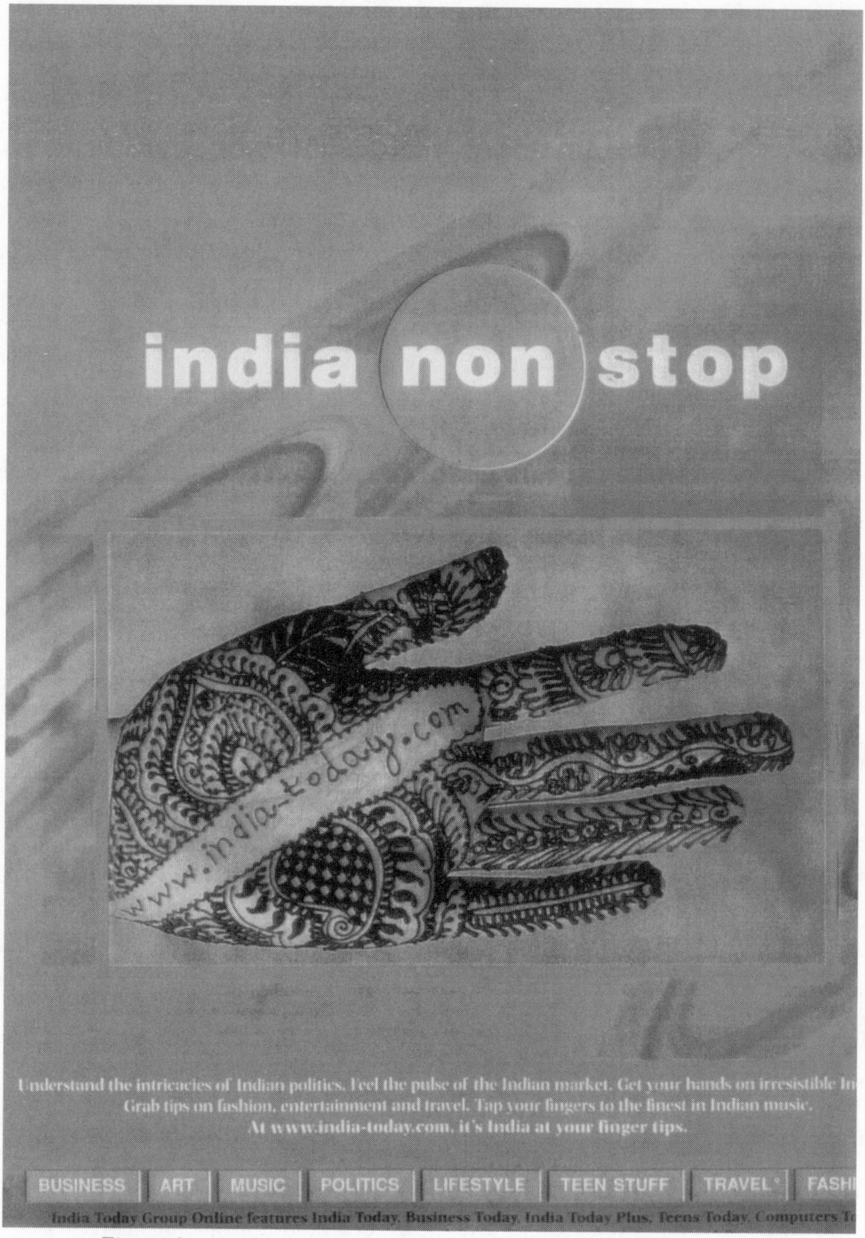

_____ *Figure 1* _____
Advertisement for *India Today*, 27 October 1997: "India non-stop."
Courtesy *India Today*.

teen "official" languages of India, the so-called Indian vernacular languages, during the same time; and, indeed, this new, and still-burgeoning "Indo-Anglian" literature represents perhaps the most valuable contribution India has yet made to the world of books. (1997a, 50).

A little later in the essay, he casually mentions that he has read the vernacular literatures mostly in translation. When the essay was reprinted in the collection *Step across This Line*, the sentence ended in "during the same time," erasing the officious claim of the last phrase—"'Indo-Anglian' literature represents the most valuable contribution India has yet made to the world of books" (2002b, 146). Rushdie explains the omission as a response to the "howls of protest and condemnation" that his initial statement had drawn from Indian writers and critics, pompously retorting in a footnote: "Readers are accordingly warned that mine is an improper view. Which doesn't necessarily mean it's wrong" (147).

To make things worse, in an interview with Christopher Hitchens in October 1997, Rushdie insisted in proto-colonial fashion that the Indian vernacular literatures have lost steam because they have failed to keep up with the twentieth century. Unabashed (and apparently unaware of urban modern vernacular literatures), Rushdie decries the "parochialism" of these Indian literatures whose worlds seem unchanged: "Village life is hard," "women are badly treated," "landlords are corrupt," and "peasants are heroic" (1997c, 40).

The reactionary edge to Rushdie's defensive valorization of the Renaissance is more striking when one considers his earlier cynicism in "'Commonwealth Literature' Does Not Exist" about the postcolonial value of Indian writing in English.[15] Carried away by the hubris of his lionization in critical circles, not to mention his political celebrity, Rushdie falls victim to generating more cultural purchase for an elite practice with economic advantage over vernacular Indian literatures. Predictably, his comment caused a furor (both praise and blame) in India. Arundhati Roy, for one, who ironically falls into the prestigious literary set privileged by Rushdie, marked her distance from his evaluations by labeling them "unnecessary" in her national self-representation in the U.S. press via the *Los Angeles Times* (1997c).

Despite condemnation of his remarks, what is even more important to our pursuit of the Renaissance as global commodity is the support that Rushdie received from commentators in the Indian press. For instance, in July 1997, a writer in *India Today* decried the parochialism behind the Indian criticism of Rushdie's comments and emphasized the fact that English *is* India's lingua franca, for it is a language that buys the nation currency in world affairs and markets ("Be Indian," 9). Elsewhere, in unabashed celebration of new linguistic pathways to India, Alex Wilber (1997), writing for the *Seattle Times* about the golden jubilee, celebrated the new explosion in Indian literature as "a literature born and informed by the Indian diaspora. It is a literature that takes the colonial language the British left behind and marries it to the vibrant 'Babu English' of the marketplace to create something new and exuberant." Since "Babu English" is the "colonial language the British left behind," Wilber's formulation makes non-sense of the historical development of English in the postcolony. In a more nationalist modality, Soumitra Das (1997) in the Delhi edition of the *Statesman* insisted on English as the linguistic glue: "It's a powerful binding agent that cuts across caste and region, it is an authentic instrument of national consciousness, no matter how hard our feelings are about colonisation." Such eagerness to enter the global economy is right on a par with global North-based productions of Indian writing in English as a tradition that contributes to a vast and plural fund of world Englishes—a cultural plethora unmarked, in this neocolonial discourse, by the historical wounds of empire and its linguistic hegemonies.

The disregard of the political girding of the literary is underlined by critics like Graham Huggan who examine the neocolonialism of literary prizes given to postcolonial writers. The targets of Huggan's censure are neoliberals who avoid "confronting structural differences in conditions of literary production and consumption across the English-speaking world" (1997, 413). Proffering a history of the Booker McConnell Company, a corporation that profited from the harshest of colonial regimes in the 1830s, Huggan goes to some lengths to show how the Booker awards attempt to contain postcolonial cultural critique by pro-moting English as a harmoniously shared common fund. In his recent book on the subject of marketing that "strategically malleable" product, the "postcolonial exotic," Huggan elaborates on the role of the Booker in consuming India in par-ticular (with 1981 and 1997 as key moments). The Booker parleys in the "com-modified eclecticism" of the "multicultural cachet," Huggan explains, effectively harnessing and value coding the "postcolonial" for furthering British cultural pluralism (2001, 110).

Huggan's critique is important to our discussion here because the symbolic recognition of prizes has built the international reputations of several of the cos-mopolitical writers, whatever their politics: Rushdie and Roy have Booker tro-phies; Vikram Chandra, the Commonwealth Prize for the Eurasia region. We know, of course, that Amitav Ghosh made big news in 2001 by turning down his nomination for the same Commonwealth Prize, thereby short-circuiting his currency within that colonial rubric. And of course, most recently, the most politically conservative of South Asian writers, V. S. Naipaul, was awarded the Nobel Prize.[16]

The iconic visual on the cover of the *New Yorker* issue on Indian writing in English, one which samples many passages to India, from E. M. Forster to

Salman Rushdie, exemplifies this neoliberal celebration of this Renaissance as simply a rich cultural legacy (see figure 2). Notice the khakhi-and-sola-topee dress of the adventurous couple who comes upon an architectural figure (in the likeness of temples) of Ganesh, the scribe of the Indian epic *Mahabharat*. An Indian temple hovers farther back to reinforce the image of an ancient civilization. The combination of surprise, fear, and excitement on the couple's faces recalls Adela Quested's delight and disquiet at Indian "ruins" in *A Passage to India*, no doubt shaded by Indiana Jones's more recent foray to the kitsch "Temple of Doom."[17] Most readers of Rushdie's *Midnight's Children* will remember the first-person narrator's resemblance to this elephant-headed, long-nosed scribe in Rushdie's self-conscious modern epic of the postcolonial nation. The *New Yorker* cover, then, transcribes literary and popular texts into painting (Owen Smith's *The Elephantine Prophecy*) and foregrounds Rushdie's place as the "father" of this Renaissance.

In fact, most global North-based accounts of India at fifty and of the Renaissance chose to ignore the materiality of South Asian writing in English. The literary phenomenon was treated as a symptom of a thriving democracy without attention to the imperial history of English in India; its continuing links to economic, social, and political power; or indeed the fact that only an elite few are conversant in its literary expressions. The golden jubilee NPR show blandly proclaimed: "In fact some critics believe that the next great novel in the English language will come from an Indian writer," given the "extraordinary renaissance in Indian fiction" (Fleming 1997). When asked why the "leading novelists" write in English and not in the "native languages," Bill Buford of the *New Yorker* chose to note merely that English has achieved such popularity and literary value through "an accident of history" (Fleming 1997).

It is precisely this dissembling about the commercial underpinnings of cultural production that trouble critics of globalism. These commentators variously theorize the impact of postmodernism and its pedagogic counterpart, multiculturalism, on postcolonial artifacts. They demonstrate how the plenitude of these other worlds is contained and managed in neat packages: exotic worlds "reflected" in the writing of equally exotic writers; delicious ethnic, racial, and religious othernesses; and a vast plural fund of variations in English.[18] Cultural agents, the translators who bring non-Western contexts into global circulation, are the target of trenchant critiques from Marxist theorists such as Gayatri Spivak and Arif Dirlik.[19] In their view, the exchange of subaltern, colonized, and disenfranchised worlds on the global market brings little compensation to the subjects in these worlds. But writers, editors, distributors, translators, and critics have everything to gain from these global exchanges.[20] To sell a Renaissance as the most interesting cultural phenomenon of the 1990,

_____ *Figure 2* _____

Cover of the *New Yorker* special issue on Indian fiction, 23 and 30 June 1997, featuring a
painting by Owen Smith, *The Elephantine Prophecy.*
Courtesy *The New Yorker.*

without attention to the materiality of that practice is precisely to exert such cultural agency.

Progressive theorists worry that this commodity production effectively empties out vast postcolonial social worlds into simulacra. They contend that the world of simulacra knows no origins. Here the "authentic" or the "nonmodern" is "countersigned" by its displacement in the hierarchies of global signification (During 1990, 30). Deepika Bahri provides an excellent example of this postmodern countersigning of the postcolonial in her analysis of a Dosa King banner (Dosa King is a multinational chain in India). India's "capitulation to capitalism," argues Bahri, is signaled by the simulacric use of an Abe Lincoln–like figure emblazoned on the banner. Lincoln's stature as the "liberator of slaves" now signifies the "freedom" that can come to the postcolony via multinational free enterprise (1996, 144).[21] All political inflections of resistance to capital (its early manifestation in the institution of slavery) are evacuated in such re-signification. During underlines this point in remarking on the "postcultural" nature of postmodern products that are "not essentially bound to the life-world that produced them." The simulacric televisual production of Nelson Mandela, for instance, During reports, circulates often in broadcasts that "forget" Mandela's revolutionary legacies (1990, 27). An interesting Indian parallel is found in the Gandhi fetishes in global circulation. Consider the huge hoardings of Gandhi marching alone in Apple computer advertisements that challenge us to "Think different" (e.g., the one on Fairfax going south on Wilshire in Los Angeles, fall 2000), a visual citation that erases Gandhi's well-known aversion to techno-consumerism. Always fervently engaged in public culture, Salman Rushdie attacked this particular "Think different" campaign in his essay "Gandhi, Now." "Fifty years after his assassination, Gandhi is modeling for Apple," writes the sardonic Rushdie. "His thoughts don't really count in this new incarnation. What counts is that he is considered to be 'on message,' in line with the corporate philosophy of the Mac" (2002c, 165). Not surprisingly, when I approached Bob Robinson of Apple's Legal Department for permission to print this advertisement for this book, he bluntly refused (for an example of the "Think different" campaign's Gandhi posters, see *www.redlightrunner.com*).

We see such disconnected simulacric use of the Renaissance in some of the commentaries on India's multilingual democracy in 1997. Consider the emptying out of any national or local reference in Edward Hochmann's reply to Shashi Tharoor's article "India's Odd, Enduring Patchwork," published in the *New York Times* 8 August 1997. In his article on the Indian polity, Tharoor exalted the flexible strength of India's multicultural democracy, despite the social schisms, political pitfalls, and business inefficiencies wrought by that nation's *multilingual* culture (my emphasis). Edward Hochmann, missing Tharoor's laudatory tenor, wrote a letter to the editor on 12 August exclaiming that Tharoor's piece "convinced me that English needs to be recognized as the official language of the United States."

If the Renaissance spoke to the political health of the Indian democracy, the "multicultural" democracy emerged as another fetishized commodity at the golden jubilee—a political triumph disconnected from the complex relations of labor that produce the national community. NPR and PBS privileged the democratic ideal as the cause célèbre at this global juncture. Articles in the *New York Times*, often written by Indians, pitched the democratic angle with rhetoric that catered to a readership versed in popular understandings of multiculturalism. For instance, Shashi Tharoor's just-cited piece celebrated the "idea" of India amid the diversities of languages, ethnicities, geographies, and religions: "Indian nationalism is the nationalism of an idea, the idea of an ever-ever land that is greater than the sum of its contradictions." Tharoor's comment presents a striking contrast to the more reflective gaze in the Indian national and local press, where the fifty-year celebrations became an occasion for ruminating on national historiography and representation. A common perception among those writing with a national public in mind was that they were recording a changed India. The writer of "Is India Suited for Democracy?", an article in the *Statesman*, 15 August 1997, started not with jubilation but with the disappointment of senior citizens on the eve of the golden jubilee. While reminiscing about August 1947, these citizens criticized India for her postindependence "blind imitation of developed democracies existing at the time" (2). Such critiques of democracy, and the marking of a change from the Nehruvian nation of midnight's children, remain untouched in the global North-based press where "democracy" is unabashedly celebrated as the institutional legacy of the colonial past.

One other fetish of the moment overwrites the signification of the Renaissance at the golden jubilee: The nation's poverty became the main source of disappointment in transnational circuits. The "poverty" of the "third world" commonly functions as a sensational object that buttresses the self-congratulation of developed nations. The introductory remarks on Indian democracy on the golden jubilee NPR show stressed "population" and "poverty," somehow making democracy even more wondrous: half a billion voters keeping "the faith" with democracy in the "world's second most populous country," despite "power-hungry" leaders and "one-third of the population" scrambling for a living "below the poverty line." Of the three interviewees, two focused attention on the issue of poverty, guided by questions on the "accuracy" of Rohinton Mistry's depiction of Bombay's squalor; on the realism of beggar masters, beggars, and untouchables; on the degree to which there was improvement in the lives of the poor (the concerned query: "Is it getting worse?"). The last interviewee, Palagummi Sainath, a journalist who lived in "India's poorest districts," was asked a series of questions on "the living conditions of the poor" and on his "exposés" of the political manufacturing of poverty (Fleming 1997). Palagummi Sainath's *Everybody Loves a Good Drought* (1997) actually deconstructs the functioning of Indian democracy, but that internal critique never quite found its way into the show.

Palagummi Sainath's reconstitution of the national-global dialectic exemplifies a cosmopolitan activism congruent with that of the writers featured here; I will pursue this comparison at greater length in chapter 4. I read his interrogations of the Indian democracy as partly a symptom of his postcolonial perspective on globalism and nationalism. As we have seen in our discussion of alternative social imaginaries, the "nation" as a strategic space remains a resonant progressive imagining in many postcolonial contexts. In fact Cheah is quite categorical about conceptualizing the "cosmopolitical" as a global force field that includes national mobilizations (Robbins and Cheah 1998). This is a marked departure from older styles of cosmopolitanism that construe nationalism as cosmopolitanism's historical other. Given the "absence of a world order" capable of ensuring equitable distribution, not to mention the persistence of colonial legacies in the neoliberal restructuring of the world, Cheah insists that the nation-state still remains a "political agent for defending the people of the South" (302). I evoke his view of a cosmopolitics from the South to evaluate what appear to be disagreements with "Western" perceptions of India and the Renaissance in local and national Indian circuits. These responses are postcolonial in their implicit historically modulated discernment of writing in English as not just an existing material practice, but a concept metaphor for a continuing cultural hegemony. They shore up different ratios between the Renaissance and the postcolonial democracy in their evaluation of South Asian writing in English. But these considerations that seek to arrest global productions of the Renaissance are not necessarily utopian by virtue of their postcoloniality—quite the contrary. As we shall see, they often result in chauvinistic emplacing performances of national or local identity *for* a global audience.

Arresting Looks

National and local chauvinism are especially apparent in the consumption of Roy as a cultural icon. Indian critics were both pleased with the recognition from the West and triumphant about the massacre of the British literary establishment. A judge for the 1997 Booker Prize, Jason Cowley, was quoted in the Indian press: "If the Booker is a mirror in which contemporary literary culture may glimpse a reflection of its own worth, then one ought to look elsewhere—to the USA or India. I once again congratulate Roy for winning; but where are the new British writers?" (1997b, 1). The cultural claims on an "Indian writer in English" who "lives in India" jostled other responses in the 27 October 1997 issue of *India Today* that acclaimed Roy's transcendence of national cultural boundaries; the cover of the same issue was emblazoned, "By winning the Booker, Arundhati Roy gives Indian writing in English global acceptance," with the smiling Roy feminized as "the princess of prose" (see figure 3).

Claims on Roy further erupted into culture wars elsewhere in the subcontinent, as we saw in the local uproar over her depiction of the Syrian Christian community in *The God of Small Things*. Soon after Roy's Booker triumph, Sabu Thomas filed suit against the book at a central Kerela court on charges of obscenity. A reporter in *India Today* compared this high-profile case with another by-now-famous transnational clash, the *Bandit Queen* legal charge against filmmaker Shekhar Kapur—a case in which Roy had raised a hullabaloo *against* Kapur's "sensational" portrayal of subaltern folk hero Phoolan Devi ("Indecent Exposure" 1997, 65). At a regional level, E. K. Nayanar, the chief minister of Kerela, writing in the Marxist daily *Deshabhimani*, criticized Roy's novel for "belittling" the revolutionary movement and for presenting an "unreal" picture of Kerela, as the 1 November 1997 *Statesman* reported under the headline "The Chief Minister of Kerela Attacks Roy." In general, both cases against Roy challenged the bourgeois commodification of Indian subalterns and local communities for global audiences. Local and regional discourses further criticized the national intelligentsia's (Roy's and Shekhar Kapur's) right to speak for cultural minorities.[22] They exemplify local limits placed on the national and transnational circulation of local subjects and their communities.

The postcoloniality of some of these responses becomes particularly evident in the one rather striking difference between the national and transnational circulation of the Renaissance, Roy, and India. Many accounts of the Roy-Booker jubilee event in the national press underlined literary popularity as made by the market, in a cynical gaze on the commercialization of culture under globalization. Where the global North-based depictions of Roy primarily focused on her contribution to a global *cultural* fund, Indian national critics demonstrated an extreme awareness of the *financial* underpinnings of celebrity. An excerpt from *India Today* typifies the kind of national coverage that she received:

It was too true to be an Indian fairytale. From the moment the manuscript of Roy's 340-page debut novel *The God of Small Things* was bought by Flamingo (a division of the publishing giant HarperCollins) for Rs. 3.5 crore, there was the bristle of eternity around the book. From the middle of last year, when literary agent David Godwin landed up in the barsati Roy and her husband

_____ *Figure 3*_____
Cover of *India Today* celebrating Arundhati Roy's Booker triumph, 27 October 1997:
"The Princess of Prose."
Courtesy *India Today.*

Pradip Krishen inhabit in Delhi's Chanakyapuri, there was a sweet tinkle of cash too. Roy's tally to date: approximately Rs. 5 crore [$10,000]. (B. John 1997, 28)

A few paragraphs later, the author returns to the question of money. Other articles in local presses obliquely approach the same issue by detailing the novel's publication history. For instance, the *Statesman*'s coverage of the Booker event painstakingly plodded through the particulars of international rights (sold to HarperCollins), national rights (the first book from the publishing house India Ink), literary agents, and monetary transactions (Wagner 1997).

In an *India Today* article, "Patriotism, Inc.," where South Asian writing in English is featured as one marketable item among others that commemorate the golden jubilee, perceptions of this corporate cannibalism of a revolutionary historical moment are laced with sarcasm. The author begins by noting that the corporate world takes advantage of history-making occasions as just another "mega-event": "In 1996 it was cricket's World Cup. This year it is patriotism which is corporate India's flavour of the season" (Bhandare 1997, 47). Later there is further opprobrium of "the efforts to cash in on the India-50 dividend [which] ranged from the banal to the extraordinary" (46). Foreign companies managed to sell products that so far had faced formidable domestic competitors: Corum, a Swiss watch manufacturer, sold a 0.4 million rupee limited-edition gold watch, while Cadbury Schweppes invited consumers to pop champagne bottles at midnight. Domestic companies, too, made merry: HMV overdosed on patriotic songs, Penguin on new Indian novels, and the Imperial hotel embarked on a four-million-rupee restoration project and offered discounts to anyone who could dig out a single British Indian currency note. Pictures of the commemorative objects with large price tags on them surround the text, drawing attention to the jubilee's commercial value (47). Unlike the *New York Times* exultation over the prodemocracy potentials of a global cultural economy, the writer of "Patriotism, Inc." was cynical about the possibilities of this emerging commercialism: "Gandhiji would never have approved. But it's 50 years too late to worry about that" (47). Here was a clear national perception of the consumer logic of flexible capital that could transform a revolutionary politics into a readily available commodity. The reference to a forgotten Gandhian moment implied a revaluation of India's promise at the dawn of independence, at the "midnight hour when the world slept" (Nehru 1997). This was not the fetishistic production of national identity but a demystified postcolonial gaze on the global cultural arena, one that noted the transformation of the citizen-subject into the consumer-subject. Such a gaze signals those local struggles over the production of modernity that are the focus of cosmopolitical writing.

In fact some national responses took the unraveling of nation as their primary concern. Predominantly in the global North-based presses, interviewers and commentators grappled with the task of understanding the object, that other world/nation as refracted through the gaze of its Renaissance writers. Yet in the national press this was a historic moment of self-interrogation for the constitution of this celebrated object, a chance to reflect on the relationship between nation and its cultural imaginary. For instance, Swapan Dasgupta noted that "the tepidness" of the fifty-year celebrations "stems from the fact that 'official' India does not know what to celebrate." The statist version of "India at fifty" is a "damp squib"—"*their* India is not [after all] *our* India." Dasgupta goes on to claim that popular films of 1997 did more toward suturing a national imaginary than the fetish that is the "India" of official nationalism (1997b).[23]

Certainly this rumination on nation is relevant for an occasion lauding the winning of sovereignty. Yet the preoccupation with constructing the nation in the face of rapidly collapsing cultural borders was indicative, I would argue, of more. It bespoke a larger progressive critique of nationalizing cultural projects forged against the social imaginary of democratic self-rule.[24] Of course, such an argument finds little support among some Marxist critics of globalism, who largely treat nation-states as violent arbiters of capital, and nationalism as a largely antagonistic reaction to global flows (Jameson 1998). But as we have seen, some of this rethinking of nation has been in the eye of the storm in the South Asian context in the last two decades. We see such commitment to democratic self-rule in some scholarly discourses of the jubilee. In the critical commemoration of the fifty-year celebration, *Wages of Freedom*, edited by Partha Chatterjee, which featured luminaries in social, economic, and cultural theory such as Prabhat Patnaik, Achin Vanaik, Madhav Prasad, Kancha Illaiah, Sudipto Kaviraj, and Tapati Guhathakurta, there is a concerted effort to make sense of India's present state of the union, and to critically explore its "historical possibilities in the real world of politics" (1998a, 17). Chatterjee locates his comments on these "historical possibilities" under the heading "Freedom Not to Choose" in a rather pointed disavowal of "free choice" ideologies spewed by the proponents of globalism intent on turning all Indians, regardless of access or income, into good consumers. Here Chatterjee elaborates on his vision of democratic promise in "political society," a reconceptualization of relations between the nation and its constituent populations.[25] Most other contributors to *Wages of Freedom*, too, draw our attention to the vast Indian populations left out of the equation, historically during the Nehru and Indira Gandhi regimes, and currently in "globalized" India. These populations cannot afford to give up on the nation-state, they argue, but that state itself requires rigorous political and cultural intervention.

So far I have attempted to illustrate how posteighties South Asian writing in English is abstracted into a commodity in the jubilee discourses. Given the unevenness of globalization in the postcolonies, I have further pursued the political implications of a more cynical gaze on these celebrations of the Renaissance that attempts to arrest global perceptions but often produces a reified local or national perspective as a result. The differences in the circulation of the Renaissance that are shored up in this comparative study of reception contexts are rather illuminating. We see exactly how (and why) writers and texts are abstracted and evaluated in these cultures of circulation, and how these cultures inflect literary value. The self-reflexive cosmopolitical writers attempt to arbitrate these discrepant values, with considerable literary consequence.

Critical Cosmopolitics

Part of my project enacts literary-critical and linguistic analyses of five key cosmopolitical novelists for reasons that I have cited in my introductory remarks. There I briefly allude to my departure from criticism that settles on identifying vertical literary traditions as its primary objective. Now I pause on this extant criticism to demarcate the critical contours of this project more sharply. The painstaking consolidation of a literary tradition is most apparent, I have argued, in the generational rhetoric that dominates discussions of the "Indian novel in English." Posteighties writers are more often than not referred to as "Rushdie's children," a descriptor worn as a badge of honor by Rushdie himself and repeated often in critical circles. In his interview with Swapan Dasgupta during the jubilee celebrations, Rushdie, characteristically, underscored his own fatherly status: "I now think there is a beginning . . . a group of writers younger than myself, many of whom have only one or two books. They may well have their best books in front of them. There is a kind of a *buzz* around this literature and any publisher, anybody in the world of books, will tell you that you cannot fake that buzz" (Rushdie 1997e, 89; my emphasis). Report of the "buzz" echoed in transnational spheres, with Adrienne Johnson describing Arundhati Roy's Booker win with the following blurb: "First-time Novelist Arundhati Roy Has Created a Buzz" (1997, 84). Given the velocities of global circulation, this assertion, self-aggrandizing as it is, has passed into common parlance. For instance, an *India Today* address from the editor-in-chief, in the 2002 issue on new Indian writers in English, echoes the earlier interview, alluding to the "buzz following Indian writers in English." Alongside the echo, the address further visually cites the *India Today* cover with Roy reigning as "the princess of prose" (figure 3).

Elsewhere, Rushdie's "fatherhood" meets critical approval. In his anniversary piece in the *New Republic*, James Wood, for one, sums up Rushdie's influence in the following way: "He was central to the new power of Indian fiction in English, so dominating that he gobbled up his predecessors, who seem like clouds to his sun" (1997, 32). And in her positioning of Rushdie as literary progenitor, Josna Rege argues that Rushdie radically reconfigured the relationship between the "Self" and the "Nation." He thus enabled Indian writers in English to think beyond the binary trap of preeighties Indo-Anglian writing.[26] In characterizing the "Post-Rushdie" novels of the 1980s as "national narratives," Rege sees the onrush of new narrations as the record of a watershed, writings that are literary markers for "the post-Emergency crisis in the Indian national idea" (1997, 187).

But looking at the writers is only a part of this project. Throughout the book I argue against treating contemporary literary production within the framework of self-evident literary traditions. A strictly vertical nation-state-oriented analysis that places literary texts under the banner of national traditions cannot lead us to evaluate exactly how literary value is produced on a global market hungry for these neatly packaged commodities. Thus my critical venture is somewhat different from present postcolonial literary analyses of Indian writing in English: from monographs such as Fawzia Afzal-Khan's *Cultural Imperialism in the Indo-English Novel* (1996) or Meenakshi Mukherjee's *Twice-born Fiction* (1971) and *Perishable Empire* (2000) that read South Asian writers in dialectical relation to each other and to their Anglo antecedents;[27] and from collections such as Vinay Kirpel's *The Postmodern Indian English Novel* (1998) that provide exemplary individual readings of literary experimentation in the posteighties Indian novel in English, but where no consolidated vocabulary emerges for considering these texts together as a distinctive literary practice.

Leela Gandhi's essay on the new South Asian writers partly represents the kind of work with which I would align this project. Gandhi notes the "deliciously 'win-win' situation" of the new "postcolonial" Indian novelist, one whose "enviable position of privilege and dissent" is rendered possible through critical discourses that assign counter-hegemonic status to this writing (1998, 1).[28] Drawing our attention to how literary value is constituted, she refutes the idea of a "Stephanian school of writing" (with Roy as its star) as a self-evident aesthetic designation; in fact this rubric is the mark of cultural capital for a certain class of metropolitan intellectuals who overtly position themselves in opposition to elite North-based literary circles (2). Her attention to the circuits of cultural globalism that underwrite literary value is the kind of analysis that I hope to bring to our lauded practice, the Renaissance.[29] Of course there are some monographic accounts of Indian English writing as it emplaces national subjects, such as Rumina Sethi's book on Rushdie, *Myths of Nation* (1999), and Teresa Hubel's perusal of the fictionalized freedom struggle in *Whose India* (1996). But these analyses of the characters and myths constitutive of national identity still remain primarily focused on literary production.

I hope to cast the net wider. First, in exploding the privileged categorization of postcolonial literary traditions, readers are borne across disciplines: The literary is placed alongside historical, sociological, ethnographic, and political discourses, which together seek to produce a minoritarian modernity. And second, in establishing the circulation of this literary practice, I shift part of the cosmopolitan responsibility for literary activism to the site of reading: To what extent does the reader (and cultural critic) bear the responsibility for cosmopolitical acts? To what respect do constant cultural translations of the local and the vernacular intervene in the global hierarchies of knowledge production?

The nature of these inquiries leads me to consolidate an archive not restricted to the novels and to literary criticism, but one that incorporates critical, journalistic, and other popular discourses across media (interviews, commentaries, advertisements, magazine covers) that influence our reading of the novels. This attention to comparative production and reception contexts impels me to locate postcolonial studies within the larger configuration that is transnational cultural studies, a move that is seen as politically efficacious for the study of cultural globalism (an ongoing effort in the journal *Public Culture*). To this end I align my work with contemporary intellectual projects that stipulate the postcolonial as one kind of critical gaze on the present global cultural arena. Some pertinent examples are two anthologies, Kuan-Hsing Chen's "inter-Asia cultural studies" volume, *Trajectories,* published in 2000 and named after the two conferences that brought together a number of international scholars at the Center for Asia-Pacific/Cultural Studies at the National Tsing Hua University, Taiwan; and Richard Dienst and Henry Schwarz's North-based *Reading the Shape of the World* (1996).

Kuan-Hsing Chen is chiefly concerned with the promise of cultural studies for ex-colonial cultures. The challenge to universal propositions that cultural studies poses in its recovery of the local historical, not to mention the cultural studies will to combat hegemonic national and global forces, makes it a particularly useful model for the continuing war against "multiple structures of global domination": "The decolonization task of a postcolonial/cultural studies would then be to deconstruct, decenter, deform, debunk, and disarticulate the colonial cultural imaginary, and to reconstruct, rearticulate, reconnect a more democratic kind of imaginative lines of flight" (2000, 29). Chen offers a fair description of my bifocal reading of the Renaissance as both a global commodity and a political intervention into aggrandizing globalism and nationalism. Dienst and Schwarz also propose a move toward internationalizing cultural studies that, in their estimation, is crucial for arresting imperialistic global flows harnessed to dominant military and financial interests. They insist that "cultural critics who know how to do things with images" should habitually interrupt the "epistemologically secure and politically deadening" dominant transmissions in the global imaginary (1996, 5).

I extend these commentaries on postcolonial critical practice in developing a notion of performative localism. The necessary textual migrations into the local privileged by the cosmopolitical writers' overt localizing strategies insist on an interactive textual politics. From the cultural critic they demand translation and, to some extent, vernacular restoration. This implies that a fair amount of labor is required for reading these cosmopolitical texts. For instance, in chapter 5 when I analyze the relationship of vernacular ghost fiction to *The Calcutta Chromosome*—notably, Rabindranath Tagore's "Kshudhita Pashaan" and Phanishwar Nath Renu's "Smells of a Primeval Night"—I demonstrate the difficulties of vernacular restoration. The Tagore story is quite easily available, but the Renu story was a rare find after a month of digging. When taken seriously, the invitation to migrate, then, demands considerable intellectual labor.

Such a task is advocated by critics preoccupied by recessive local knowledges in contemporary globality. In *Out of Place: Englishness, Empire, and the Locations of Identity*, Ian Baucom (1999) insists that we counter the "nostalgic celebrations of the local" (what I name "fetishistic localism") with a commitment to recessive "global cultural vernaculars"—local idioms of the sort that Rushdie foregrounds in *The Satanic Verses*. Baucom's spatial metaphor envisions the translation of local knowledges as an active conjoining of the familiar hearth with its (postcolonial) *unheimlich*, a politics of postcolonial migrancy that renews England. But to underline the violence of translation that makes the local globally communicable, I describe such acts of conjoining as "cultural grafting"—the suture on the skin of text ever a reminder of incommensurable local idioms, transmuted but always in process when being borne across. Despite my divergence from Baucom, his point on the regenerative power of translation or textual migrations is well taken, for in the Benjaminian sense the translation ensures the "continued life of the original" (Benjamin 1923, 16). Thus I emphasize contingent cultural translations as efficacious postcolonial literary cosmopolitics.

The current global hierarchies of knowledge that frame the beleaguered acts of translation demand such a readerly cosmopolitics. Much has been said on translation lately, so I will restrict myself to a few comments pertinent to my own critical acts and those of the cosmopolitical writers.[30] In her introduction to the *Public Culture* issue "Translation on the Global Market," Emily Apter highlights some of the problems of cultural translation and cautions us against the assumed political neutrality of these acts. Translators engender cultural currencies, warns Apter, and therefore the greater the need for sustained attention to their role as arbiters of a putative international canon (2001, 2–3). Some of the contributors to this issue record viable means for writers and artists to resist the linguistic hierarchies of the global marketplace. Michael North's perusal of "rotten English" as an act of political resistance and Rainer Ganahal's evocation of "auditory strangeness" in linguistic transfers speak to the projects of the cosmopolitical writers—the vernacularization of English that both "breaks" the standardized tongue and registers the awkwardness of an other syntax. Other contributors like Gayatri Spivak and Timothy Brennan flesh out Apter's reservations about critics' translation of other worlds on the global market, both linguistic transfers and the implicit cultural translation of "reading" vernacular and supplemental knowledge.[31]

In my migratory politics of reading, I try to shore up my own critical limits whenever possible. This edges close to Kalpana Seshadri-Crooks's stipulation of critical practices in her "preoccupation" with the current melancholia of postcolonial studies. Seshadri-Crooks valorizes supplementarity in spatial terms: a margin that is the "irreducible remainder—that which is necessarily excluded by every regime of power/knowledge" (2000, 13). In her view, the postcolonial look must always register the mark of the incommensurable and the nonrecuperable, even in the process of translating these local knowledges for global consumption. Throughout the book, then, I highlight my own moments of critical failure in acts of cultural translation. For instance, in not being able to access the idiomatic untranslated Malayalam in Roy's work, I foreground that irreducible supplementarity of Roy's linguistic localism that undercuts my "specialized" knowledge as postcolonial critic in the North-based academy.

Given this critical landscape, *When Borne Across* finally seeks to establish cultural translation as constant motility. The "when" of the title connotes the everyday and performative aspect of the cultural migrations required of the critic. Performative cultural translation both deconstructs the essentialized "native informant" position and recognizes the limited arc of the critic's gaze. For instance, in chapter 3, I discuss one of Upamanyu Chatterjee's experiments in Bengali-English that draws on the *spoken* grammatical registers of Bengali; and in my elucidation of vernacular literary traditions in chapter 5, we see how Amitav Ghosh draws from Bengali literature (ghost fiction) in the uncanny narration of *The Calcutta Chromosome*. But these two examples precisely illustrate the unevenness of my own acts of translation. As a Bengali speaker I am able more substantially to decode Chatterjee and Ghosh than I am Roy's Malayalam-English. So finally, my linguistic limitation not only undercuts my efficacy as cultural translator, but also governs my choice of literary examples.

Two

Passages and Passports

Globalism, Language, Migration

In a Call Center College, hundreds of young English-speaking Indians are being groomed to staff the backroom operations of giant transnational companies. They are trained to answer telephone queries from the United States and the United Kingdom (on subjects ranging from credit card inquiry to advice about a malfunctioning washing machine or the availability of cinema tickets). On no account must the caller know that his or her inquiry is being attended to by an Indian sitting at a desk on the outskirts of Delhi. . . . The Call Center Colleges train their students to speak in American and British accents. They have to read foreign papers so that they can chitchat about the news or the weather. On duty they have to change their given names. Sushma becomes Susie, Govind becomes Jerry, Advani becomes Andy.
—Arundhati Roy, Power Politics

So goes Arundhati Roy's sardonic sketch of a corporate reach that transforms quotidian forms of postcolonial life. Linguistic demand now makes good corporate citizens of Indians, albeit of a certain class ("English-speaking") and age. Since "older employees" might find the nocturnal hours difficult (a requirement for U.S.-based companies), Roy notes, the call centers prefer younger workers. Service-sector employees, these workers are paid "one-tenth of the salaries of their counterparts abroad" (2001, 84). In this emergent global landscape, English, the tongue that has ever had the power to nationally and globally emplace the Indian modern subject, finds renewal as once more the passage to becoming "global."

It is against this "global English" that cosmopolitical writers pitch their local-izing linguistic praxis. They fracture any prevailing standardized literary English with the specific aim of grounding English use in local contexts. At the same time, the writers facilitate new passages to India in their wide cosmopol-itan address, making the most of the excitement over different global Englishes. And in their creation of specific English vernaculars, the cosmopolitical writers target heterogeneous markets: They demand cultural passports for linguistic migrations—privileged knowledge of local vernacular resonance—from regional, local, and translocal readers. Such practices of attachment are glob-alism's localisms and do not necessarily constitute a progressive intervention into linguistic globalism. How then to evaluate these cosmopolitical practices of localism? How to separate the market success of cosmopolitical novels from their progressive politics?

I suspect the answers lie in our ability to situate these literary acts within the larger intellectual debates that concern, enthuse, or mortify these cosmopolit-ical writers. Two discursive contexts seem particularly relevant to our literary practice at hand: the furor over globalization, and its corollary, linguistic glob-alism. Here I attempt to carve out the intellectual terrain that the cosmopoliti-cal writers traverse in their literary experiments, positioning this terrain at a historical juncture marked by large structural changes in markets, media, and migration. The cosmopolitical writers remain critically cognizant of these changes, quite vociferously engaging in the cultures of circulation constituted by (and constitutive of) contemporary South Asian writing in English.

Wrenching Circulation

Joining dissenting voices against certain aggrandizing global flows, the South Asian cosmopolitical writers actively enter into conversations on their own circulation and currency. We shall see how they deliberately attempt to con-strain, buttress, or manipulate the refracted image of the glamorous South Asian writer in English filtered in print culture and in audiovisual mass media. The glamour of the Indian writer in English, of course, has a long and some-times difficult history in the postcolony. That historical anguish comes home to roost in the brouhaha over the Renaissance. We see this quite plainly at moments of fracture when a celebratory event, like the ICCR Indian writers fes-tival of February 2002, can turn sour because of the embattled status of Indian writing in English as an "Indian" tradition. Many regional writers at the festival complained of the "unfair advantage" that English had over the Indian vernac-ulars. "Just like a fair-skinned woman has in our society," surmised Bengali Sunil Gangopadhyay, alluding to the colonial clout of English that has been ever a sore point in the subcontinent (Ramaswamy 2002). Gangopadhyay has had his own brush with cultural globalism in a lawsuit (brought by his publisher in 2000) against the internationally known Deepa Mehta. Mehta had reportedly "plagiarized" (or used without permission or acknowledgment) Gangopadhyay's tale of a young Bengali widow (from *Those Days*) in Mehta's screenplay for *Water*. In that encounter with the global scavenging of regional literary archives, Gangopadhyay had done the generous thing: He had allowed the film to proceed.

Gangopadhyay's irritation at the fêted IWE was equally matched by that of other regional writers at the meet. "The IWE come from a rich circle which has money to buy books," grumbled Punjabi writer Gurdial Singh. "It's all a commercialized industry: a publisher gets his books reviewed in English magazines and newspapers, then it becomes a status symbol for people who read these journals to buy that book even if it costs Rs.500 or Rs.1,000" (Ramaswamy 2002). By such commentary, Singh signaled the thriving culture of circulation that underwrites South Asian writing in English. Cosmopolitical writers who take these accusations of commercialism seriously, then, must necessarily reexamine the language in which they make their bread and butter—English.

English has ever had anomalous status in postcolonial India. Historically the "outsider's tongue," it had marked the colonial subject as a privileged yet alienated migrant. It was also always a concept-metaphor for linguistic hegemony, a language apposite to the Indian "vernaculars"—the colonial category for the eighteen recognized Indian regional languages. It is in this context that I attempt to situate the new claim on localized English as a vernacular (thus reappropriating the term), one perhaps more organic to heterogeneous Indian contexts than Hindi (a dominant language refueled by the nationalizing linguistic drive of the Hindu right). I argue that English is now the insider's tongue, a distended space of linguistic migration from the global to the local.

In the cosmopolitical novels, each protagonist's direct engagement with the idea that language is constitutive of one's social relation to the world frames the particular English vernacular. They imply that global standard literary English affords only subjective alienation. A localized English, however, properly offers the postcolonial subject recompense. Further, the cosmopolitical writers quite self-reflexively foreground the process of constructing an English vernacular for each locale sketched in the novels. These locales, like Roy's Ayemenem, are linguistically layered worlds in which an idiomatic Malayalam English becomes an everyday performance rather than a stable language. It is the self-conscious constructedness of these English vernaculars that makes each performance of language use temporary, contingent, and irreducible to any other context. There is no stable linguistic world to which one returns in full-blown nostalgia.

Passages to India

The cosmopolitical writers render India "communicable" to a global audience, acting as cultural translators who cater to a global market for world Englishes. This literary production of Indian locales and subjects is partly annexed to economic communicational globalism. Progressive politics notwithstanding, the celebrated Renaissance that fuels the circulation of these literary texts became possible because of India's gradual economic liberalization since the late eighties. Recent data show how new financial networks created the conditions for the outpouring of writing from the subcontinent. Languishing national publishing houses such as Rupa and Ananda Bazaar Patrika have merged with HarperCollins and Penguin to become multinational conglomerates with considerable clout. Foreign investors anticipated a huge readership for English books. As David Davidar, chief editor of Penguin India, notes: "Books published by Penguin had been selling in India for over 50 years, and selling well, too. It was Peter Mayer, chairman of Penguin books, who deduced from this that there must be a large readership for general books in English, both fiction and non-fiction, in India and decided to set up a company here. The company would both publish for a home market and serve as an outpost to find writers for the international market. In Ananda Bazaar's Aveek Sarkar, he found a perfect partner. Both were, in a sense, visionaries" ("Area of Brightness" 1998). And those visions were made possible by the economic reforms that allowed multinational corporations such as Penguin to enter into joint ventures with Indian corporations, and to be taxed at the much lower domestic rate. Penguin India's success in publishing Indian writers in English soon became legendary. By 1995 the press had featured fifteen debuts and was publishing ten titles in Indian writing in English on the average every month (Bahal 1995). By 2002 *Outlook* reported five hundred titles—fifty a year!—from Penguin India, born of the happy marriage of "desi" (home) talent to "pardesi" (abroad) capital (Bibliofile 2002). The huge structural changes in the publishing industry made it feasible for South Asian writers in English to now write for an English-speaking audience both at home and abroad.[1] Earlier South Asian writers in English, such as R. K. Narayan, were widely published abroad, but only sporadically in India.

Such free-market expansionism was regarded with alarm by commentators on globalism. Some of these critiques of globalism constitute the intellectual terrain for the cosmopolitical writers' postcolonial reworking of the national-global dialectic. One lucid account of India's economic globalization is found in Amit Bhaduri and Deepak Nayyar's popular and widely read *Intelligent Person's Guide to Liberalisation*.[2] Bhaduri and Nayyar explain that it was India's external debt crisis of 1991 that propelled the government to introduce a number of reforms, a stabilization program guided by the economic policy of the International Monetary Fund (IMF), which raised $1.8 billion to prevent India from defaulting on debt payments. The reforms included dismantling a complex set of controls both in industrial licensing and in trade taxes and tariffs. By September 1992, the government had decided to allow foreign institutional investors to enter the stock market. A corresponding set of public-sector reforms were set in motion, and a policy regime for foreign investment and foreign technology was set up to accommodate multinational investment in India—now with full realization that India was particularly attractive to foreign investors because of its wealth of natural resources and low labor costs, and its contribution to technological research and development.[3]

As progressive economists, Bhaduri and Nayyar perceive these reforms, reflecting the "orthodox wisdom" of the IMF and World Bank, as somewhat short-sighted—particularly the IMF's reliance on market logic to bring equilibrium to the country, at the cost of financing state-regulated long-term development objectives essential in countries with large poor populations. When the marketplace is arbiter of stability and economic mobility, they argue, those with greater purchasing power will always control political goals. In societies with large-scale gaps between the rich and poor, reason the authors, the underprivileged cannot afford to give up on the state to protect their interests. In short: "While better quality consumer goods are highly desirable, we must show a sense of proportion. They are not and cannot be the highest priority for our society. Better cars are desirable, but surely better buses for our public transport system, which provide comfort to passengers and cause less pollution on the roads, are more so. Cellular phones and better soft drinks are desirable, but surely better quality ploughs or pump-sets to irrigate land and provide safe drinking water are more so. We could multiply these examples" (1996, 7). In arguing that the poor cannot afford to give up on the democratic state, Bhaduri and Nayyar invoke Pheng Cheah's premise that in postcolonial contexts the nation-state can still be seen as a strategic, and perhaps contingent, bulwark against neocolonial encroachment.

We find such emphases everywhere in economic analyses of globalism originating in the global South, tracts that are part of the discursive context for the cosmopolitical novels. Writing about India's economic liberalization, Ajit Roy stressed needful attention to the global North-South divide despite all the deterritorializing effects of globalization. Observing the political dangers of the emergent transnational landscapes, he underlined the close alliance of multinational corporations with centers of financial credit based in the global North. Flexing financial muscle through global networks such as the IMF, these corporations can now "bypass the regulations of national states and can manipulate the movement of finance, credit and various other resources" for their own gains (1995, 2006). Given cheap labor and lax pollution laws in the developing world, multinational corporations such as Enron (whose tussle with the Maharashtrian government I examine in chapter 4) relegate most of their manufacturing functions to the developing world, while the service sector is largely located in the developed world. The lion's share of profits is fueled back to the global North through the service sector. Ajit Roy describes a divide implicitly acknowledged by progressive global North-based social theorists concerned over the renewed draining of the South by the ex-colonial and neocolonial North. Fredric Jameson's and Masao Miyoshi's commentaries exemplify some of these critiques that target global capital flows originating in the global North. Miyoshi (1995), for instance, has painstakingly pointed out that, for the majority of the earth's 5.5 billion inhabitants, globalization has offered only overpopulation, poverty, and civil violence.

Such a critique acquires postcolonial valence in other, less known, voices. A particularly trenchant example may be found in Ziauddin Sardar's *Postmodernism and the Other*, often regarded as a perspective on globalism from the global South. Sardar has peculiar relevance to our analysis when we remember him as the British Islamic scholar who wrote a book-length "reply to Rushdie" during the *Satanic Verses* controversy (Sardar and Davis 1990). In *Postmodernism and the Other*, Sardar provides specific instantiation of the pernicious effects of globalization for non-Western countries in the cataclysmic transformations of people's work, life, and habitats. For instance, the economic cannibalism of corporate multinationals has wreaked havoc on indigenous medical practices. To make his case, Sardar examines the uproar over the *neem* case, in which U.S.-based multinationals attempted to patent this medicinal plant used in folk medicine all over India and some parts of Africa, and the consumer targeting of Body Shop that recycles folk remedies in skin and hair products. His elucidation of biopiracy finds support from other postcolonial activists like Rustom Barucha, who documents the eco-feminist resistance to corporate piracy that mobilizes nongovernmental forms of international alliance (1994a, 1). Arundhati Roy joins this growing alarm over subaltern populations left out of the new world order in a poignant portrait of the "cost of living" in globalizing India: "In a lane behind my house, every night I walk past road gangs of emaciated laborers digging a trench to lay fiber-optic cables to speed up our digital revolution. In the bitter winter cold, they work by the light of a few candles" (2002b, 16).

In this condemnation of economic globalism, cultural globalism receives a fair share of attention. Given fundamental dissymmetries in the global economy, world cultures serve an apprenticeship to U.S. mass culture and to the English language. Cultural globalism, or what is often understood as "cultural imperialism," for much of the world has largely meant Americanization. Fredric Jameson underscores the economic drive of cultural flows in his analysis of the GATT meetings, where the opening of quota barriers on Hollywood films in foreign countries nakedly exposed the economic expansionism of U.S. cultural policies.[4] Sardar concretizes this observation: "One doesn't see an Indian Michael Jackson, a Chinese Madonna, a Malaysian Arnold Schwarzenegger, a Morrocan Julia Roberts, Filipino 'New Kids on the Block,' a Brazilian Shakespeare, an Egyptian Barbara Cartland, a Tanzanian *Cheers*, a Nigerian *Dallas*, a Chilean *Wheel of Fortune*, or Chinese opera, Urdu poetry, Egyptian drama etc. on the global stage" (1998, 22). And when non-Western products do reach the global stage, they are often expensive global commodities unavailable to those very cultures they seek to represent. Citing the example of Peter Brooks's *Mahabharata*, fashioned "within an orientalist framework of representation endorsed by the Indian government as part of its propagation of "festival culture" in the world," Barucha scathingly notes that no one in India saw this much-touted production, as it was too expensive to "transport" back home (1994b, 106).

The general fear of cultural globalism that frames reconsiderations of the national-global dialectic explodes on the Indian scene following the gradual privatization of television. As early as 1989, Arvind Singhal and Everett Rogers published *India's Information Revolution,* cataloging the dominance of public culture by electronic media. In a country of eight hundred million, with approximately 65 per cent illiterate, electronic media has the distinct advantage over print. Television access (but not viewing) grew from 167 million in 1981 to 500 million in 1988 (62 percent of the population). While the Asian Games of 1982 had 156 million viewers, by 1988 Purnima Mankekar (1999) notes a jump to 500 million viewers. The big change, notes Lloyd Rudolph, came in 1983 when the satellite INSAT-B was launched; the satellite broadcast television signals to ground stations which could then rebroadcast them to surrounding areas. By 1989 Doordarshan, the state-sponsored televisual organization created in 1977, had transformed electoral politics from party-based campaigns to U.S.-style national televisual addresses, and Rajiv Gandhi became India's first TV prime minister, reaching 62 percent of the population on television and fulfilling his mother's dream of making television an instrument of mass persuasion and political influence (Rudolph 1992, 1489). Ironically, television received a boost again in 1990, not from the strengthening of state controls, but from the privatization of television channels. The Prashar Bharati bill that argued for functional autonomy for a national broadcasting enterprise was passed in May 1990 (an early version had languished since its introduction in 1979).

With economic liberalization well under way, and the Internet revolution on the horizon, by the early nineties hitherto "foreign" popular and mass cultural forms became part of quotidian Indian life. The dominance of U.S. channels on Indian television (often featuring Hollywood films dubbed in Hindi or the regional languages) made it possible to sell the U.S. way of life to an avid Indian public. After the privatization of televisual media, India it seemed had become satellite crazed, and signs of extraterrestrial national life were everywhere. Consider, for instance, the Amul butter advertisement that appeared in the golden jubilee issue of *India Today* (figure 4). The little-girl icon of the Amul butter ads was beloved by the nation's middle-class consumers through the seventies and eighties, alluring them with promises of nationally manufactured "foreign" food items ("Kraft cheese") in a protectionist economy. In those decades Amul advertisements featured witty asides on national and local issues, presided over by the little girl. She lit sparklers for Diwali, the national festival of lights; mourned the loss of the Indian Airlines maharajah icon; slopped butter on the Mumbai street food Pau-bhaji; played delightedly with the popular god "Ganapati-moriya"; and spoofed Bollywood hits like *Pati, Patni, Aur Wo* (see *www.amul.com* for visuals). In many ways, her shenanigans were an index of prevailing national concerns and debates. In the 1997 advertisement featured here, her attention has turned toward new galaxies, with butter and cheese— "the taste of India"—relegated to a small logo in the left-hand corner of the visual display. Also unmistakable is the advertisement's address to the "global Indian" in the coy play on an "ellite connection," alongside the national essentializing of a "dish" that works better than cheap but readily available new technologies (notice the comically frazzled satellite in the right-hand corner).

More importantly, changes in televisual address now transformed linguistic terrain. In "The Channel Babble," an article in the 9 September 1995 *Times of India*, Bharat Bhushan points out a negative effect of televisual languages now inflected by marketing paradigms. Noting the prevalence of channel babble in the Hindi spoken on television, Bhushan sketched the creation of new exclusions and inclusions in Hindi language communities that did not exist before. The sea change in language use finds further explication in Peggy Mohan's analysis of the morphing "four-tier" language structure in India (1995, 887). The distinctions between tribal languages, the dialects of village India, the standardized regional languages of the economic epicenters of large regions, and English (the language of a "literate" city culture) had stabilized with televisual address. Given economic liberalization, the English-speaking layer had clearly expanded, but quite paradoxically, English was less and less solely a metropolitan language. It had become a more dispersed and interpenetrative vehicle for global-local communications.

_____ *Figure 4* _____
Advertisement for Amul butter from *India Today*, 27 October 1997: "The Shut-ellite Connection."
Courtesy Amul.

To "be Indian" in the merging marketplace was also to "write English," said one enthusiast, insisting that information and capital flows had radically changed the vertical hierarchies of English use in India ("Be Indian" 1997). Emphasizing the emergence of new linguistic pathways, this commentator pitches the national consensus "to globalize" in this way: To survive "in today's world," India "must absorb the capacity to exist at various planes—local, national, and global." In such an equation, English is the linguistic pathway to new jobs, goods, and information—the language of global exchange. Taking this linguistic pulse, the *Times of India* headlined an article on 27 March 1996: "English Has Become Asia's Language of Opportunity." The Asia Pacific Economic Corporation Forum and Association of South-East Asian Nations, after all, uses English for its interactions, as do customs officers, air traffic controllers, and technicians. Given the renewed economic muscle, census data from the late eighties showed that of 2.4 million urban workers in India, more than half, approximately 1.7 million, were employed in jobs requiring a working knowledge of English (Sen 1995, 654).[5] Cataloging the new "linguistic cacophony" in India, the golden-jubilee issue of *India Today* claimed English to be a dominant lingua franca in the subcontinent. The publication's polls show the astounding fact that one in three Indians understands English, while at least 20 percent are confident speaking it—a monumental percentage of English speakers given India's population. No surprise though, since one of the least-documented changes in the last few decades has been a quiet revolution in newspaper consumption and distribution. Robin Jeffery carefully catalogs this revolution, offering some striking numbers. In 1976, daily circulation was calculated at 9.3 million, but 1992 saw 40.2 million (Jeffery 2000, 1).[6] English-language newspapers still continue to have the largest circulations, despite the greater numbers of Hindi speakers.

Yet my discussion of linguistic globalism and of the renewed force of English in the context of a larger cultural globalism departs from considering literary production only in terms of print circulation. The days of rational bourgeois reading publics bounded by print circulation are long gone, as we have seen in the case of the *Satanic Verses* controversy. Hence the "production of locality" by cosmopolitical South Asian writers in English is as much a part of the larger contested "public culture" as are television, billboards, calendar art, and such. Most recently, Arvind Rajagopal's meticulous investigation of the work of media in transforming national politics makes this crucial connection between electronic and print capitalism: "If the impact of newspapers may be pre-empted by radio and TV, print itself is communicated via telephone, computer, and fax, so that the gap in information velocity is narrowed. Thus the dissemination of print media may be electronic even if its forms hark back to an older era" (2001a, 155).

Rajagopal makes his point by tracking the new relations between the two dominant Indian language cultures of English and Hindi, historically alienated domains. He goes on to demonstrate how the BJP (Bharatiya Janata Party) used this "historical cleavage" to its advantage, by militant posturing in the Hindi press and feeding off frictions in the English press. As a new system of representation, television offered new circuits for the exchange between the English and Hindi language publics. This scenario has had a radical effect, Rajagopal argues, on the split publics of an "incomplete modern polity"—that is, publics stratified by language, caste, region, and sociocultural domains (2001a, 153). In the case of coverage of the Ramjanmabhumi movement, a Hindu right-wing mobilization, the chasm between the English and Hindi language publics widened in the respective language presses.[7] Yet it was television, with its large electronic public, that suddenly made these English and Hindi language publics mutually aware of each other. Now their historical frictions gained new salience.

By consistently privileging the local and the everyday, the cosmopolitical writers effectively battle the televisually consolidated univocal Hindu national culture. In her manifesto against globalization, for instance, Arundhati Roy describes the inroads of globalism as a creeping insidious force that requires minute attentiveness every day from the activist: "On the face of it, it's just ordinary business. It lacks the *drama*, the *large-format*, *epic magnificence* of war or genocide or famine. It makes *bad TV*. It has to do with boring things like jobs, money, water supply, electricity, irrigation. But it also has to do with a process of barbaric dispossession on a scale with few parallels in history. You may have guessed by now what I'm talking about is the modern version of globalization" (2002b, 16; my emphases). And Roy demands another kind of globalization: the globalizing of dissent. Her view fairly typifies the cosmopolitical writers' discomforts with cultural nationalism and globalism, and they challenge representative phenomena in their provisional linguistic localisms. The writers further indirectly participate in the debates over market-driven media in their novels, self-consciously staging narrative situations where print circulation and electronic or other visual media are often pitched against each other. As we shall see, in their often ambivalent relationships to literary cultures, the cosmopolitical writers posit a need for a larger canvas for forging collective agency against nationalism and globalism.

Also cognizant of the limitations of literary acts, generally perceived as more individual than collective performances, the writers further pose questions of reception in their novels, nonfiction, and interviews. Translocal reading constituencies and critical fraternities become the locus of anxiety, sometimes censure. These anxieties become more attenuated given increasing migratory flows, the third major structural change that historically impacts South Asian writing in English. We now turn to an overview of these changes, crucial to our understanding the cosmopolitical writers' professed politics of localism.

Cultural Passports

To some extent the localizing linguistic strategies of these cosmopolitical novels resist global unmoorings, only to reterritorialize global cultural space. Recent evocations of cultural citizenship exemplify such acts of cultural reentrenchment, although most of these accounts recuperate a progressive politics in these border drawings. As I have noted, in *Consumers and Citizens*, Nestor García Canclini, for one, insists that the complex terrain of contemporary cultural globalization demands a deconstruction of the received dichotomy between the global "consumer" (predominantly market driven) and the global "citizen" (predominantly politics driven) (2001, 20). He demonstrates how the availability of global commodities in Latin America has enabled certain political stagings of social and cultural belonging aimed at challenging the view of a common global order. Canclini, together with theorists such as May Joseph, are preoccupied with defining cultural citizenships as political, and not necessarily just reactionary, responses to migration. As a mode of participatory politics in an era of inauthentic national citizenship, the performances of cultural citizenship gesture toward alternative social imaginaries.

But other theorists, like Aihwa Ong, depart from such a utopian reading, contending that political and economic circumstances underwrite the progressive politics of cultural citizenships. Ong (1999) examines the transnational Chinese performances of cultural citizenship as elite mobilizations against the cultural discomforts over dislocation. These performances do not aim at global citizenship for everyone but seek to lodge elite Chinese transnational subjects more firmly in the networks of global capital. The migrant's relation to global flows emerges as the key issue in these conversations on the emplacing capacities of cultural performances. Taking Ong's caution seriously, I pause on the exigencies of South Asian migration, navigating recent discussions where the Indian "migrant" has often emerged as an embattled figure. The reconstitution of the Indian diaspora, now most visible in the plush figure of the NRI (the nonresident Indian), is essential for our purposes because we are in pursuit of a literary cosmopolitics aimed at dismantling the elite "global Indian" subject. As in the case of elite Chinese transnationals, contemporary debates on the elite mobile "global" *Indian* subject (to whom the moniker "cosmopolitan" often attaches, in a narrowly economic sense) circle around South Asian valences of cultural belonging urgent to diaspora cultures.

Performances of cultural belonging have ever been at the heart of inquiries into migrant cultures. A particularly fine example of scholarship on belonging is James Clifford's (1994) investigation of diasporas, which he defines as migrant cultures that share originary narratives of dispersal and metonymically reach for forms of regathering. Diasporic cultures retain attachments outside their nation-state of residence, to imaginative loci differently constituted in each case: a place, an ideology, a religion, a kinship, or a memory. And they rely on cultural practices to constitute a social imaginary of regathering. One of Clifford's major examples draws from Paul Gilroy's "black Atlantic," the transnational social imaginary where historical memory is reconstituted through written and oral texts. This return to the nation finds an echo in R. Radhakrishnan's (1996) description of contradictions in the diasporic social imaginary. While diasporic cultures are truly the nation's "other," explains Radhakrishnan, it is in this imaginary that the nation as homeland is reinvented every day.[8] These discussions compel us to consider the remaking of "nation," quixotically from the point of its dispersal—our case in point is the reinscription of "Indianness" in the "global Indian."

The dispersal of peoples is everywhere the story of globalization, and India is no exception. It is estimated that currently over ten million "Indians" live in communities outside the Indian nation-state (George 1996b, 179). In providing a history of the Indian diaspora, Robin Cohen distinguishes between the labor, trade, and imperial/colonial diaspora. Indians workers indentured in British, Dutch, and French tropical plantations from the 1830s to the 1920s invented an India that stabilized their world in relation to other hostile national and migrant groups, especially in Guyana, Fiji, Uganda, and South Africa (1997, 62). These are very different diaspora from the two other kinds of Indian diaspora emergent in the era of late capital: the migrant labor diaspora and the professional diaspora of the last twenty years. Both these groups are mobile and deterritorialized, and their existence is made possible by expanding markets, flexible manufacturing sites, cheaper forms of transportation, and communicational networks. Presenting a detailed "archaeology" of Indian diaspora, Vijay Mishra differentiates these two historically separate communities as "the old labor diaspora" and the new "border diaspora" (1996, 421). The distinction is immensely pertinent to our discussion here, because the social imaginaries of these two diasporas differ significantly: In the case of the labor diaspora, the homeland is imagined as plentitude, a purity that represses the hyphen of belonging elsewhere. But in the second case, the hyphen creates vibrant hybrid and cross-cultural spaces where British Asian *bhangra* influences Caribbean reggae and soul. Such hybridity is often read as resistance to the "controlling social, political and cultural myths" of belonging (434). It is this latter "border diaspora" that best describes the readers and writers of the cosmopolitical novels, while the migrant subjects of the texts sometimes include the labor diaspora.

Since the late eighties, the corporate global Indian as representative of the border diaspora has dominated the significations of the migrant Indian subject. We have witnessed the emergence of a new commercial elite with seasonal work abroad, creating a powerful third culture. They overlap with large-scale transversal and asynchronous flows of people visiting other worlds for study, tourism, or occasional jobs (Cohen 1997, 28). So the upwardly mobile and electronically connected migrant now defines the modern Indian subject at ease at home and in the world. Consider, for example, the figure of the successful male global Indian in a cellular communications advertisement that appeared among the jubilee discourses of 1997, one of many such images (see figure 5). Here there are emphatic references to a "one-world culture," while the colonial-Moorish architecture of Mumbai situates the corporate cell-phone-wielding employee in a specific Indian metropolitan locale. The idea of the global Indian is encrypted in the third blurb on the right: Sunil Bhatt's corporate credentials are impeccable in subscribing to "World 1 National Roaming."

The global Indian represents a growing network of mobile migrants, more nomadic than ever, who differ widely in interest and affiliation from the poor migrant laborers working for global North-based manufacturers (employed in sweatshops, factories, or fruit-picking units, for example), or sex workers who drift between borders—those migrant networks that comprise Saskia Sassen's "discontents" of globalization (1998).[9] The category of the "cosmopolitan" comes to define these elite mobile transnationals, categorically demarcating them from the equally mobile but disenfranchised subjects of globalization (these migrant workers, but also refugees and illegal immigrants). The latter often have little control over either their travels or their living and working conditions.

_____ *Figure 5* _____
Advertisement for World 1 Roaming *India Today*, 27 October 1997: "A World of Just One Number."
Courtesy One World Cellular

When used in this narrowly economic sense, "cosmopolitan" masks crucial ideological disjunctures within mobile diaspora and other transnational cultures. The progressive intellectuals and activists who practice a situated cosmopolitics may overlap in lifestyles and location with the national and global Indian elites. Yet they do not necessarily share the ideological frameworks of these elites, especially the corporate advocates of free-market fundamentalism. The latter "new" cosmopolitan, sometimes referred to as the "critical cosmopolitan," habitually attacks and attempts to destabilize the emplacing capacities of a given "majority" culture, national and global. I reserve the term "cosmopolitan" for these latter politically heterogeneous migrant cultures. The distinction requires highlighting here because more often than not there is a metonymic slide where all cosmopolitans come to be either purveyors of the global market or nostalgic nomads. Hence the commercial success of South Asian writing in English is too quickly understood as a canny play to global demand: a scene where bourgeois cosmopolitan writers market India for an increasingly mobile and dispersed Indian bourgeoisie, by fashioning narratives that ameliorate the discomforts of migration.[10]

Producing the Local

In committing to the local, all cosmopolitan writing does not steer clear of the fetishistic localisms that underpin the new world order. In fact such localism is to be found everywhere in the conversations about writing during the jubilee celebrations of 1997. Consider Suketu Mehta's "From the Outside: Should NRIs Be Celebrating Indian Independence?" A novelist and journalist based in New York, Mehta recalls a question he was asked regarding the fifty-year celebrations: "On 15 August, will you be celebrating or mourning?" (1997, 39). The writer self-reflexively remembers his own befuddled responses, stumbling slippages between "their achievements" and "our failures," a fraught confusion about belonging produced in his twenty years abroad: "What right do I have to talk about our country? Does India belong to those whose forefathers left in the last century for Guyana, Fiji, Africa; does it belong to those who left last year for Jackson Heights or Southall? Is there a greater India, dispersed around the world?" To these self-posed questions, Mehta answers in the affirmative—that he will definitely be celebrating a country that has made it possible for him always to return. And he makes an emphatic claim:

> The global Indian community is useful to India for more than just remittances. We have an enormous amount to contribute in what in an earlier, more hopeful age would be called nation building. After all, the leader of the

Independence movement was also an NRI—Gandhiji lived for 26 years in England and South Africa before coming back. Some of us may never come back, but we would like to think that the door opens both ways. The most important gift we can give the land we left behind is the gift of reconciliation, of re-gathering. (39)

Mehta poses the possibility that abiding fractures in national political imaginaries may be better healed from elsewhere; hence the "right" of the diasporic communities to celebrate the cultural idea of India. But Mehta's self-defensive claims also stem from the refracted images of diasporic writers (writing in English) in all manner of media. These images, which often raise questions of belonging and attachment, regulate the cosmopolitical writers' arbitration of their politics, especially the ramifications of producing locality.

In much of the golden-jubilee discourse, commentators consistently circled back to geographic location as definitive of cultural performance. This is most evident in the furor over Arundhati Roy's celebrity. The *India Today* issue of 27 October 1997, featuring several pieces on Roy's winning the Booker, introduces her as the "first Indian" to win the trophy, despite the success of the two previous diasporic South Asian winners, Salman Rushdie and V. S. Naipaul (John 1998, 23). And the news clip from the *Statesman* of 6 October 1997 reiterated the national angle: "Roy becomes the third writer from India to win the Booker, after Salman Rushdie and V. S. Naipaul. And she is the first winner who lives in India and who wrote in India" (Wagner 1997). John Updike also raises the issue of physical location as a sign of authenticity with special reference to Arundhati Roy. Comparing Roy to Ardashir Vakil in his essay in the *New Yorker* jubilee issue, Updike is precisely concerned with the dislocation of these metropolitan writers from their milieu: "Arundhati Roy lives in New Delhi, as far from Cochin as Bombay is from Miami. . . . These two writers certainly have a past—vivid, problematical, precious—but where is their future?" (1997, 156). For Updike, this distance spells trouble.

As we have seen in the last chapter, on the national scene, "owning" Roy stemmed from acute postcolonial sensitivity to the troubling significations in transnational media of "India" as an ancient culture, a "multicultural" conglomeration of regions and ethnicities, and a modern democracy caught in the garish limelight of the fifty-year celebrations. The regional and national claims therefore signify efforts to constrain the circulation of these representations through a politics of location: Roy knows India for she lives there, and she can speak for Kerala since she was brought up there. By the same token, Updike's concern about Roy's dislocation can be read into the Western need to map the non-Western world by relegating roots and niches.

_____ *Figure 6* _____

India Today "Personality" section spread on Arundhati Roy, 5 January 1998.
Courtesy *India Today.*

A spectacular version of the battle over how these writers represent India is
found in the 5 January 1998 *India Today* "Personality" section spread on Arundhati Roy, where she is showcased as one of the most important people of 1997
(see figure 6). Notice the gendered, glossy, but also homely presentation of Roy
in a vegetable market, while the text drools over the fact that she can now "buy
her own damn market." In the accompanying blurb, droll references to non-U.S.
or British readers exalt her international celebrity; and there is a nod to national
readers and local obscenity charges in comparisons to the soft-porn writer
Shobha De and Rushdie. The latter is positioned as the outsider whose giant
reputation is now matched by this "thin, black and clever" home girl. The blurb
repeats the consistent visualization of Roy as a feminized elite icon, a refraction
that she has been at pains to arbitrate. "The New Deity of Prose," the Binoo K.
John cover story on Roy in the *India Today* 27 October 1997 issue, for instance,
goes to some lengths in describing the "slim-hipped" Roy with a head full of
curls and a nose ring, winking "naughtily" as she claimed her Booker (23). A
passage on Roy's Booker triumph of 1997 reported in a 6 May 2002 *India Today*
feature, "The New Word Power," on "more" new writers in English encapsulates
these refractions in rather telling ways: "Still, the post-Rushdie event was

Arundhati Roy—Booker for the first novel, an international cover girl, and in a eulogy from John Updike, a Tiger Woodsian performance in fiction" (6). Published in the section "The Global Indian," the article in its title deliberately links contemporary South Asian writing in English to globalism. Then there is the ever-present reference to Rushdie, the toting of Roy as visual fetish in the "cover-girl" allusion, the veiled citing of a Western writer's "eulogy," and the quick gloss on Tiger Woods as the iconic black success in games played by the rich.

One way in which Roy arbitrates her many refractions shores up her politics of the local. On several occasions following her Booker triumph, Roy studiously unlinked herself from Rushdie's celebrity by highlighting her physical location in India. Veering close to a claim for authenticity—surprising in a writer who combats most emplacing drives of globalism and nationalism—Roy argued that India is an everyday experience for her, not the extraordinary, hyperbolic, and fantastic India vibrant in Rushdie's writing: "And he [Rushdie] said, 'The trouble with Arundhati is that she thinks that India is an ordinary place.' Well, I ask, 'Why the hell not? It is my ordinary life.' The difference between me and Rushdie begins there." Roy makes this claim despite her abrogation of "any brownie points" for living in India, and her vow not to "trade on the currency of cultural specificity." In fact on occasion Roy was quick to recount how Americans have come up to her and exclaimed that they too had an "aunt like Baby Kochamma" (Cowley 1997b).

I contend that the claim must be understood partly as a defensive response—as Roy's contestation of her refracted image disseminated by critical fraternities and by the popular English-language press and electronic media. Roy overtly references this circulation when she prefaces her remark with an aside: "When I was in America I went on a couple of TV shows with Rushdie. And he said," and so on. We find clues to Roy understandable reaction to relentless comparisons between the two Booker-winning writers in comments where Roy suffers in comparison to Rushdie. James Wood, for instance, characterizes Roy to be "not as ideological as Rushdie, and not as magic-realist. She is essentially an extremely talented anecdotalist. Every so often, she displays the inflammations of infection by Rushdie in this regard" (1997, 34). Tellingly enough, Rushdie, although never dismissive of Roy, seldom speaks of her literary talent. In 2001, after Roy's arrest, Rushdie wrote his strongest piece on Roy's behalf, supporting her political activism in a veiled address to the Indian Supreme Court (2002a, 332).

This authenticating gesture on Roy's part is at odds with her production of the local in political essays, and in her linguistic experiments that are the subject of chapter 3. Writing polemically against globalism in the print media, Roy privileges the local as the site of everyday and contingent struggles—over jobs, money, irrigation, water supply. Such everyday performance of localism further underwrites her linguistic politics. For instance, acknowledging the position of English as the language of the elite in one interview, Roy categorically refutes the idea of speaking for other Indians or for all Indians: "And what happens is in that situation it is not so easy, you're not writing the literature of the oppressed, which is powerful but simple, you're struggling to see why society works in this way. [Literature] cannot hold one simple position" (1997c).

Exhorting us to pay more attention to contemporary power struggles (where language is always implicated), Roy foregrounds the need "to see why society works this way" as the locus of postcolonial inquiry (1997a). Her chosen subject is the "practice of everyday life," and so she devotes a whole chapter in *The God of Small Things* to the experience of being caught at a traffic light. For Roy, linguistic heterogeneity is inevitable to inhabiting the local: "You can't just say, 'This language is more important.' Why should that be? There is no one language that can claim to represent all of India, but there are stories. If no one else, at least writers must believe that they govern language" (1997c). She claims to dream in English, and her novel intersperses English with untranslated Malayalam, an idiomatic mix that has a very specific regional location in India.

Such a production of an everyday localism speaks to the situatedness of the cosmopolitical writer, in contrast to other writers in English who often localize the national in resisting globalism. We see such a border emerge in Shashi Deshpande's defense of South Asian writing in English in her piece titled "Language No Bar" that appeared in the *Times of India* 28 April 1995. Evoking colonial racist policies, Deshpande warns of a new linguistic racism against "Indian writers in English," and she celebrates the resurgence of English at the present moment: the "language of access to a global community," English now has both "vertical" and "horizontal" mobility. Reacting to a critical tradition that has historically pitched English against the vernaculars, Deshpande cautions: "It is wrong to pit English writing against the whole of regional writing: how can you compare a part with a whole? How can you put a literature that is over a thousand years against one that is scarcely 100 years old and only just finding its true voice?" But the only line she does draw is one based on migration. While writers living in India draw on the same source as regional vernacular writers, argues Deshpande, nonresident Indian writing is "another category" altogether. Here the "national" is construed as a different kind habitation that inflects the content, rather than the language, of South Asian writers.

But language troubles are ever at the heart of cosmopolitical endeavors, especially in the context of linguistic globalism and nationalism. In the next chapter, I will demonstrate how a complex linguistic localism is in fact a distinctive feature of the cosmopolitical novel. While each cosmopolitical writer professes a slightly different politics of the local, mostly in response to their own circulating refractions, all remain remarkably similar in their linguistic experiments. In their self-conscious politics of the local that we find in interviews, letters, and nonfiction, there are definite divergences in the situated localism of the cosmopolitical writers—what they do share, however, is situatedness. Amitav Ghosh, for instance, performs a migrant writer's politics of the local, exemplifying what R. Radhakrishnan designates as the repoliticized migrant: one who "cannot live, earn, pay taxes, raise a family, produce scholarship, teach and take passionate and vigorous political stances here, and still continue to call it [the host nation] 'not-home'" (1996, xiii–xiv). Hence in Ghosh's nonfiction, the Twin Tower tragedy is as much his concern as is the carnage in Godhra. Ghosh lives and teaches in the global North (New York), and his politics of the everyday logically involve undercutting his own institutional privileges that impart global currency. The withdrawal of his novel *The Glass Palace* from consideration for the Commonwealth Writers Prize (in the category of the Eurasia regional winner) provides a spectacular example of this situated cosmopolitics, a self-conscious resistance to his circulation in global markets. Ghosh is further known for his championing of heterogeneous local histories, languages, and cultures, threaded together to offer a contrapuntal vision of globality that combats corporate or military global design. Ghosh tracks diasporic links elided in the glare of the visible migrant elites of our contemporary moment, such as the historical connections between Egyptian and Indian subjects in his *In An Antique Land* (1992), and Indo-Myanmar traffic in the recent *Glass Palace* (2001).

This grappling with globality is rather different from Upamanyu Chatterjee's explicit interventions into national hegemonies reinforced by global capital flows. In a jubilee interview, Chatterjee quips: "As one of the world's largest corporations, government, the microcosm is uniting. . . . Ditto for the tongues that one will hear. Stray Hindi phrases in Tamil accent . . . there wouldn't be any language barriers in India if one followed certain ground rules, . . . for example, the simple principle that the language of the people, should be the language of governance. Nothing alienates like a familiar face rendering a familiar tongue alien . . . whether it be Hindi or English" (1996, 6). In his novels Chatterjee takes up the challenge of linguistic heterogeneity, a practice recognized even in critical commentaries not explicitly engaged in defining Chatterjee's production of locality. For example, Amitav Kumar writes of Chatterjee's prose: "Rather, the heterogeneity of the scenarios suggests not only a variety of uses but also a variety of languages, registers, and sociolects dividing and bringing into tension what could be only *reductively* described as English" (1996, 316; my emphasis).

There is here no "purity of cultures," but an English vernacular that is historically organic to the local user.

Yet other cosmopolitical writers—as we have seen in the case of Roy—often
find themselves at odds with critical fraternities, particularly when their work
is filtered through the received image of the migrant South Asian writer in
English. In "The Cult of Authenticity," an essay in which Chandra provocatively
recounts his brush with an "ethnic-bindi wearing lady" (who turns out to be
Meenakshi Mukherjee, the veteran critic of South Asian writing in English),
Chandra builds a defense against that reified image (2000, 3). Like Roy, he
acknowledges the privileged position of English, its undeniable emplacing
capacities: "To those who have never had English, who don't have it, the advantages that flow from it are as palpable as the healing effects of *amrit*, ambrosia,
and the struggle to acquire it frequently lacerating and painful: you can swallow
the poisonous metallic mass of this sharp language, but it will cut your throat
and linger in the skin like a blue bruise" (9). But for those for whom English has
become a vernacular, the situation is somewhat different. Hence it is deceptive
to treat English as "alien" to the Indian experience: "Indians have lived in many
languages simultaneously for thousands of years," says Chandra. "If Hindi is my
mother-tongue, then English is my father-tongue. I write in English, and I have
forgotten nothing, and I have given up nothing. And I know the tastes and
quirks and nuances of my regional audience, of the people who live in the locality of Andheri, in the colony of Lokhandwalla, as well as a Bengali poet knows
her regional audience" (8).

Quite overtly challenging his national reception, Chandra remains deeply
critical of the Indian bourgeoisie who wave their glasses of scotch at the NRIs
and speak of the "real India"—an essentializing gesture from critics who decry
the fetishized India that nonresident writers sell on global markets.[11] And given
his long and embattled relationship to critical fraternities, Rushdie follows suit,
characterizing the paucity of the critical vision itself as a function of the market,
where Indian critics try to "beat the local product" (literature): "English writers
are being constantly criticized by English critics for the smallness of their
vision. You endlessly read reviews which say that if only these writers had a
larger canvas, the greater ambition of the writers coming out of India. I think
that's an unfair criticism but it is an indication of a kind of respect for this writing which one might say is misplaced or overstated. But excitement is excitement and different literatures have generated that kind of excitement" (Rushdie
1997d, 88). I will not belabor Rushdie's obvious politics of the local here, a gesture characteristically dismissive of criticisms leveled at his privileged economic and political position. Here I want to foreground the one lens that refracts
every received image of the cosmopolitical writer, a dominant image to which

each writer responds with discrimination or exasperation: the historically constituted signification of "the Indian writer in English."

Given that this signification constrains almost any discussion of these writers' politics, it is imperative to pause on it here. If these cosmopolitical writers are doing something "different," if indeed there is a rupture in literary production after *Midnight's Children*, what constituted normative South Asian writing in English before the eighties? How did the pre-eighties writers politicize English somewhat differently from the cosmopolitical writers under scrutiny? These questions will etch the backdrop for our investigation of the cosmopolitical linguistic experiments in chapter 3.

The Migrant's Tongue

The change in linguistic politics inheres in a shift from earlier perceptions of English as the outsider's tongue, the mark of migrancy and alienation, to the new claims of English as the space of migration—of being borne across to new globalities. As we have seen in many of the discourses of 1997, the nationalist injunction to be a global Indian celebrates fluency in English as a national value; the linguistic migrant is now the cultural insider. But in the hands of the cosmopolitical writers, the migratory powers of invented English vernaculars achieve something else. English is still the marker of migrancy, but now wedded to regional and local Indian vernaculars. An English in flight now becomes the postcolonial native tongue. Given the hierarchical connotations of the English-vernacular dichotomy, turning English *into* a vernacular levels the linguistic playing field. These writers privilege situated local performances of linguistic identity over any homogenized articulation of Indian English. The political valence of these linguistic migrations becomes clear when one reads it in the context of historical debates over English in the Indian postcolony.

It has become a commonplace to start the story of Indian English with the Charter Act of 1813, when the British government was newly invested with educational responsibility and saw its role as the guardian of the natives' "moral and intellectual improvement" (Viswanathan 1989, 17). The most acclaimed work on the subject is Gauri Viswanathan's influential study *Masks of Conquest*, which starts with a consideration of Thomas Macaulay's now infamous minute on Indian education: "We must do our best to form a class . . . of persons, Indian in blood and colour, but English in taste, in opinions, in morals, and in intellect" (Macaulay [1835] 1965). Viswanathan examines the political strategies of containment that governed education, the humanistic program of enlightenment in the Indian postcolony from 1813. She proceeds to demonstrate how the narrow requirements of political and social control gradually cut off English literary cultures from the social contexts of India by the late nineteenth century.[12]

Her exposé of British instrumental use of English literary studies has become the touchstone for subsequent analyses of the subject. Rajeswari Sunder Rajan notes that Viswanathan's elaboration of how English literature was gradually disassociated from its national origins "made possible its [English's] unproblematic retention and continuance in the post-Independence education syllabus in India" (1992, 12). Contributors to the volume on English literary study in India edited by Sunder Rajan explore the institutional rubrics that sustained English use in the period following decolonization—in schools and universities, but also via printing presses (Rukun Advani elaborates on Oxford University Press) and societies like the British Council.[13] These institutions attempted to "fix language" in the decolonizing years, an effort most visible in the hotly contested "three-language formula" advocated by the Indian government. English and Hindi were posed as the two official languages, with optional learning of Sanskrit, Urdu, or another regional language deemed necessary in most major administrative and educational arenas. Nandita Ghosh reads this policy as a systematic attempt to "standardize a linguistic practice of translation by trying to control the way in which translation is to occur between communities and to fix the value of each linking language" (2001). Given their commitment to local heterogeneity, these emplacing agendas become the cosmopolitical writers' targets of critique.

The official travails of English in India are, of course, the tip of the iceberg. From the very beginning, English had entered a linguistic fray already rife with tensions between Sanskrit, Persian, Urdu, and Hindusthani.[14] The language debates that have polarized English and the Indian regional vernaculars first emerged in the twenties and thirties as a part of nation-making agendas. Gandhi's *Hind Swaraj* (1909) asserted the need to valorize indigenous literatures and to establish a nation language, inspiring groups of vernacular writers who protested against the "foreign tongue." In 1933, surveying Indian verse in English, Latika Basu concluded: "As long as the vernaculars in India are . . . alive it should be the aim of Indians to develop them, for writing in a foreign tongue can serve no useful purpose" (qtd. in Dharwadkar and Dharwadkar 1996, 91). On the other side of the issue, cultural practitioners such as Raja Rao embarked on disciplining an "alien" tongue. The battle continued into the fifties and sixties, with the English poet P. Lal commenting in 1966: "The real writer in English not only thinks, but makes love in English. English is at the tips of his senses" (92). Reacting to Lal, the Bengali author Jyotirmoy Datta proclaimed English to be a "dead" language in postcolonial India, a vehicle for information, not ideas and feelings (92). But by the seventies, Indian writing in English had become a recognizable cultural practice: Ten excellent books of English poetry, and the consequent publication of *Midnight's Children* in 1981, propelled Indian English to international recognition. Yet this mirror effect of doubling and othering—English versus the *bhasha* or vernacular literatures—persisted in critical discourse through the Nehruvian era (see, for instance, Mukherjee 1993).

The outsider status of English in criticism on the Indian novel in English was soon at odds with the growing usefulness of English for diversely inflected regional political movements. This is nowhere more evident than in one of the most culturally and linguistically heterogeneous parts of India—the Northeast. John Samuel divides Northeast India into several linguistic communities with common political aspirations and affiliations: "well-formed nationalities" who share linguistic, cultural, and literary traditions (Bengali and Assamiya); emerging "minority nationalities" who are moving through different phases of nationality formation (e.g., Mizo, Tripuri, Naga, Khasi-Garo); "sub-nationalities" who exist as satellites in the shadow of the dominant groups (e.g., Bodo, Lakher, Hmar); "ethno-political collectivities" who engage in common dialects and adhere to ethnic affiliations (some thirty communities in Arunachal Pradesh); and "migrant speech communities" like Nepali and Chakma (Samuel 1993, 91–92).[15] Samuel goes to great lengths to show how these linguistic nationalities are the result of language policies under British administrators who "ideologically manipulated the language situation" to suit their own ends. Between 1837 and 1874, they actively suppressed the Assimaya language in favor of Bengali, using a divisive language policy to stratify speech communities into labor groups (91). At the same time, the inner-line system of 1873 and the Excluded Area Act of 1935 separated the tribal communities of the hills from the plains civilization; this, coupled with missionary efforts at assimilating manageable groups, created nascent ethnopolitical identities. The postindependence Nehruvian policies of noninterference with the cultural traditions of the tribal peoples, argues Samuel, further led to the "emergence of alienated and mutually alienating minority nationalisms" (92). As a result, several communities in the Northeast felt removed from the nation-making process.[16] The effect of this cultural and political alienation has been a strong anti-Hindi rather than anti-English sentiment: For example, among Mizos, Hindi is still known as Vaitwang, the language of intruders or foreigners. As late as 1997, Assam's deputy speaker, Nurul Hussain, strongly supported English over Hindi as a unifying force: "Adoption of English will remove the hang-ups people have with dominant vernaculars like Assamese" (Namboodri 1997, 42).

In fact the history of Hindi in the subcontinent has always been associated with cultural and religious hegemonies. Focusing on the linguistic conflicts in Tamilnadu, Rajeswari Sunder Rajan explains how English emerged as a "lesser evil" in the regional language riots of 1965 that exiled the Congress Party from power and brought in the DMK (Dravida Munnetra Kazagham) and the AIADMK (All India Anna Dravida Munnetra Kazagham) on an anti-Hindi platform (1992, 15).[17] And in "How AIR Killed Hindi," Madan Gopal (1996) catalogues the prolonged debates over Hindusthani (Persianized Hindi), and the "needful Sankritisation" of Hindi (under B. V. Keskar, the freedom fighter), in the postindependence years—debates that testify to the communal anxieties over Hindi. In most Indian regional contexts, Hindi has always been the language of the North Indian belt. The years following independence saw the rise of Hindi use and the decline of Urdu use; more recently, policy makers have attempted to address this lapse by reconstituting the National Council for the Promotion of Urdu (which has turned to computer literacy to standardize and modernize the tongue).[18] Hindi became part of the national agenda again when the Hindu right wing, especially the Swadeshi Jagaran Manch of the RSS (Rashtriya Swayamsevak Sangh), called for the vernacularization of education to promote "national self-esteem."[19] Such privileging of Hindi elicited several subnational linguistic backlashes against the strong languages (including English). For instance, the Mumbai-based Hindu right-wing Shiv Sena's localized use of Marathi targeted both Hindi and English; the anti-Hindi agitations of the DMK ("English is the language of the absent other, while Hindi is the language of the present other") waged an Indian North-South war; and the silent war of Konkani speakers of Goa against the neighboring Marathi state broke down around caste lines.[20]

Across regional polities in India, anti-Hindi sentiments gave rise to calls to vernacularize regional education: J. B. Patnaik planned to make Oriya compulsory in English medium schools in Orissa, according to "Report in Education" in *The Pioneer,* 28 April 1997, while the Bishnupriya Manipuri called for the inclusion of their version of Manipuri in school curricula, demonstrating against the regional Assamiya government. In Andhra Pradesh, demands to allow non-Hindi speakers to write Civil Service exams in Telegu and English surfaced in 1995, as *The Hindu* reported on 26 June under the headline "The Use of Telegu in Civil Service Exams Urged." The heterogeneity of the vernaculars as they enter the English spoken in India is recorded in the 1996 edition of the *Advanced Learner's Dictionary* (compiled by members of the English Department at Jadavpur University, Calcutta), where Indianized English words are cataloged as regional Indianizations alongside the more commonly known Hindi-ized English words. And both Arvind Rajagopal and Robin Jeffrey attribute the robust growth of Indian vernaculars since the 1970s to increasing print circulation—of newspapers, periodicals, and magazines. Jeffrey tracks the gradual movement of newspapers out of the metropolitan centers to small towns and rural areas, a shift matched by corresponding alterations in print languages as successful newspapers "searched for local styles and idioms" to target their local audiences.

These accounts chart a rather complex linguistic terrain as backdrop to the linguistic cosmopolitics that concern us. Since English, Hindi, and the other regional vernaculars have always existed in shifting and often discordant relation to institutionalized language policies, it is a misconception to see English in blanket opposition to the "vernacular" or regional language cultures. But this is *the* national-global linguistic dialectic inhabited by Indian writers in English of the first few generations, working with critics who promoted such a dichotomy. Who are these generations and how do their politics of language deviate from the cosmopolitical experiments analyzed in this book?

Priya Joshi (2002) outlines the "indigenization" of the English novel in India, starting with the Bengali writer Bankimchandra Chatterjee's *Rajmohun's Wife* (1864)—the first Indian novel in English. Labeled "the Scott of Bengal," Chatterjee spearheaded the first generation of South Asian writers in English but abandoned the colonial tongue after this literary venture. Meenakshi Mukherjee notes that these early novels (written by regional writers in the Indian vernaculars) are hardly self-reflexive about the language they deploy, so we have to turn to vernacular fiction to understand the "complex function of English" in these literary practices (2000, 20–22).[21] The second generation of writers took English to be their cultural heritage but remained ambivalent about the suitability of English for the representation of native contexts. In the author's foreword to *Kanthapura*, Raja Rao insisted that, like Sanskrit and Persian, English remained "the language of our intellectual make-up," but "not of our emotional make-up" (1967, vii). Underscoring his subjective distance from the colonizer's tongue, Rao wrote: "One has to convey in a language that is not one's own spirit that's one's own. One has to convey the various shades and omissions of certain thought-movement that looks maltreated in an alien language" (vii). In Rao's estimation, the writer who sought to represent Indian subjects wreaked havoc on English. So, keeping syntactical revision to a minimum, Rao buttressed his novel by providing fifty-nine pages of notes that explained linguistic, cultural, and historical references unfamiliar to global readers of English texts. In similar vein, juxtaposing his own linguistic practice against a phantom "pure" English, Mulk Raj Anand, one of the luminaries of this second generation, says of his "Pigeon-Indian": "Even when Indians know English grammar, and have been used to speaking the alien tongue for a long time, they tend to feel and think in their own mother tongue. Often, the native speech enters into the shell of the sentence in the foreign language" (1982, 328). In Anand's view, English is definitively an alien tongue whose shape and structure remain intact, only mildly altered by the inflections of the Indian vernaculars.

Even G. V. Desani's "bent and kneaded" English is overtly conscious of the foreign tongue bearing down on an Indian soul. A rogue novel of its time, *All About Hatterr* (1949) offers a rather self-conscious linguistic project, a transcription of the Babu English idiom in a somewhat modernist Joycean vein.[22] In this bildungsroman, Desani features a grotesque but memorable autodidact who migrates between languages, but with a clear perception of the purity of each. But the protagonist's confusion of linguistic boundaries is the subject of parody, not of valorization. Hatterr slowly builds up a vocabulary with the aid of an English dictionary and French and Latin primers, combining curiosities like "colloquialisms of Calcutta and London, Shakespearian archaisms, bazaar whinings, quack spiels, references to the Hindu pantheon, [and] the jargon of Hindu litigation" (Desani 1986, 10). Every vernacular reference is subsequently translated into standardized English, either directly or through the unfolding of narrative situations. In one scene, Banerji, Hatterr's Bengali friend, compliments the latter's "knowledge" of India in complete seriousness: "Mr. H. Hatterr, India owes you a heavy debt! I humbly say, it is overdue! You are spiritual. You speak the vernacular as any Indian savant. We love the spiritually inclined and the linguists from the bottom of our hearts. Excuse me, you are more Indian than a sahib" (233). Banerji's rhetorical flourishes, his fetishized love of the spiritual and the linguistic, and his authenticating gestures ("you are more Indian than a sahib") are the butt of the joke. This becomes evident when Banerji's outburst is followed by Hatter's demand that Banerji translate "Sangita Kala Sagara"—the very cultural "honor" that Banerji bestows on Hatterr for the latter's knowledge of India. An Indian knighthood in Banerji's view, the nonsensically Sanskritic "Sangita Kala Sagara" translates into "Ocean of Musical Art" in hyperbolic colonial babuspeak.

On these occasions and others, the purity of the colonial tongue remains the centerpiece of all Hatterr's creative endeavors, as he ostentatiously strains "[your] goodly godly tongue" (35). Desani's self-reflexive parody that in Bhabha's words "distends the space between self and other" through exaggeration is evident in the failed rhetorical act staged by an author well-versed in the British oratorical tradition. The sense of world Hatterr cannot capture through his "rigmarole" English, the protagonist's social and cultural alienation through language, the centrality of the colonial as it doubles back to see its distorted image, are all modernist gestures that end in political aporia. One needs little knowledge of Indian locales and contexts to understand the parody.

Similar translations of vernacular reference into a standardized English can be found in both the mythic and realist fiction of the thirties and forties. Even when English is the subject of narration, as we see in R. K. Narayan's early novel *The English Teacher* (1945, reprinted in 1980), the alienating powers of English are addressed at the level of content. This novel commences with the first-person narrator's irritation at the fossilized English of Indian educational institutions: "Mr. Gajapathy," exclaims our narrator, "there are blacker sins than a dropped vowel" (6). His own imbrication in English literary studies weighs heavily on the narrator as he struggles toward a vocation more organic to him. He finds some sustenance in the example of indigenous education (a headmaster who runs a *gurukul*), and in poetic expression beyond university walls.[23] Narayan's thematic approach to the English-vernacular question is fairly representative of the second generation of South Asian writers in English. In linguistic practice, his English is immensely readable in its standardization. This remains the trend in the writing of the third generation as well, with some change in the subjects of narration.

Most of the novels of the sixties, seventies, and early eighties retreat into private worlds, a fiction best exemplified by Anita Desai's work. Here the linguistic effort seems to be primarily about producing a language of interiority, of family relationships, and of personal matters. Indian words and phrases are translated or assimilated into standardized English, and the English of British academies is still the sacrosanct measure. For example, even in her novel on language, *In Custody* (1984), Desai writes the Urdu phrases recited by the illustrious Nur (the reigning monarch of Urdu poetry in the novel) into English: "a verse of Nur's fell into Deven's mind as casually as a discarded bus ticket: 'Night ends, dawn breaks, and sorrow reappears, / Addressing us in the morning light with cock's shrill crow'" (65). Here the rhetorical flair of Urdu is transcribed into poetic English, transparent in its meanings with little allusive resonance. Of course, the poetic constructions appear more florid in their English translation, despite Desai's graceful style: "'My body no more than a reed pen cut by the sword's tip, / Useless and dry till dipped in the ink of life's blood'" (129). At other points, vernacular words are translated dexterously in the very paragraphs where they appear italicized: "Truly all our poets will become singing birds to us then. We will be able to hear the voice of the *koel*, the *bul-bul*, whichever songster we wish to hear." Sarla's *puja* is similarly explained as the sentence progresses—"Sarla regularly performed *puja* before the tinted oleograph of the goddess Lakshmi that hung in the corner of her dressing table, offering it flowers, incense and candles"—with the second half of the sentence elaborating on the rituals of *puja* (100).

In Custody stages the declining fortunes of Urdu in the face of the official policies privileging Hindi and English. The protagonist, Deven, is another university professor trapped in a stifling marriage and a mundane career. Deven's passions are ignited when he agrees to write a piece on Nur for an Urdu journal's special issue on poetry. Desai underlines the materiality that underwrites the life of languages in her poignant sketch of Deven's lack of resources—the cheap tape recorder, the inexperienced research assistant, the grueling paucity of money, the difficulty of travel from small-town Mirpore to metropolitan Delhi. She is equally attentive to the communal affiliations of Hindi and Urdu, reaching a utopian solution when the Hindu Deven enlists his Muslim colleague Siddiqui's help. Together, they hold a vanishing culture "in custody," as Deven muses in the predawn darkness that brings the novel to a close.

Most notably in this novel about language, there is little vernacular play. Desai in fact makes note of this in a long interview, where she signals changes in her own use of English:

> I grew up with three languages—we spoke German to our parents, Hindi to our friends and neighbors and, once we went to school, learned to read and write in English. So we patched together a family language and simply seized whatever word or phrase seemed appropriate to the moment. In my earlier writing, I tried to achieve a purity of language—the English language since that was what I was writing—but increasingly I find myself concerned with amalgamating the languages of my childhood and the languages of India in my prose: not to dissolve them all into one bland tongue but to differentiate between them and use their different qualities, rhythms, tones. Of course, each is loaded with its own cultural references and that makes the writing denser, to my mind, richer. (1988, 532)

From a "pure" English, Desai moves to the "natural idiom," but she continues to make clear the distinctions between "literary" and "spoken" Englishes. She seldom alludes to the spoken vernaculars and their interpenetration with spoken and literary English, thereby keeping the English-vernacular divide intact at the level of linguistic practice. In his interview with Swapan Dasgupta in which Rushdie floats the "buzz" about a new writing, Rushdie aligns Desai, along with Ved Mehta, Kamala Markandaya, and others, as the "middle generation" of writers who clearly separate the spheres of English and Indian languages, experiences, and cultures. Commenting on Desai's "best book," Rushdie admires the manner in which Desai uses "English to represent a crisis in another language [Urdu]" (1997e, 90). Yet there is no mixing of the linguistic idioms at play in her text: Urdu poetry, whose cultural demise is at the heart of *In Custody*, is present in complete translation.

But Desai's comments on her English use intimate a perceptible shift in Indian English after the publication of *Midnight's Children* in 1981. *Midnight's Children* really broke the mold of the presiding linguistic registers of the South Asian novel in English. Critically hailed as the progenitor of the new writing in English, the novel features the multivalent English characteristic of the English vernaculars that I examine here.[24] In retrospect 1981 and 1982 appear as water-shed years, literally marking the birth of a new generation of writers. Such transcription resounds in Meenakshi Mukherjee's description of her first encounter with Rushdie, at a 1982 conference at the Commonwealth Institute in London: "Nobody could have thought then that this vibrant young man would one day turn into a staid literary oracle, pronouncing judgment on Indian books he had never read" (2000, 119). The two Rushdies in Mukherjee's account speak to Rushdie's labored arbitration of his refracted image in the popular and critical press in the decades that followed. In fact Mukherjee buttresses her comment on Rushdie in 1982 with two other observations of relevance to the global circulation of contemporary South Asian cosmopolitical writing: the publication of the first volume of *Subaltern Studies* in 1982, and the fact that at that moment the term "postcolonial" had not yet gained critical currency.[25]

In his more recent introduction to *Mirrorwork*, a collection of South Asian writing that commemorated the golden jubilee, Rushdie adopts a humble posture. He writes of his luck (no doubt made good by economic and institutional support!) at publishing the "midnight's children" idea. Soon after its publication, he recounts meeting several other writers who had similar (aborted) projects in Indian vernaculars (Rushdie 1997b, ix).

Midnight's Children achieved its stature as a publishing event and literary birth only after the currency of postcolonial studies had gained ground in the West, reaching new proportions in the aftermath of the *Satanic Verses* controversy. Sketching Rushdie's literary reputation in his introductory remarks to a collection of critical essays on Rushdie, M. Keith Booker offers a telling statistic: Most of the 267 articles on Rushdie were published after the *Satanic Verses* affair and, of these, 219 appeared between 1989 and 1993—at the height of the controversy. In fact sixty-three of the ninety-three items that spring up under the entry "Midnight's Children" in a search of the online MLA database were published after 1989 (1999a, 6).

But Rushdie had claimed new ground for Indian Englishes quite early, in his 1983 "'Commonwealth Literature' does not exist": "What seems to be happening is that those people who were once colonized by the language are now rapidly remaking it, domesticating it, becoming more and more relaxed about they way they use it—assisted by the English language's enormous flexibility and size, they are carving out large territories for themselves within its frontiers" (1991a, 64). Not only had English become an Indian tongue—now it was a place of linguistic migration, of translation, of mobility. The cosmopolitical writers who follow showcase this constant motility between linguistic registers in Indian locales. Hence "idlis and ratatouille" appear together in italics and remain untranslated in a short story in which Upamanyu Chatterjee's much-traveled protagonist vertiginously hybridizes Hindi, Punjabi, and English (1996, 21). And Arundhati Roy's prose appears dotted with Malayalam and Hindi, a hybrid English that she describes as "the skin on my thought," the "unselfconscious medium of dreams, speech, emotions and logic" (1997c).

The English vernaculars of the cosmopolitical novels not only invite readers to "return" to local contexts, but also galvanize the recessive epistemologies of a globalizing world. The linguistic projects described in chapter 3, then, must be understood as visionary linguistic geography aimed at dismantling colonial and new imperial worlding. Rushdie concludes his essay on new Indian writing in the golden-jubilee *New Yorker* issue with a map: "The map of the world in standard Mercator projection is not kind to India, making it look substantially smaller than, say, Greenland. On the map of world literature, too, India has been undersized too long. Fifty years after India's independence, however, that age of obscurity is coming to an end. Indian writers have torn up the old map and are busily drawing their own" (1997a, 61).

An Other World

My emphasis on the linguistic contours of recessive vernacular knowledges continues a contemporary line of thinking on "globalization from below." The phrase is invoked in the *Public Culture* issue on globalization, when Arjun Appadurai writes persuasively of the need for a "new architecture" for producing and sharing knowledge about globalization, given the threat of the "globalization of knowledge" where all critical practices follow global North-based institutional and epistemological norms and vocabularies (2000, 13). While recognizing the significant mobilization against transcolonial processes by TANS ("transnational advocacy networks"), Appadurai remarks that one of the clear disadvantages for these struggles is a paucity of vocabulary used to characterize the defects of globalization—hence the need for critical (academic) analysts to form alliances of knowledge that will enable these efforts at "globalization from below." But how exactly can this be done? One of the research models that draws Appadurai's ire is the U.S. Cold War area studies model, in which certain regions are written into geographies that conceptually contain and manage them for security reasons. As analysts, argues Appadurai, we continue to reproduce this "world-generating optic" where knowledge of world regions is generated from the disciplinary limits of global North-based institutions. We need to attend to a varied set of public spheres so that a critical dialogue on these "world-pictures" ensues, generating another optic that will destabilize the primacy of neoliberal and neocolonial imaginaries. Appadurai prompts us to ask different questions of texts visible and recessive: "How do people in Taiwan, Korea, or Japan think about the Pacific Rim, if they think in those terms at all? What is their topology of Pacific traffic?" (2000, 8).

If one follows Appadurai's argument, one of the issues implied in his insistence on multifarious world pictures is the question of language: the global hierarchies of language highlighting some epistemologies and foreclosing the potentials of others. It is linguistic limitation in fact that prevents many global North-based progressive critics from accessing the public intellectual repertoire of other cultures where these resistant "world-pictures" may be found. What is required for these critical efforts at globalization from below is a pedagogic commitment to world vernaculars beyond the politically and economically viable modern languages.

One critic who explicitly pitches such an argument for globalization from below from the linguistic angle is Walter Mignolo, whose geographic metaphors for linguistic worlds destabilized by cultural transgression resonate with my critical imperatives. Linguistic "impurities," in Mignolo's view, are politically destructive of economic (market) and political (nation-state) re-inscriptions of geopolitical boundaries (2000, 219). The very notion of national languages, literatures, and cultures are the epistemological equivalents or maps of geographic colonial and (later) postcolonial nation-state borders, still caught within imperial geopolitical hierarchies (219). Literary geographies, linguistic maps, and cultural landscapes, along with the scholarship on these objects, remain firmly within such vertical national rubrics. For example, Mignolo notes the disciplinary striations of "foreign languages" in the global North-based academies in colonial difference from English, and the equally dichotomized frame of "bilingual education" dividing languages along national borders (in the former colonies) as cases in point. These rubrics fail to resist these colonial and neocolonial ways of knowing the world, despite the "sociohistorical transformations" of the last twenty years.

Keeping alive the political will to decolonization, Mignolo foregrounds a series of texts that challenge the geohistorical epicenters of power: specifically, the work of Jose Maria Arguedas, Michelle Cliff, and Gloria Anzaldúa, who create unstable language hierarchies and multiple linguistic addresses in their texts. All of these writers participate in what Mignolo characterizes as the act of "languaging." They not only present mobile linguistic landscapes but subsequently, via discussion or narration, quite self-consciously challenge the radical asymmetries of the languages in the text. Moving between Quechua and Castilian (Argueda), English and the Creole Englishes (Cliff), and Spanish, English, and Nahuatl (Anzaldúa), the writers therefore present a theory of languages in their linguistic innovations.

I find evidence of similar linguistic migration in the cosmopolitical writers' language "theories," and their self-conscious attention to political relations between languages. As we shall see in chapter 3, all these writers either infuse standard English with the lexicon, grammar, and syntax of the Indian vernaculars of choice, or record the local variant (Bombay, Malayalam, or Bengali English) of spoken speech in their novelistic heteroglossia. Their linguistic "maps" have unstable, layered, collusive contours that throw into confusion the established geopolitical borders of modern languages.

The presence of an English vernacular "native" only to a locale shifts the reader's eye to different registers of knowledge—to popular culture, street slang, folklore, and the syntax of regional vernaculars. These English vernaculars can be best translated by readers familiar with particular tongues such as Bombay English, spoken and literary Bengali, or Malayalam. As cultural insiders, these readers know most of the languages at play in the text. But even among such translocal publics, further divisions emerge: between those familiar only with spoken variants of the vernaculars, and those who have both the spoken and literary aspects of the vernaculars (often a generational divide between first- and second-generation immigrants). For the nonexpert reader, these English vernaculars require "surrender" to the irreducible supplementarity of the text; the activist reader willing to be borne across might turn to vernacular archives in print and in electronic media readily available in the information economies of the global North. In the final analysis, what these English vernaculars call for is a critical gesture, an adequate readerly cosmopolitics: the self-reflexive performance of reading on the "border," always at the edge of comprehension but never fully at ease with the entire linguistic register of a text.

Three

Linguistic Migrations

Experiments in English Vernaculars

If I was going to face an audience which could, at any moment, become my executioner, I wanted the odds stacked in my favour. I wanted an audience full of young faces eager for tales of adventure and passion and honour, full of young minds still susceptible to the lures of unearthly horrors and epic loves; even as Yama settled himself into his black throne and Hanuman found a perch on top of the doorway, I heard the murmur of young voices in the courtyard, speaking Hindi and English accented with the rhythms of Punjabi, Gujarati, Tamil, Bengali, and a dozen other languages.

"how many," I typed.

"Four teams," she said, "maybe fifty. It wasn't easy, I tell you."

"The whole courtyard is filled," said Mrinalini, opening the door a crack.

"thank you," I said to (typed at) Saira, who was clearly not to be underestimated. "what did you tell them."

"What you said to tell: secret-secret, a story, nothing about you. Here," she said, "this is how you make capital letters. The shift key, you know."

A, she typed, AB, ABC.

—*Vikram Chandra,* Red Earth and Pouring Rain

So commences Sanjay or Parashar's epic tale in Vikram Chandra's *Red Earth and Pouring Rain* (1995). Exhorted to suspend disbelief, the reader finds Sanjay, the warrior poet reincarnated as a monkey, on the verge of death in the first pages of the novel. A narrative pact is immediately established. Scheherazade-like, the bleeding Parashar desperately holds Yama, the god of death, at bay with circuitous stories. Soon other gods, as well as realist characters, join the fray: Hanuman, the great dialectician, cleverly proposes meandering and circular tales, while Abhay and Saira arbitrate the procedures for transmitting the monkey-narrator's typescript. Here stories live only in their circulation; in fact they depend on the public gathered in the courtyard by the redoubtable Saira, Chandra's exemplary reader/listener. Depicting mainly youthful listeners, Chandra appeals to a modern audience generationally distant from India's oral cultures. They constitute the public whose inhabiting of the epic story—of passion, heroism, and betrayal—will lodge it firmly in the contemporary social imaginary.

In foregrounding a culture of circulation—the speakers, writers, literary predecessors (Ganesha and Hanuman), critics, listeners, distributors, and growing culture industry in the text—Chandra is clearly self-reflexive about his own act of cultural translation in writing a modern novel in epic mode.[1] Astutely, he fleshes out the means of transmission that will enable the passing of the epic into quotidian modern life. Sanjay turns to type (which he learns from Saira) in his efforts to disperse the Indian story to a multilingual polity, thereby surpassing the concrete limits of oral transmission. Print culture, then, offers new possibilities for the epic. The text printed in English, which signifies cosmopolitan address in this postcolonial milieu, quite effectively translates the classical vernacular. But that act of translation brings irreducible supplementarity to the cosmopolitan text. It is this conscious supplementarity—the turn to the vernacular in localizing cosmopolitan address—that is the subject of this chapter. The scene staged in *Red Earth and Pouring Rain* is enacted elsewhere in the cosmopolitical novels under scrutiny.

Vernacularism as a Situated Cosmopolitanism

Embarking on a fuller investigation of linguistic migration as a situated literary cosmopolitics, I focus here on the very different vernacularizing strategies of three writers: Salman Rushdie, Arundhati Roy, and Upamanyu Chatterjee. Each writer presents a theory of language that revises older postcolonial language debates, most famously remembered as the Ngugi–Achebe conflict over authenticity and hybridity.[2] The cosmopolitical writers featured here actively promote language as formative of the postcolonial subject's social and political engagement in the world, Ngugi's Marxist invocation become commonplace. But now the native tongue, socially enabling in postcolonial locales marked by cataclysmic cultural interpenetration, is the "hybrid" tongue of Achebe's prescription. The representational worlds of metropolitan, small-town, and village India—Rushdie's Bombay, Chatterjee's Madna, and Roy's Ayemenem—are layered linguistic topoi whose migrant subjects construct idioms that allow them to overcome cultural and political alienation.[3] We shall examine such linguistic processes in *The Moor's Last Sigh* (1995), *English, August* (1988), *The Last Burden* (1993), and *The God of Small Things* (1997). I spend a considerable amount of time on my readings of each novel's philosophical and political frame because I attempt to illustrate the organicity of these evolving linguistic idioms to these representational worlds. By "organic," I do not mean to imply a naturalized relation to the world; quite the contrary. I claim that in each configuration of linguistic layering we encounter, one linguistic idiom (be it an English burlesque or a polysyllabic English vernacular) seems best suited as the narrator's chosen tongue born of this historical moment. In staging this connection of language to social and political action in the world, these cosmopolitical writers nativize their idioms.

The writers bring the postcoloniality of these linguistic innovations into sharp focus through pitched arguments that directly critique national and global linguistic hegemonies. Moreover, the overt artificiality of these English vernaculars as local "places" in a new world order emphasizes historical contingency and performance over any reified production of the local. Ostensibly these worlds seem to offer a microcosmic India to global audiences, as many of the jubilee discourses suggest; yet entry into those representational worlds and their linguistically confused subjects demands constant linguistic motility, and resists replication for purposes of commodity fetishism. Thus Rushdie's, Chatterjee's, and Roy's projects both render India communicable (the local fetishized as national) and undercut full communicative access.

In such vernacularity, then, the cosmopolitical writers seem most aware of the ramifications of their own circulation. The global hegemony of English, historically amplified in the Anglophone postcolonies, certainly implies high cost to the eighteen Indian vernaculars. But there is more. As my perusal of vernacular recessive knowledges in chapter 5 will show, linguistic losses further denude epistemological resources for alternative social imaginaries—those "other" world-generating optics aimed at combating globalism. Hence a politics honed to translocal solidarities need necessarily take into account existing structures of circulation—the buying, selling, and distribution, as well as the institutional and market privileges of reading publics. All the cosmopolitical writers I investigate therefore demand cultural translation rather deliberately, while also manipulating emerging (linguistically stratified) reading publics. Critics, as well as specialized and general readers, are all invited to migrate in varying degrees to the subjectively rendered linguistic locales of these novels.

With such linguistic acts, the writers emphasize *vernacularity* as a responsible cosmopolitanism. And in turn, the modality of their praxes enjoins critics

to rethink the prevalent oppositions between the vernacular and the cosmopolitan. Such an opposition is the rubric for the special winter 2000 issue of *Public Culture*. Of the many complex arguments on these categories, Sheldon
Pollock's historical essay, "The Cosmopolitan and the Vernacular in History,"
best exemplifies this vernacular-cosmopolitan divide. I am not treating his as a
representative view for this volume by any means.[4] Rather, Pollock's reading of
a widening abyss between the vernacular and the cosmopolitan at our current
global moment does illustrate the critical extreme with which I take issue. Pollock argues for a renewed critical focus on the vernacular in our age of beleaguered cultural belonging: "And it is only now for the first time, when this
epoch seems to be drawing to a close as vernacular modes of cultural and political belonging are everywhere coming under powerful pressures from an altogether new universalizing order of culture-power (call it globalization, or
liberalization, or Americanization), that we may conceive of this past history as
a whole and make sense of it for cultural and political theory" (2002, 16). These
new universalizing orders find form in "cosmopolitan" literary modes that, in
Pollock's view, are directed toward "unbounded" and "infinite" audiences; in
contrast, the "vernacular" binds communication by addressing a finite audience
(17). What emerges is a succinct opposition between the cosmopolitan and the
vernacular as communicative modes, as "a language that travels far and one that
travels little" (18). My coinage of "English vernaculars" runs against the grain
of such a binary.

The word "vernacular"—derived from the Latin *vernaculus,* meaning
"domestic" or "native" (alluding to the native of the house, a "home-born
slave")—entered the English language in 1601. Such an etymology continues to
define the two contemporary applications of "vernacular" as a noun: a descriptor for the everyday speech of people, or a term designating the characteristic
language of a particular group. My use of "vernacular" when I speak of English
vernaculars stands against the implications of common lexical descriptions of
the term. *Webster's Collegiate Dictionary* characterizes the vernacular as: "(a)
Using a language or dialect native to a region or country rather than a literary,
cultured or foreign tongue; (b) non-standard language or dialect; (c) being the
normal spoken form of a language." The first two categories—"native" dialect
and "non-standard" language—oppose the vernacular to literary, foreign, and
standard tongues, all of which have historically been the cultural matrices of
cosmopolitanism. Such a definition does not capture the colonial categorization
of the Indian languages as the "vernaculars" historically set in opposition to
English. The eighteen official Indian regional vernaculars are, of course, spoken, but they also have unified and standardized fields of written communication. Extant postcolonial scholarship has shown how colonial education and
language policies in fact consolidated and unified the prominent Indian lan-

guages from the 1830s.[5] The last lexical category—"the normal spoken form of the language"—is even less successful in accounting for the Indian vernaculars as modern standardized languages. Therefore the literary traditions of the Indian vernaculars are elided in a lexicon that tags the "vernacular" as nonstandard.

When one begins to designate English as a vernacular, one is forced to revise the globally and nationally prevalent hierarchies of language. The representational worlds of the cosmopolitical novels are rife with multifarious linguistic performances that stage asymmetrical relationships between languages and their variants. We hear colonial English and the old "babu English"; contemporary standardized literary English; colloquial corporate and other workaday global Englishes of the marketplace; national vernaculars, in their formal and popular/mass cultural variants; regional vernaculars, both literary and spoken; and the several English vernaculars that are the subject of my tale. Following Mignolo's lead, I spatialize these linguistic relations that geopolitically order our world. The cosmopolitical writers therefore emplace postcolonial subjects through their "linguistic geographies" that rewrite global cultural space.

Bombayspeak in Rushdie's Moor's Last Sigh *(1995)*

While *Midnight's Children* narrates the evolution of nation, *The Moor's Last Sigh* targets the subaltern politics of representation. The *Moor* unflaggingly pursues the question of a suitable representational apparatus for national minority communities. While many critics have celebrated Rushdie's famous wordplays as manifestations of Bombay English, few have examined the politics of such vernacularization. So in the ensuing analysis, I attempt to make good that critical lacuna. Consider, for example, Suchismita Sen's persuasive essay on *Haroun and the Sea of Stories*, in which she examines "Rushdie's use of the South Asian variety of English," a language that "evokes a lost childhood for Rushdie and for many of his generation":

> Despite political opposition from non-Hindi-speaking regions to the language policy, the Bombay film industry has quite successfully spread Hindi to the farthest reaches of the subcontinent. Resistance to Hindi nonetheless remains strong in many parts of the country. As a result of the ambiguous position of Hindi, a typically South Asian variant of English has developed that is highly Indianized in incorporating speech patterns from not only Hindi but also other Indian languages. (1995, 660)

Sen scrutinizes Rushdie's deployment of Bombay English as a layering of different varieties of "South Asian" English. The resonance of the magical land of Alifbay, in "corny poems" often posted behind Indian trucks or buses ("Drive like hell and you will get there") that Haroun encounters on the road, situates the allegorical landscape in Bombay. Sen notes that at other points in *Haroun*, Rushdie directly records common Hindized usage of English: "Have a care! It is my goodwife you are insulting!" (qtd. in Sen 1995, 655). In these cases, Rushdie does invent the literal translation of Hindi syntax into English, but he writes (from memory) a spoken variant of that vernacular. Such drawing out of locale-specific reference is indeed laudatory, yet Sen does not elaborate on the politics of such overt linguistic localism—a localism that Rushdie more recently fine-tunes in *The Ground Beneath Her Feet* as a HUG-ME English, a hybrid Bombay mix of Hindi, Urdu, Gujarati, Marathi, and English.

In essays and interviews, Rushdie asserts linguistic authenticity when he remembers Bombay of the fifties and sixties: "I found myself remembering . . . whole passages of Bombay dialogue *verbatim*" (1991, 11; my emphasis). In *Moor*, his linguistic localism becomes a polemic against majoritarian cultural politics. First, the variety of spoken English vernaculars that constitutes the linguistic geography of *Moor* designates Bombay as plural locale, undercutting the fetishized Mumbai-for-Marathis vibrant in Shiv Sena Hindu Right discourses. If language politically emplaces subjects, then Rushdie's Bombay is a cosmopolitan linguistic home. Yet Rushdie's is a very particular weave of Bombay-specific idiomatic phrases, one that insists on the reader's excavation of Bombayspeak, an idiom linked to Rushdie's beloved Bollywood. A phrase like "the godfather, the dada of dadas" ("dada" colloquially signifying the urban Mafioso who have a stranglehold on the Bollywood film industry), for example, sutures Hollywood and Bollywood terminologies and occurs in the text without quotation marks. By reusing such phrases in the space of this novel, and sometimes across his oeuvre, Rushdie renders passing phrases familiar. As his own extensive unpacking of these references suggests, he enjoins critics to habitually migrate to his linguistic locale to render it communicable to global readers. Over time, such activity would facilitate the readerly processes of learning abstruse vernacular resonance as global idiom.

Finally, in *Moor* there is a further localizing of cultural citations that are also not directly quoted. These are available only to those readers who can access the subtext in question, be it film gossip or popular memory, a decoding especially important in *Moor* to get the full drift of Rushdie's political critique. Thus the phrase "boys who dream of golden fortresses" may seem of the same temper as Rushdie's magical prose, but I will show how this passing phrase actually cites Satyajit Ray's lesser-known children's fantasy films that have considerable relevance to the culture wars over representation waged in *Moor*.

Turning to Rushdie's politics of linguistic migrancy in *Moor*, I isolate four distinct strategies in the text that define Rushdie's intervention into linguistic globalism: direct recorded speech patterns in recognizable colloquialisms and street slang drawn from several oral registers; popular cultural resonances that harness context-specific vernacular knowledge, becoming learned idiom through iteration; (globally) circulating mass cultural signs that are recoded for the Bombay milieu; and citations that require historical knowledge of local milieux.[6]

In *Moor* the central concern is the nation's/world's romance with its representation: cinema, popular cultures, and folklore are under investigation, even though ostensibly the text provides a commentary only on painting. The real quest in the novel is for a sustained imaginary that will help heal the political fractures of reactionary majoritarian power. The narrator's mother, as the figure of the artist, is the one who squarely faces the problem of representing the clan's "real" stories: "Our deepest mysteries usually ended up oils-on-canvas," says our sardonic Moor (1995, 13). By contrast the narrator, the Moor who is finally expelled from his Bombay and imprisoned, gives birth to the narrative: "I sigh therefore I am" (53). The visual idiom dominates the novel. The Moor's fate, for one, is foretold in paintings: Aurora's angst-filled painting of the mother-son dyad, and Vasco Miranda's eroticized portrait of Aurora as mother (which he paints over with a kitsch of Sultan Boadbil leaving Alhambra). These paintings, both named *The Moor's Last Sigh*, are stolen from art galleries in Bombay; they are, of course, indexes of the Moor's secret identity, and therefore are the objects of his search in the tale's denouement.

The novel quite explicitly showcases the textual acts of worlding that Rushdie pitches as necessary for a minoritarian politics. If there is a community envisioned, it is a collection of minority communities always in danger of being steamrolled by the (Hindu) majority. A family saga of what Rushdie names "our far from ordinary clan" (Portuguese, Jewish, Catholics, and others) unfolds, not allegorically as in the case of *Midnight's Children*, but as yarns that dovetail into the legends of the nation. That is, the fortunes of the Da Gama Zogoiby clan parallel those of the nation. Members of the clan debate, barter, and part ways on the philosophies that shaped the nation. For instance, Francisco Da Gama's modernist scientific India emerges in the 1920s, paralleling (but not allegorizing) the historical founding of the Communist Party of India by M. N. Roy in 1923. The difficulty of translating the Marxist dream is recounted in a hilarious episode in which several officially sanctioned Lenin thespians arrive from Russia and overwhelm the Goan crowd with their esoteric "babel" (30–31). Francisco Da Gama's dream collapses, generating several other lines of action in the novel with no homology to the continuing saga of Indian Marxisms.

The heterogeneous "minority" communities in *Moor* face imminent erasure under the majoritarian drive of Hindutva (the drive toward establishing the kingdom of Ram). Marking the national-global moment, Rushdie cleverly characterizes the age as the rule of Ram/RAM (RAM signifying India's software revolution). Moorish Spain and its moment of disintegration becomes a mirror for another moment of collapse: the possible decomposition of the Nehruvian secular pluralist India that Aurora bequeaths to her son as "Mooristan" (directly opposing both Hindusthan and Pakistan).[7] It is no accident that the Moor has Jewish blood, a refraction of a European other, the Moors. Hindutva and its corresponding forms of politicized religion are the targets of Rushdie's critique, and the novel stages the fundamentalists' (ethnic) cleansing of all otherness from Indian soil through violence. In the culminating chapters of the novel, bomb blasts dismember Bombay, directly referencing the 1993 Bombay blasts in the unrest following the Babri Masjid destruction:

> Bombay was central; had always been. Just as the fanatical "Catholic Kings" had besieged Granada and awaited the Alhambra's fall, so now barbarism was standing at our gates. . . . We were both the bombers and the bombs. The explosions were our own evil—no need to look for foreign explanations, though there was and is evil beyond our frontiers as well as within. . . . –Excuse, please, the outburst. Got carried away. Old Moor will sigh no more. (372–373)

Rushdie's own comments on secular India in his essay "In Good Faith" were prescient of the crumbling Nehruvian dream under divisive politics:

> To be an Indian of my generation was also to be convinced of the vital importance of Jawaharlal Nehru's vision of secular India. Secularism, for India, is simply not a point of view; it is a question of survival. If what Indians' call "communalism," sectarian religious politics, were allowed to take control of the polity, the results would be too horrifying to imagine. . . .
>
> To be a Bombayite (and afterwards a Londoner) was also to fall in love with the metropolis. The city as a reality and as metaphor is at the heart of all my work. "The modern city," says a character in *The Satanic Verses*, "is the locus classicus of incompatible realities." Well that turned out to be true. "As long as they pass in the night, it's not so bad. But if they meet! It's uranium and plutonium, each makes the other decompose, boom." (1994c, 404)

In *Moor* Rushdie makes his critique of sectarian politics through the voice of a painter, the arbiter of visual idiom. Aurora is at once representative of Mother India and her best historian. She is the epic fabulist painter who takes on a task similar to the narrator in *Midnight's Children*. Most eloquent among her paintings of the country is the protean sea-city Mooristan (multivalently, the land of the Moor, or Spain, the country of *mórs* or peacocks, the national bird of India, and place of mother-son *amor)*:

> "Call it Mooristan," Aurora told me. "This seaside, this hill, with the fort on top. Water-gardens and hanging gardens, watchtowers and towers of silence too. Place where worlds collide, flow in and out of one another, and washofy away. Place where an air-man can drowno in water, or else grow gills; where a water-creature can get drunk, but also chokeofy, on air. One universe, one dimension, one country, one dream, bumpo'ing into another, or being under, or on top of. Call it Palimpstine. And above it all, in the palace, you." (Rushdie 1995, 226)

As a national icon of this fabulous Mooristan, Aurora performs as a secular god in challenging Bombay's celebration of its beloved Hindu deity Ganesh. Her annual dance on the cliffs attracts more attention, notes her besotted son, than the immersion rituals of Mumbai's Ganapati festival at the water's edge.

Central to the acts of visual and written worlding is the question of the migrant's desire for origins, the impulse toward the fullness of return. In *Moor* this is best articulated through Aurora's erotic relationship with her son, the Moor whose history she paints in her famed "Moor paintings" that feature the Sultan Boadbil and Axya. The mother-son duo, duplicated in the Bollywood film world by the Nargis–Sunil Dutt pairing and captured in the witticism "the entire country has a mother-son problem," is at the heart of this Indian story.[8] Rushdie suggests that the mother-son symbiosis depicts the central social imaginary of Indian nationalism. But as the narrative progresses, Rushdie implies that what such a representational matrix elides is the real source of national power—economics and political self-interest—embodied in the father figure, one who represents the death drive in the nation's vitalist ontologies. In a paternalistic India of fundamentalist resurgence and urban Mafia, the hidden godfather looms to destroy the social imaginary. With Abraham Zogoiby's rise, Aurora's fortunes decline. Her paintings, like the nation's ideals, are corrupted when commercialized ("sold" in art galleries and by art critics) and politicized (Raman Fielding begins to characterize her as a "Christian" artist).[9]

Rushdie approaches the subject of majoritarian rule linguistically in the localism of his Bombayspeak. Perhaps the easiest markers to identify are speech patterns that deviate from standard written English. Hindi and Urdu syntax molds many conversations: "Where is the air to breathe?" says one character, instead of the more standard, "Where is there any air to breathe?" (23). And we find an English that echoes general Hindi phrases and idioms littering the speech of several characters in usage like "Hate me, don't hate me but . . . ," "my goodwife," or "wallow-pallow" and "art-shart." The more ethnic variants of Bombay

English are heard among Goan Christians and Anglo-Indians, often mouthed by the narrator's family. "Shutofy" and "washofy," for instance, are recognizable constructions that mean "will shut up" or "will wash away/out" (in the imperative). These specifics identify minority subjects within the larger linguistic Hindi/Gujarati/Marathi-ized English as Rushdie repeatedly emphasizes different linguistic idioms to stratify classes or groups. Adam Sinai, who turns out to be Saleem Sinai's big-eared son born at the close of *Midnight's Children*, claims his place in the sun as Adam Zogoiby's surrogate heir. This manifestation of the global Indian, with satellite ears and sold on RAM, spouts a memorable example of a class-distinct vernacular, the corporate spiel of the new global marketplace. Mockingly parodied by the jealous and weary narrator, Adam Sinai scrambles to please or impress in "a positive tizzy of social-climbing panic":

> Should we go Polynesian at the Oberoi Outrigger? No, no, it was only a buffet luncheon, and one did so appreciate a little fawning. Maybe just a bite at the Taj Sea Lounge? But, on second thoughts, too many old buffers reliving fading glories. How about the Sorryno? Close to home, and nice view, but darling, how to tolerate that old *groucho* of a proprietor? A quick businesslike in-and-out at an Irani joint—Bombay AI or Pyrke's at Flora Fountain? No, we need less noise, and to talk properly one must be able to *linger*. Chinese, then?—Yes, but *impossible* to choose between the Nanking and the Kamling. The Village? All that fake-rustic themeing, baby: *so passé*. (353)

The ease with which Adam drops the ritzy names of the social spaces traversed by rich Bombayites, and the manner of his delivery, identify him as one of the global elite. *The* "Nanking," in this outburst, connotes a unique restaurant, while *an* Irani "joint" suggests an ethnically cool eatery. The verbal accentuations on "linger," "impossible," and "passé" imitate the speech rhythms of the Indian metropolitan sophisticate; and "baby" and "darling" seem to float up from the gossip columns of Bombay's glossy magazines (like the widely distributed *Stardust*), which constitute a large part of the city's mass culture.

Sometimes the narrator's humor, disdain, or anguish can be located in the nuances of accented speech. For example, the Zogoiby–Da Gama clan's spice factory is administered by a "trinity of controllers" whose names are Mr. Elaichipillai Kalonjee, Mr. V. S. Mirchandalchini, and Mr. Karipattam Tejpattam. Any reader familiar with Indian spices will easily catch the silliness of naming the spice factory officers after popular spices such as cardamoms (*elaichi*), red chili pepper (*mirch*), cinnamon (*dalchini*), and bay leaves (*tejpatta*), and lesser-known, and sometimes region-specific, spices such as *karipatta* and *kalonjee*. The regional valence added to these names is more difficult to catch: the "pattam" in the last name, for instance, marks this gentleman as a South Indian, while the "pillai" and "kalonjee" have a definite Parsi ring. We know that in Maharashtra of recent years there have been major labor clashes over ethnicity and jobs. The Hindu Shiv Sena has inflicted violence on non-Marathi ethnic workers in Bombay, claiming "Maharashtra for Marathis." South Indians and Parsis have long been a part of the Bombay middle class, a point the Shiv Sena uses to its advantage in inciting violence among the unemployed. The business, family, friends, and artistic community gathered at Malabar Hill in *Moor* hail from the heterogeneous India, Aurora's little India of ethnic, regional, and religious pluralities. The narrator's humorous labeling of the spice factory trinity, then, carries a political edge that pleads for secular pluralism.

If Rushdie refuses to translate such "Indian" material for his Western audience, he does the same for varying cosmopolitan references recognizable only to certain cultures of print circulation. For instance, we remember Dr. Zeeny Vakil, art critic/doctor and the chief spokesperson for cross-cultural translations in *The Satanic Verses*, who attacks authenticity and essentialism (in her book *The Only Good Indian*). Vakil, complete with the sexy signifier "Zeeny" (a common name for the Indian sex bomb Zeenat Aman), reappears as an art historian in *Moor*. Here she is once again the mouthpiece for hybridity, writing critical works reminiscent of Homi Bhabha and Roland Barthes. Rushdie lightly parodies the complexity of Bhabha's significant oeuvre on migration by the length of Zeeny Vakil's book title, *Imperso-Nation and Dis/Semi/nation: Dialogics of Eclecticism and Interrogations of Authenticity in A.Z.*, the excessive use of slashes between words of the title mimicking verbal conventions of poststructuralism.[10] Examples like these point to Rushdie's multivalent linguistic address, for clearly this dig is pitched at a group of critics who form one part of his literary readership.

Rushdie's seasoned rampage of what Arjun Appadurai (1990) has called the "cultural warehouses" of the postmodern era creates a network of cross-cultural references in the text. He draws extensively on cultural signs that would be part of the popular culture and memory of Bombayites, and these signifiers are sometimes simply inserted into the text without explanation or further elucidation, creating an extraordinarily dense and resonant prose. The range of these references is impressive: Hollywood film knowledge, a staple for Bombayites' obsessive interest in commercial film industries, is juxtaposed with Indian preferences. Audrey Hepburn, for instance, has been a popular female Hollywood icon in India, a cultural preference that comes into play when Minnie, the Moor's sister who becomes a nun, "appeared at the door looking like Audrey Hepburn" (211). This in turn jogs the cosmopolitan's memory of Audrey Hepburn's less-known role in the 1959 Hollywood flick *The Nun's Story*.

On other occasions, the net of cultural signs is cast wider. Buñuel is implicitly cited when we are told of Vasco Miranda's "spiced-up rehash of the European surrealists" in the latter's short film *Kutta Kashmir Ka*, "a 'Kashmiri'—rather than Andalusian—'Dog'" (148); but *Kutta Kashmir Ka* further references the 1977 Bollywood *Kissa Kursi Ka*, a biting satire of the 1975–1977 Emergency (the original print of the film was reportedly destroyed by Indira Gandhi's son Sanjay Gandhi's goons). The well-known Indian disdain for Nehru's compulsive speechmaking finds expression in the name of a dog, "jaw-jaw Jawaharlal," a national-level in-joke; Miltonic phrases soar just as easily when the Moor sees himself "hurled from the garden" (5); and several other insider quips, such as the phrase "bleddy Macaulay Minutemen" to connote a colonized consciousness, abound in this close-packed prose. In these cultural references Rushdie seems actively to create a hybrid transnational cultural landscape where phrases like "the godfather, the dada of dadas" become received idiom.

More difficult to fully excavate are the cultural signs that Rushdie recodes to fit his Bombay milieu. Take, for example, the character named Jimmy Cashondeliveri, a country-and-Eastern singer who marries one of the Moor's sisters. The Moor's Mafioso black-marketeer father, Abraham Zogoiby, destroys the "great [industrial] houses" that previously had their grip on Bombay's and, to a large extent, the nation's financial nerve: "In the mid-Fifties, he made his spectacular takeover of the House of Cashondeliveri," the name in part parodically denoting a Parsi ethnicity (181). Abraham Zogoiby's ousting of the "old Parsi" business networks heralds a new globally oriented financial era for Bombay, a financial turn that dislocates one of the "great clan's weakling scions," Jamshedjee Jamibhoy Lifebhoy Cashondeliveri—Jimmy Cash for short. The narrator wryly notes that the irresponsible Jimmy Cash is only too happy to sell his "birthright," "ill-equipped" as he is to shoulder the responsibilities of the business. Given any knowledge of Bombay's commercial history, the decline of old business houses slowly replaced by new corporate and black markets has an instant resonance with the Parsi name. The Parsis constituted the premier business community in the post-1947 period. The name Jamshedjee resonates with that of Jamshedjee Tata, one of the greatest industrialists from the most prominent industrial family in India. In this half of Jimmy Cash's background, Rushdie draws on historical knowledge of Bombay's (and India's) communities. But in the other half of this quick and dirty portrait, Rushdie borrows just as easily from Western popular cultural references. Starting on a career of country-and-Eastern music in Nashville, Tennessee, the birthplace of some of the most exciting country-western music, the fictitious character Jamibhoy Cashondeliveri takes on a stage name that imitates that of the famous Johnny Cash. The carefree, partially on-the-road and at-home-in-the-world image of the country-western singer—"yodeling rhinestone cowboys," according to our caustic narrator—acquires recoded value as a signifier of this uprooted Parsi boy's angst and nostalgia. The signification of displacement through the country-western singer provides a clear instance of the recoding of contextual knowledge that depends on one's familiarity with global, national, and local Indian cultures and histories.

To this Jimmy Cash episode Rushdie adds another unexplained reference drawn from Bollywood mass culture that perhaps only Bollywood film buffs would notice. Ina, the sister who marries Jimmy Cash, begins to sing with him on tour: "She, who had become a legend by remaining silent, now opened her mouth and sang" and took the stage name "Gooddy." *Guddi* (meaning "doll" or "little girl" in Hindi, anglicized into "Gooddy" in *Moor*) is a 1971 Hrishikesh Mukherjee film starring the young actress Jaya Bhaduri, who went on to marry the Indian megastar, Amitabh Bachchan. The public often accused the Bachchan family for not allowing Bhaduri to reenter the film industry after their marriage. This restriction, the mark of an antiquated gender ideology, was anticipated by another film, *Abhiman* (1973), in which the two starred as husband and wife. In a story in which the husband mistreats the wife who outclasses him as a singer, the wife "loses" her voice and becomes hysterically silent until forgiveness and reconciliation ensue. *Abhiman* now seems prescient, because the film staged Jaya Bhaduri's subsequent disappearance from public view—no mean irony, given that it was Bhaduri who had been the bigger star in the couple's early films, hailing from a renowned theatrical lineage. Ina's stage name, Gooddy, in *Moor*, recalls Bhaduri's young screen persona (in *Guddi*) and sutures that memory to Bhaduri (the wife), who makes a way for her husband's career in *Abhiman*. Ina simulates that later performance, where the singing-legend wife breaks her silence and grief by bursting into song. Given the Bachchan-Badhuri contretemps in real life, the citation in *Moor* draws to our attention the reality effect of Bollywood tales on the Jimmy Cash–Ina relationship, a point that Rushdie is at pains to make in this novel. After Jaya Bhaduri retired early from Bollywood, she remained frozen for almost two decades in cultural memory as young, lovable, and girlish, all qualities that endeared the character Guddi to national audiences when the film came out (Ina occupies just such a place in the Moor's heart). Notable in this instance is Rushdie's use of popular and mass cultural references from national and global cultures, knowledge that might well be frowned on by erudite readers who scorn such global mediascapes.

On other occasions, Rushdie depends entirely on local and translocal engagements with local city politics, and it is precisely the intricacies of these vernacular citations that enact his most incisive political critique. Consider, for instance, the strange hyperbolic figure of Lambajan Chandiwala. Evoking the lame pirate Long John Silver from Robert Louis Stevenson's adventure fiction *Treasure Island*, in the one-legged character Lambajan Chandiwala (the Hindi name translates as "the silver fellow who lives long"), Rushdie examples a Western signifier reinterpreted for the Indian context. Yet the particularities of Lambajan's function in the novel completely depend on our knowledge of Hindi slang, Bombay's indigenous religious festivals, and the contemporary myth making of the local Hindu fundamentalists. Lambajan, referred to as "our personal pirate" by Aurora, who furnishes the former with a parrot to complete her westernized myth, is the gatekeeper for the Zogoiby family. As gatekeeper he guards the "treasure," Aurora and her secular pluralistic India on Malabar Hill. Colonial fiction like Stevenson's adventure is woven into the fabric of Indian storytelling. Yet the boyish tale of search, betrayal, and loss is recoded to fit the young Moor's imaginative Indian landscape. He will pursue that lost treasure, Aurora, and immortalize her until his last asthmatic breath.

While this Western allusion provides one key to reading Lambajan, the vigilant reader can decode further the complex weave of Bombay references attached to this character. Lambajan tells legendary tales of an older India, exerting a hypnotic fascination on the adolescent Moor. The Elephanta caves, renowned for ancient cave paintings, are Lambajan's other treasure island off the coast of Bombay:[11]

> "Once in that place there were elephant kings, baba," he confided. "Why do you think-so god Ganesha is popular in Bombay City? It is because in the days before men there were elephants sitting on thrones and arguing philosophy, and it was the monkeys who were their servants. It is said that when men first came to Elephanta Island in the days after the elephants' fall they found statues of mammoths higher than the Qutub Minar in Delhi, and they were so afraid that they smashed up the whole lot." (127)

The fact that this other world, a mythic India, threatened men who knew the Qutub Minar indicates that Lambajan is speaking of a precolonial (perhaps Hindu) India. Bombay's indigenous Hindu traditions derive from this earlier time, a different Hinduism from the "monkey worshippers" of Hindutva. Northern Indian Hindu fundamentalist traditions often celebrate the monkey-god Hanuman, who fought for Ram in the epic *Ramayana*, while Bombay's most popular Hindu festival invokes Ganesh, the elephant-god.[12] Lambajan is therefore claiming that these are fallen times of sectarian politics, when Hindu fundamentalists (the monkeys) now harness the power of ancient local traditions (the elephants) specific to Bombay. Lambajan's tale of the monuments ("statues of mammoths") on Elephanta implies that the monkey worshippers of politicized Hinduism have slowly effaced the heterogeneous mythic Hindu past. In such a parable, Lambajan parodies the Hindu Right's predilection for smashing up monuments like the sixteenth-century Babri Masjid, supposedly built over the birthplace of the god Ram. As a mythmaker, Lambajan bewails the loss of local knowledge, and the appropriation of all tales by Hindutva politicos. Later in the novel, quite tragically Lambajan himself becomes a henchman for Raman Fielding, the Shiv Sena doyen Bal Thackeray figure in *Moor*.

This complex fabric is spiced up by the ongoing conflict between Aurora and Lambajan's parrot, Totah, who screams "Peesay—saféd—hathi!" This is a witty distortion of the Stevenson parrot's "pieces of eight," the colonial English phrase which Aurora fails to teach the ever recalcitrant Totah. "Peesay—saféd—hathi" translates into "mashed white elephants," perhaps indicating Totah's cultural memory of the death of elephants and the smashed monuments on Elephanta island. More interesting is the fact that Aurora, while dancing on the cliffs during the Ganapati festival, plunges to her death screaming, "mashed white elephants" (127). The suggestion here is that Aurora understands the "stupid" parrot's cultural memory at the moment of her own death— that earlier traumatic memory of a lost time, the death of the secular/magical India that she sought to embody, recapture, and valorize in her art. Equally pertinent to this nexus of meaning is Totah's reluctance to learn the Anglo version of "pieces of eight," and the parrot's Hindization of the Stevenson line. While this could be a reference to a pre-Anglicized India, it also resonates with the Shiv Sena's rejection of English as the language of political struggle. The fact that Totah's words can signify a Hindu fundamentalist cultural agenda in turn points to the Hindu Right's renarrativizations and appropriation of a precolonial past. Totah's line becomes prophetic when pagan, secular, magical India (Aurora) is "mashed" by the power of a newly designed elephant of majoritarian mobilization:

> Christians, Portuguese and Jews; Chinese tiles promoting godless views; pushy ladies, skirts-not-saris, Spanish shenanigans, Moorish crowns . . . can this really be India? . . . Majority, that mighty elephant, and her sidekick, Major-Minority, will not crush my tale beneath her feet. Are not my personages Indian, every one? Well, then: this too is an Indian yarn. . . . Elephants are promised for much later. Majority and Major-Minority [read "communalism"] will have their day, and much that has been beautiful will be tusked & trampled by their flap-eared, trumpeting herds. (87)

Communalism, the day of the majority and major-minority, will end the Moor's world and text, but until then this "yarn" becomes Rushdie's lament for the old secular India. One can comprehend Rushdie's palimpsestine swings at the majoritarian cultural politics of the religious Right only when the reader decodes and recodes cultural meanings specific to his Bombay regional milieu.

To move to our last category, another set of long and involved encodings are drawn from the world of Indian art and painting. Although impossible to recount fully here, these are fairly important in a novel about artists, their relationship to their work, and the role of representation in the political life of a nation. The various stages in Aurora's career as a painter—her folk murals, realism, and abstract art—roughly follow developments in the history of Indian painting.[13] Rushdie scrutinizes the exhibition, distribution, and consumption of Aurora's art as part of his argument on the varying roles of mass, popular, folk, and high culture in creating viable national representations. As Abraham Zogoiby, the man with a finger on the pulse of Bombay's underworld, scornfully notes: "'You art-wallahs'. . . . Always so certain of your impact. Since when do the masses come to such shows?" (131). In reading Rushdie's excursions into the Indian art world, one encounters the last category of cultural specificity, local citations, which function as critical commentaries on national and global politics.

One of the projects of *Moor* is to ask quite directly: To what extent does the artist bear some degree of responsibility in generating social imaginaries? For without the critical counterpoint to political power present in art, sheer economic and political self-interest or majority rule—the rule of the flap-eared herd—extinguishes all democratic possibilities. Mass-produced cultural forms that consolidate national identity, exemplified in Bollywood successes such as *Mother India* (1962), are definitely dangerous when they are the *only* representations of nation. Ashis Nandy's characterizations of the various categories of postindependent Indian national culture provide a vocabulary for salvaging Rushdie's complicated exegesis on bourgeois art. Bourgeois art, in *Moor*, bears the responsibility for maintaining a democratic polity. Nandy first differentiates between "folk" culture as artisan nonmodern cultures, and "mass" culture as urban mass-produced forms that serve dominant economic and political interests. He then adds "popular" culture to the scene: the creative output of the haute bourgeois or the urban middle class who have enormous "economic muscle" and a "huge pool of professional skills" (Nandy 1995b, 196). This class, exemplified by a Satyajit Ray, an Maqbool Fida Husain, or an Amrita Sher Gil, "mediates" the classical traditions and the old colonial culture for the more "low-brow" mass cultural realm. Popular culture, in its accessibility and historical role of vanguardist political criticism, can offer alternatives to mass culture while partially funneling and diffusing the complexities of high art.

Aurora, who paints lively pan-Indian murals (and styles herself as Ravi Varma in the Chipkali paintings), is a bourgeois artist from a business family with political connections. She is deeply critical of commercial Bombay movies: Her bitchy interchange with Nargis, the actress who plays *Mother India* and later becomes a member of Parliament (as Nargis actually did), marks Aurora's dislike for artistes who serve dominant political interests. In *Moor* Bollywood is the dream factory for the nation's major social imaginaries, but also painting's visual other. Aurora's tumultuous life-filled murals invoke the active visual language of cinema rather than the more eclectic high art of galleries and private collections; yet the complexity of her art escapes reification. This initial cultural battle between Nargis and Aurora recurs in the text when Aurora weighs her ability to represent India, struggling against the major currents of her age:

> It was easy for an artist to lose her identity at the time when so many thinkers believed that the poignancy and passion of the country's immense life could only be represented by a kind of selfless, dedicated—even patriotic—mimesis. Abraham was by no means the only advocate of such ideas. The great Bengali film director Sukumar Sen, Aurora's friend and, of all her contemporaries, perhaps her only artistic equal, was the best of these realists, and in a series of haunting, humane films brought to Indian cinema—Indian cinema, that raddled old tart!—a fusion of heart and mind that went a long way towards justifying his aesthetic. Yet these realist movies were never popular—in a moment of bitter irony they were attacked by Nargis Dutt, Mother India herself, for their Westernised élitism—and Vasco (openly) and Aurora (secretly) preferred the series of films for children in which Sen let his fantasy rip, in which fish talked, carpets flew and young boys dreamed of previous incarnations in fortresses of gold. (Rushdie 1995, 173)

I would argue that the citation of Nargis's remark about "Sukumar Sen" is the cornerstone for understanding Rushdie's larger argument about national culture. To begin with: The film director here is, of course, Satyajit Ray, best known for his realist *Apu Trilogy*, films which remain defining moments for Indian "art cinema." Ray was also well loved in Bengal for his children's fiction written in the vernacular, a role in which he was no longer the elite artist but a popular writer whose stories were formative childhood influences. Ray's fabulist films, the ones that Aurora "secretly" liked, such as the 1968 *Goopi Gyne, Bagha Byne* (where carpets fly) and the 1975 *Sonar Khella* (where young boys dream of previous incarnations), are based on his grandfather, the renowned Upendrakishore Ray-Choudhury, as well as on Satyajit Ray's own stories written for children and young adults.[14] These films remain less known outside Bengal mostly because of their culture-specific humor, depictions of familial relationships, and prototypical local characters. Therefore, these films are constructed in a cinematic regional vernacular that eludes most national or global registers. Perhaps it is this vernacularism that attracts Aurora; she is drawn to plural particularities constitutive of her Mooristan, rather than universal stories. Moreover, in her vision, India is hyperbole and excess, best captured in fantastic and epic dimension. Further, the name "Sukumar Sen" is no accident, for it sutures two other popular cultural figures in Bengal: Ray's father, Sukumar Ray, most famous as a poet of nonsense verse, and the other great Bengali director (often regarded as Ray's antithesis), Mrinal Sen, whose politicized "art cinema" continues to mediate popular Bengali Marxist sentiments.[15] Aurora's "equal," then, constitutes a composite of three luminaries who greatly influenced, even fashioned, the Bengali social imaginary; her evocation of this regional composite marks her desire to influence the national social imaginary by drawing on "minority" cultural sources.

The reference to Nargis in this passage alludes to her now infamous remark as a member of parliament about Satyajit Ray's films: Nargis decried Ray's realist exposé of India's poverty to the world, insisting his films therefore should not be considered the best of Indian cinema.[16] The "bitter irony" of Nargis's nationalistic prescription inheres in the fact that Ray's films put Indian cinema on a par with Western art cinema, acquiring critical acclaim for his country. Aurora's re-invocation of Nargis functions as a certain kind of self-fashioning: She remains the artist who paints with a commitment and passion unadulterated by political agendas, while Nargis plays the politics of global markets where "selling" the nation's image acquires paramount importance.

The specific speech patterns, cultural resonances, recoding, and citationality of Rushdie's prose require contextual knowledge without which much of Rushdie's political and cultural critique is effaced.[17] Rushdie's English is that space of migration where "pieces of eight" can become the politically relevant "peesay—saféd—hathi." When one has to actively research every context-specific reference, the process of reading can become a prodigious task. Hence the standard response in the global North-based press, epitomized in James Wood's dismissive description of *Moor* as a "little sickening" in its plethora (2001, 5). This emphasis on contextual recessive knowledges begs the question of how to read Rushdie: Do we read him for his cosmopolitan address, his highly patterned literary and philosophical allusions? Or do we read him as a vernacularist, a down-to-earth critic of nationalizing and globalizing agendas through his sustained local citation?

Burlesque Idiom and Reflexified English: Two Projects in Upamanyu Chatterjee

Upamanyu Chatterjee's pithy quip midway through *English, August*— "What is Jane Austen doing in Meerut?"—poses the central problematic of the novel, the protagonist's cultural alienation from contemporary small-town

India.[18] The Jane Austen reference is, of course, symptomatic of the larger issue:

"Dr. Prem Krishen of Meerut University has written a book on E. M. Forster, India's darling Englishman—most of us seem so *grateful* that he wrote a novel about India. Dr. Prem Krishen holds a Ph.D. on Jane Austen from Meerut University. Have you ever been to Meerut? A vile place, but comfortably Indian. What is Jane Austen doing in Meerut?" . . . "Why is some Jat teenager in Meerut reading Jane Austen? Why does a place like Meerut have a course in English at all? Only because the Prem Krishens of the country need a place where they can teach this rubbish?" . . . "That's why education is a real challenge. And in the years to come, as a bureaucrat you'll be in a position to do something about these things, things that matter." (1989, 170)

Amitava Kumar reads this exchange as simply another addition to the "narrow and futile debates about the relevance of English in the Indian context," although he acknowledges Chatterjee's "refreshing" language, the "boisterous, blasphemous mixing of words and world views to lampoon the hollow pieties of post-independence India." On examining the Rabelaisian carnival of language in *English, August*, Kumar asks: "What is this irreverence and debunking in interest of? or, put it another way, what does this laughter hide?" (1996, 316). Apparently not much, according to Kumar's calculations. His critique of Chatterjee is that the writer's discourse, "the brilliance and newness of the satirical wit" aimed at the troubled relations between Indian bureaucrats, servants, and adivasis, leads precisely nowhere, unlike the more sustained and committed work of activist writers like Mahasweta Devi (318). Mahasweta Devi is specifically chosen as a contrast because of her long solidarity with adivasis, a subject that Chatterjee problematically broaches as the metropolitan man's subliminal encounter with India's "deepest" and most impoverished "other."[19]

Yet I would argue that Chatterjee's perusal of othering in *English, August* is linguistically, rather than thematically, effected: an ideological critique of national languages, both of formal Hindi and standardized Indian public school English. For Chatterjee these languages constitute a metropolitan national subjectivity that not only "others" Indian subalterns, but also enacts violence on both the self and the other. Linguistic and cultural alienation is the center of this sketch of administrative chaos and political inertia. Chatterjee poses an enunciative language of the body, an English burlesque, as the last frontier to sanity.

In part the body is the stage for the violence of linguistic inscription. But the language of the body is also the space of migration between the disjunctive representational worlds of the metropolitan subject. Individualized and immediate, this English burlesque is not an idiom that can be reproduced. So while I agree with Kumar's characterization of this new burlesque as a Rabelaisian adventure, I do see that carnivalesque muscular use of English leading somewhere, if only to a fragile stasis for Chatterjee's alienated protagonist of *English, August*, displaced in small-town Madna. But it is really in Chatterjee's less successful and somewhat tiresome *Last Burden* (1993) that Chatterjee makes a more radical move—a stab at creating a vernacularized English whose syntactical innovations are "heard" by Bengali speakers. In short, *English, August* stages a political critique of linguistic nationalism and globalism, while *The Last Burden* carries such critique into the linguistic performance of an English vernacular. Hence the two texts should be read together as a continuous linguistic project.

English, August features a middle-class Anglicized protagonist alienated from his small-town milieu on his first administrative assignment in the Indian Civil Service. Agastya, named after the great sage, Agastya Muni (composer of some Vedic verses), in *Ramayana*, is labeled "August" at the elite boarding school in Darjeeling; the Tibetan local students scornfully refer to him as "hey English" because of the accented English he speaks with his Anglo-Indian friends. Part Bengali and part Goanese in ethnicity, Agastya/August is constantly reminded of the absurdity of the cultural and linguistic worlds that collide in him: "You are an absurd combination, a boarding-school-English-literature education and an obscure name from a Hindu myth" (Chatterjee 1989, 129). Converted by his English education into a Macaulay effect, Agastya finds it impossible to fit into the "real" India, rural and small-town India removed from the metropoles. Chatterjee's novel effects a critique of the stark disjunctures between the India of privilege and the India of the "interior," the latter variously constructed as small towns, villages, and adivasi settlements in the jungles of the Indian *Deccan*. Agastya belongs to a "defunct" bureaucracy, the Indian Administrative Service that, in Chatterjee's view, has failed to bring the promises of Nehruvian socialism to the "interior." Layered over prevalent rural-metropolitan hegemonies are asymmetries of regional identity: between Bengalis and Tibetans in Darjeeling; between Agastya's own Bengali heritage from his father (which always seems to take precedence over his other ethnicity) and his mother's Goan background; and between South Indians and North Indians working together in the bureaucracy.

But born in the Coca-Cola generation, Agastya is less concerned over issues of vernacular preference than over the status of English, the linguistic prison house of his alienation in small-town Madna, eighteen hours away from Delhi in the Indian Deccan region. Agastya dreamily represents Madna in the following manner: "Glimpses of Madna *en route*; cigarette-and-*paan dhabas*, disreputable food stalls, both lit by fierce kerosene lamps, cattle and clanging *rickshaws* on the road, and the rich sound of trucks in the slush from the overflowing drain; he felt as though he was living someone else's life" (5). Describing himself as a "fallen Adam," Agastya spends most of his days in Madna in a small darkened room masturbating and smoking marijuana, with occasional interactions with various colleagues, his servant, and other dislocated souls such as himself (the corporate Dhrubo, or the T-shirt and Calvin Klein–loving Bhatia). With a great deal of irony in a novel subtitled "an Indian story," Agastya tells us that his is not a "typical Indian story," since the "typical" story narrates migrations to the global North—no doubt a reference to his diasporic counterparts who had begun to dominate the Indian novel in English in the eighties. Agastya's migration is centripetal, journeying to the "underdeveloped" parts, the "third world" in the "third world." Here the radio tragically and incongruously blares "doctored information" (73), while adivasis in Jompanna working with die-hard leftists, the Naxalites, live by their own rules and still fight for basic amenities such as uncontaminated drinking water. Agastya, imprisoned in his cosmopolitan sensibility, sees his bizarre discordant existence in Madna as existentially absurd and hyperbolically incongruous.

But Chatterjee's canny political project will not let his protagonist ease into the pleasures of excessive angst. Immense landscapes collide in Agastya: "Madna and Delhi seemed two extreme points of an unreal existence; the only palpable thing was the rhythm of the beast beneath him, a wonder, that could link such disparate worlds together" (177). Agastya escapes to the body, avoiding human contact and longing for "one place, any place, with no consciousness in his mind of any other" (177). Writhing on his bed, our protagonist emotes: "He could even make do with Madna, if his mind would not burgeon with the images of Delhi, or of Calcutta, walks with Neera in the Lake Gardens, long chats about life and books and sex, and her hesitant revelation of her virginity; and beyond that Singapore, where everything was ordered, and Illinois, with its infinite varieties of ham. It was convulsing, the agony of worlds in his head" (177). In these collisions, every kind of language fails, inadequate to the concentric and hybrid contours of Agastya's postcolonial experience. He converts a serious Dryden text into lascivious carnivalesque in a gratuitously sexist fantasy: "Tell her [a new female teacher who exposes them to *Absalom and Achitophel*], Yes, my lovely bitch, when my hands are full with your flat buttocks, my mouth on each breast, I shall give you lust-gnaws between your absalom and achitophel" (14); he is equally disrespectful of Sanskrit "verses of some venerable Hindi epic" (15). Here is an example of Chatterjee's English burlesque, the Dryden reference resonating with Agastya's general satirical take on English in India: "At my old University I used to teach *Macbeth* to my M.A. English classes in Hindi. English in India is burlesque" (24).

The burlesque capacities of Agastya's language are used for several ends. First, for Agastya, the collision of worlds creates not luxurious sorrow and alienation, but irony and incongruity. Second, this irony satirizes the languages that flounder in the Indian interior. And third, Agastya's brand of burlesque is harnessed to a masturbating, itching, laughing, languorous body—the "beast underneath"—which becomes his only bridge between the colliding worlds. Hence it becomes the material basis of Agastya's linguistic idiom, a shifting space between conflicting vernacular and English tongues.

The intrusion of bodily functions, fluids, and movements breaks and twists Chatterjee's lively use of English. Part of the argument seems to posit the body as the only stable thing one really owns in this rush of colliding worlds. Yet the notations of the body are also hybrid, melding sometimes English and Hindi, sometimes Bengali and English, and sometimes Urdu and American. The first page records the "amazing mix, the English we speak," in Agastya's self-conscious use of the term "hazaar fucked" or "a thousand fucked" (1). The Americanism "fucked," or messed up really badly, is combined with "hazaar" in its Urdu connotative meaning of "extremely" or "a thousand times over." Chatterjee's hybrid burlesque use of English does to some extent record an existing English vernacular: an Indianized public-school English of his generation in the eighties and nineties which Agastya shares with dislocated metropolitan subjects like himself. But it is also the language that is exaggerated and overused, becoming his chosen idiom in his new milieu. It remains his linguistic recourse to a violently discordant world in which he fails to place himself, politically and culturally.

But what are these linguistic and cultural worlds that the protagonist inhabits and encounters? The cerebral Agastya offers us a vibrant commentary on the incongruity of any "officialese," the language of bureaucracy in India (254). District administration, "like the railways and the English language," is largely a British creation, now Indianized by the use of regional languages. Nation-making vernacular Hindi is placed at the next level of foreignness in this Indian interior. Agastya's inadequacy in Madna has much to do with the fact that he has to learn formal Hindi from a tutor, a stretch from the colloquial idioms of Hindi mass culture like Bollywood cinema or popular rags such as Madna's local *Dainik.* Of course learning Hindi is further satirized, as Agastya slowly comes to realize the sterility of the standard tongue in these "underdeveloped areas"— the Madna locals speak only in dialects incomprehensible to Hindi-speaking bureaucrats. Alienated because of his lack of the local vernacular, Agastya parodies the English-vernacular dichotomies:

"Didn't they teach you Gas-Cylinder Operations at Yale or Citibank?"

"But why're the instructions in English? The language of the bloodsucking imperialists, they made our hearts weep, and crippled us from appreciating our glorious heritage. I object, and like a good Bengali I'm going to write to

the 'Grievances' column of the *Statesman*, that the instructions on the gas
cylinder should be in *all* the fourteen Indian languages recognized by the
Constitution." (159–160)

Thus incongruity and irony soon turn to parody when Agastya is in a serious
satirical mode.

This satirical edge further undercuts global and national cultural myths. We
see this in his parody of continuing colonial fantasies in postcolonial times. In
the margins of Ruth Parwar Jhabvala's *Heat and Dust*, Agastya finds cryptic
scribbles in red ballpoint pen by an Assistant Collector, possibly his predecessor in Madna: "'Not necessary these days to wear *sola topee*. Relic of the Raj. The
bureaucracy to be 'Indianized,' and 'Difficult question. An officer's wife *should*
mix with others, but not without jeopardizing the dignity of the office'" (39).
While the utilitarian nature of the bureaucrat's notes are ridiculed here, later in
the novel we have an equally critical sketch of a young Britisher who material-
izes, complete with a sola topee, on the "trail of a grandfather who had been
mauled by a tiger two generations ago" (196). For Agastya, the Britisher's
enthusiasm for India seems "infinitely bizarre": "All those Englishmen who
came to India looking for a soul, any foreigner actually, who came looking for
anything, soon found some native *and* his country had wrapped their thighs
around him, and that he was getting it in the balls" (186). The incongruities of
colonial fantasy are partly captured in the iconic sola topee, an accouterment
that, we are told, had not been seen since 1947 (128). The young Britisher's donning of the sola topee links him to the Assistant Collector's anxious notes on
Jhabvala. And our self-conscious narrator worries about the impact of colonial
fiction, with its prescriptive functions for the hapless assistant collector (the
postcolonial inheritor of the nation-state).

Dominant national myths meet with equal censure. Agastya's commentary
on Gandhi's statue in Madna is an important one, for here the burlesque prose
of the body enacts a critique not so much of Gandhi as of the production of
Gandhi as the hero of the masses in the national imaginary. When Agastya
comes to Madna, he is struck by a statue of the Mahatma as "a short fat bespec-
tacled man with a rod coming out of his arse" (21). He soon learns that the rod
is simply there to hold the statue up, since it is in disrepair. But the disrespect
to Gandhi, and Agastya's perception of Gandhi's failed "vision" in the interior of
independent India, is certainly intentional. Much later, the protagonist demonstrates some confusion as to whether it was Gandhi or Wittgenstein who was
the author of the Gandhian adage, "India lives in her villages" (169). While
part of this chuckle could be put down to the Bengali antipathy toward the
Gandhization of the freedom struggle in postindependent India, the critique

becomes more serious when the climax of the novel features Agastya's friend Mohan Gandhi (no less!), whose arms are cut off for his rape of an adivasi woman. This last incident is divested of the customary humor of Agastya's other encounters, and it most clearly raises the question of political responsibility within class asymmetries.

In political terms, this communication of and through the body becomes resistance to exploitative national and global rhetoric. In an early comic instance, a taxi driver defiantly offers an opinion: "[He] fisted his cock and said, '*This* is what I think of you Government types'" (146). "This" remains gestural and funny at this early moment in the text. But later, the adivasis, dependent on the bureaucracy for water, electricity, wells, and other basic necessities, a people bereft of "the forests too ruined to sustain them," violently punish Mohan Gandhi. This time the message is inscribed on the violator's body when Mohan Gandhi's arms are amputated in revenge. At this point, he is Agastya's tragic double, acting on the various sexual urges that grip Agastya throughout the story, and he is punished through physical means. In fact Agastya feels the news of Mohan's tragedy as a bodily effect: "A light breeze, forest whispers of leaves and dust, the faint discomfort of *armpits*, something crackling in his *hand*, and some warm fluid outward from the base of his *spine*" (260; my emphasis). Mohan's body here becomes a template of political communication. The violence to different bodies—rape and amputation—exposes the violent reality effect of the bureaucratic system. Chatterjee continues this critique of an ultimately deadly sexual and political violence in his portrait of the sodomized and murdered adivasi, Chamundi, in his most recent novel, *Mammaries of the Welfare State* (2000). In these instances of violence, the body is not simply a bridge between conflicting linguistic, cultural, and political worlds, but the site where epistemological violences are felt, fought, and recorded. The question we are left with in *English, August* is: Does Chatterjee provide us a way out of this political inertia, an effect of the migrant's entrapment in disjunctive worlds?

As in other cosmopolitical novels, in *English, August,* Chatterjee makes his argument about subaltern subjects under erasure through his overt theory of language. Language is linked to bureaucracy: to practical necessities (like gas cylinders); to political rhetoric (of the Naxalities whom Agastya meets at the village of Chipanthi); and to patriotic legends (Multani's father's story of revolutionary heroism that fails to impress Agastya, the new generation). Even more trenchant is Agastya's critique of the missionary endeavor:

> As the jeep skirted the hospital, he again marvelled at its incongruity. . . . He wondered at motivation: what had induced the Dutch to build a hospital of charity in an obscure corner of India, or the Germans to fund an Indian curer

of lepers? But he was greatly amused, a few weeks later, to learn that the Dutch missionaries at the hospital were converting tribals to Christianity. But his laughter at the news wasn't cynical, it was mildly incredulous, because it sounded so *absurd*, that in this day of AIDS and the atom, some missionaries were converting the heathens to the Lord's Path before healing them. God, he laughed, when will these Christians ever grow up? (245)

In Jompanna, where the tragedy of ruined adivasi cultures seems the key problem, the clean sanitized leper facility/health farm run by a "male Mother Teresa" seems strangely out of sync. The facility is peppered with Gandhi's political aphorisms: "Real leprosy is attached to an unclean mind" (233), and "The weak became strong on Tolstoy Farm and labour proved to be a toil for all" (237). For Agastya this focused and ordered act of service simply avoids the more difficult problems of development and adivasi autonomy in the area. The missionary ideal overlaid with Gandhian slogans all point to dated rhetoric that has little to do with the complexities of the contemporary milieu.

Given these examples of political manipulation through both standardized English and the national vernaculars, Agastya searches for a socially enabling idiom for living in this part of the postcolonial world. His ability to encounter his milieu physically through the body—to feel, for example, the amputation from another's body—effects a certain kind of communication where all available languages have failed. In this capacity, Chatterjee's deployment of a boisterous carnivalesque linguistic register is the answer that cannot be voiced and, given the theme of cultural alienation in the novel, this is a burlesque that functions beyond its purposes of debunking and irreverence. Where Rushdie focuses on linguistic epistemology, Chatterjee radically poses a phenomenological grounding for linguistic praxes.

The body is of course mortal—its marks disappear over time—so its urges change in other milieus. Hence Agastya's found idiom in Madna cannot be translated, even for him, into a philosophy for living. It remains, at best, experiential and performative. In fact Chatterjee refuses to offer a sustained philosophy of living. This refusal is evident in Agastya's inability to find answers in the two texts, drawn from the West and East respectively. In Madna, Agastya reads Marcus Aurelius's *Meditations* and the *Bhagavad Gita* intermittently. Chattily referring to the philosopher as "Marcus," his role model ("like Marcus he kept a desultory diary that year, for like Marcus, he meditated"), Agastya is immersed in "exhilarating abstract problems" (69). Yet it is not Aurelius's insights about human existence, but his daily act of writing, that Agastya emulates:

Marcus Aurelius indirectly taught him the magic of catharsis, that writing assisted thought and clarity of mind, that it was good to be rational. The littlest things became significant. That a pen could move across a page and that its trail, as it were, could make sense—suddenly this seemed magical. A squiggle and a curve, they hold meaning. He wrote: "What are your problems?" and laughed, God, there were so many, and all so totally vague, but analysis helped, or seemed to help, that was why it was good to be rational. (70)

Notable here is the lack of the Aurelius text; rather, writing as a physical activity, its graphic imprint, has more relevance to our body-oriented sensual protagonist. By the end of the novel, on a train back to Calcutta, Agastya realizes that Marcus Aurelius's apparent calm and detachment were actually a sham: "He lied, he lied so well, this sad Roman who had looked for happiness in living more than one life, and had failed, but with such grace" (288). In a similar way, Krishna's call to action over inaction, the discipline over the mind in the *Bhagvad Gita*—"the mind is restless, Krishna, impetuous, self-willed, hard to train" (83)—proves an equally inadequate philosophy for living in Madna. Agastya understands his own mind as a "restless centre" for overlapping worlds, a "movement without purpose, an endless ebb and flow, from one world to another" (278). Instead of sublimating desire to achieve objective detachment, he approaches the world *through* desire, deploying the body and its urges, its intuitions, expressions, and pain. Agastya's refusal of two major philosophical systems implies that the purity of any one cultural landscape cannot enable political action in Madna. It is only the daily experiential negotiation of the world through the body and its desires that provides a viable idiom.

The Last Burden (1993) continues the argument on the English burlesque, but to a less sophisticated effect. Here, too, Chatterjee continues his complex linguistic geographies in layering his metropolitan locale, Calcutta: the public-school-educated sons speak colloquial idiomatic English, with a smattering of expletives; other characters combine vernaculars like Bengali-Marathi or Punjabi-Hindi; the doctor litters his language with hyperbolic technojargon like "angina," "infraction," "coronary thrombosis," and "phlebitic arteriosclerosis"; and erudite English is pointedly showcased in words such as "putative" and "phenomenal." In this direct record of existing speech, Chatterjee habitually exaggerates, parodies, mimics, and criticizes these variants of English. But more than parody, Chatterjee's project in this novel seems to be an attempt to catch vernacular (Bengali) syntax in English, an English that James Wood summarily describes as "a painfully jumbled and arrhythmic language," spoken by a "madcap family" who are "apparently speaking Bengali, here rendered in English" (1997, 33).

While I agree with the general perception that the novel tires the reader in its content—the long, vicious harangues of father, mother, and son spill enormous amounts of Bengali bourgeois guts and guilt over three hundred pages—I would pitch the linguistic project a little differently. The exhaustion one feels toward the uneven prose arises from the constant syntactical translation that one undertakes while reading this English. One can actually hear Bengali idioms, phrasings, syntactical constructions, and cultural resonances within the English spoken by the family, a deeply vernacularized English that is the ghost of its other. Perhaps this style is what seems uneven, for this is not English interspersed with vernacular words but galvanized in memory of Bengali. Above all the other cosmopolitical novels that pitch specific local, regional, and translocal address by harnessing a specific vernacular (like Bengali or Malayalam), this novel's English as a vernacular is least communicable to readers unfamiliar with the syntactical structures of Bengali; this may well account for the novel's unavoidable unpopularity.

The closest critical paradigm that could capture this linguistic experiment is what Chantal Zabus characterizes as indigenized African English in *The African Palimpsest: Indigenization of Language in the West African Europhone Novel*. Zabus explains that relexification produces "neither the target European language or the indigenous source language," but "an *unfamiliar* European language that constantly suggests another language" (1991, 315; my emphasis). Giving examples from African fiction, such as a phrase from Gabriel Okara, "my insides smell with anger," Zabus argues that, unlike translations where there is an original and a secondary text, relexified language places the reader in middle passage—always in the process of transcoding the European text into the African original. The source language is "imperfectly erased" and visible within the European language, effecting a "ghostly mobility" between languages in the very act of reading; I will return to this discursive ghostliness more fully in chapter 5. As a Bengali, while reading *The Last Burden* I caught myself not translating the words back to Bengali, but hearing Bengali words, phrases, and idioms alongside the English.

This relexified English vernacular makes for a florid, figurative prose. Take, for instance, the saying: "For where in the womb of time will she meet another son like you?" (Chatterjee 1993, 11). The exact phrase "the womb of time" translates into a spoken Bengali idiom—*kaler garbha*, an ambivalent phrase that connotes a nurturing womb or a devouring stomach (the valence shifts in positive or negative contexts of use). When the father deploys it in (ironical) reference to the immemorial relation between mother and son, this context-specific phrasing jolts cultural memory of idiomatic Bengali usage. The formulation of "fallen time" as *kal*, often understood as foreboding, adds a further nuance to the conflict between Jamun, the son, and his aged parents, who see themselves in decline. The problem of correctly translating often-used Bengali phrases is thematized in the "non-Bengali" doctor's incomprehension of Jamun's mother's slurred speech when she is recovering from general anesthesia.[20] She has, the doctor reports to the concerned family, "asked after some Kishori and one Ratna Garbha—your maidservant or something, I presume" (227–228). *Ratna garba*, or one who has borne a jewel in her womb, is a term the doctor misinterprets as someone's name. Yet in the context of a story about a son's rejection of his aged parents, the mother's delirious reference speaks to her tragic recognition of her lost jewel.

Another set of phrasings records idiomatic everyday expressions: "That shirt you've been rotting in for ages, why don't you send it to the *dhobi?*" (179) captures the Bengali catechism, "Je shirt-tai tumi poachcho, sheta dhopar kachche pathachchona kano?" This exemplifies everyday idiomatic Bengali phrases that are transcoded into a clumsy English construction. The Bengali penchant for melodrama is recorded in conventional phrases of accusation and guilt: "Blame me! Taunt me! Day in and day out, till the death of time, all of you jeering at me, thwacking me over the knuckles, licking your lips at every pinch" (181). There are also inscriptions of those fluid movements that Bengalis often make between high-flown sentiment and practical concerns: "When the Brahmin sees the son of his son, he is to perceive that the day that has arrived for him does not exist. Rather, it too has its season, and immortality is only continued in one's issue, and the seed of one's issue. . . . Will you ever get hold of this house again if you lease it to a Marwari? They'll battle you in court for fifteen years, bribe everyone in sight and romp home" (279). Chatterjee uses this switch in linguistic modality well, for when it comes to Calcutta's nouveau riche, the Marwaris, the Bengali habit of waxing philosophical and bitchy in the same breath is well known—especially since the Marwaris have acquired the reputation of buying up Bengali property.

Finally, Chatterjee's bending of English is sometimes just directly syntactical. Sentences are fractured through the interspersion of broken phrases that mimic the everyday speech patterns of Bengali conversation: "Savour your handiwork, *our sons*, fostered for decades to hate me. Like a perfect mother, you have kneaded them against me. You're a saint and I'm the demon, *but notice*, they damn you too" (52; my emphasis). "Kneaded" (*gorechho*) is a particularly Bengali way of referring to molding children, and "but notice" (*kintu dekhho*) is a common admonition found in the bitterest of conversations. Overemphasized familial relations interspersed throughout, in phrases like "our sons," "your mother and me," "you, your mother's son," are recurrent speech patterns in spoken Bengali familial interchanges. In these instances, Chatterjee's incorporation

of the everyday of Bengali into English articulates as a situated literary cosmopolitics: the tuning of English to *sound* like idiomatic Bengali.

In *The Last Burden* the project of relexification takes precedence over the
English burlesque of *English, August*. Of the two idioms explored in Chatterjee's
work, the English vernacular of *The Last Burden* with its syntactical shadow
remains the more daring linguistic gesture; the reader is caught in constant linguistic motility, transcoding English with heightened awareness of the gaps
between spoken (and literary) English and Bengali. *English, August* is more
overt in its commentary on language and subjectivity: Agastya's conflicting cultural worlds are incongruously irreconcilable, and he can encounter these
worlds only with his one immutable instrument, the body.

An Idiom of Sound in Arundhati Roy's The God of Small Things

No account of South Asian writing in English is complete without what
has been produced (and hotly debated) as its crowning glory, *The God of Small
Things* (1997). I have argued throughout that the new English vernaculars cannot be fully decoded outside of their local or translocal contexts, and this
remains true of Roy's linguistic experiment in her only novel. As Binoo K. John
notes of Roy:

> She remains a Kottayam girl. . . . Ayemenem and Kottayam and the sur-
> rounding regions form the country where the community was for over a cen-
> tury, trying to find a place for itself. The Syrian Christians, who populate the
> region in large numbers, found quite an unlikely ally in their quest—the
> English language and the Empire. Geographically insulated from the larger
> context of the national movement, the community tried to master the lan-
> guage and send its children to proper English colleges. . . . It needed a writer
> of Roy's impish humor and feel of the language to see the irony—and
> pathos—here. It is out of this tragic grandeur that Roy wove her novel. Twist-
> ing the language to suit her own story telling. She managed to make the
> whole world a stage for Ayemenem and its people. (26)

English is the primary language for the Syrian Christian community, a fact
that is represented on several occasions in the novel with sharp wit and sym-
pathy. Thus Roy does not have to relexify English to catch the idioms of the
vernacular. Rather, she intersperses untranslated Malayalam phrases (creating bilingual sentences) and catches its rhythms, accentuations, and intonations in English, for the Syrian Christians also speak Malayalam. Like
Rushdie's choice of a Goan minority in *The Moor's Last Sigh*, Roy chooses a
small ethnicity with its own regional relationship to the national languages and
to the colonial past.

In other words, the story's specificity of location stipulates the use of a certain kind of English. *The God of Small Things* is the family saga of a Syrian Christian family in Ayemenem, recorded through the consciousness of dizygotic telepathic twins, childishly described by the narrators as "two-egg" twins. It is of course impossible not to remember Saleem and Shiva of *Midnight's Children*, but the twins are not politically affiliated nor do they function as national allegories. There is a point to the "small" stature of the twins in the philosophical scope of the novel: Roy privileges the everyday and the intimate over larger political and social exchanges. Insignificant people, stories, and events are always seen in relation to a greater plenitude. I deliberately use the sufficiently vague characterization of "plenitude" here, for this greater whole is left uncharted by Roy; as a postmodern writer she does not claim to surmise its shape but focuses on the small and particular. On several occasions people and animals are described as "holes" in the universe—"a school-teacher shaped hole" or an "elephant-shaped hole" (1997b, 179, 235)—making being a form of *absence* from plenitude, rather than the form of a *present* ego. In death, people disappear into the greater whole, they achieve presence; but this is commonly felt as a loss or absence. Hence their disappearance is exquisitely rendered as fullness, a "darkness" that "poured like liquid tar" through the hole: "He left behind a hole in the Universe through which darkness poured like liquid tar. Through which their mother followed without even turning to say goodbye. She left them behind, spinning in the dark, with no moorings, in a place with no foundation" (191–192). The darkness speaks of fullness and loss, while the liquid signifies the twins' ebb and flow of emotions.

This ontological premise of merging into a greater whole underwrites the twins' desire for each other, a longing for their original symbiotic fullness expressed physically and mentally. For instance, Rahel "has a memory of waking up one night giggling at Estha's funny dream" (2). Like their birth, their growing up details a slow and tragic separation: "Edges, Borders, Brinks and Limits" appear as Estha is "returned" to his father and physically separated from Rahel. The loss of the other enacts psychic damage for both, a withdrawal from the world and silence for Estha, and a sense of always being somewhere else for Rahel—a fact that leads to her failed marriage: "But when they made love he [Rahel's American husband] was offended by her eyes. They behaved as though they belonged to someone else. Someone watching" (19). When the twins meet again after years of separation, they are overwhelmed by the plenitude their consciousness offers them:

> It had been quiet in Estha's head until Rahel came. But with her she had
> brought the sound of passing trains, and the light and shade that falls on you

if you have a window seat. The world, locked out for years, suddenly flooded in, and now Estha couldn't hear himself for the noise. Trains. Traffic. Music. The Stock Market. A dam had burst and savage waters swept everything up in a swirling. Comets, violins, parades, loneliness, clouds, beards, bigots, lists, flags, earthquakes, despair were all swept up in a scrambled swirling. (14–15)

This notion of "small" and separate things being inevitably reabsorbed and redefined by a larger whole is the grounding philosophical premise of the novel. The "larger whole" is variously posited as history, geological time, a mythic past, the "great" stories of collective knowledge, death, and symbiotic unions of bodies and minds.[21] Roy formalizes the philosophical girding through a narrative structure of concentric circles. The first of these is the twins' tale as it unfolds into that of their riotous family: long-suffering violin-playing grandmothers, violent grandfathers, sexually promiscuous erudite uncles, vindictive aunts, an adventurous but tragic mother, and an English aunt and cousin. They all share a house and the profits of the family business, Paradise Pickles and Preserves. Chacko "owns" the concern as the male heir, but it is his mother's recipes that make the business. The patriarchal inequity here directly references Arundhati Roy's mother's famous legal battle over women's rights to inheritance (enshrined in the Christian Succession Act) in 1986, a step that had earned Mary Roy social ostracism from the more orthodox echelons of the Syrian Christian community. The family saga expands into the world: Roy catalogs the Syrian Christian arrival in Kerala, Chacko's study abroad and marriage to an Englishwoman, Rahel's marriage to an American and Ammu's marriage to a Bengali. The family, in turn, has varying relationships to others in the community: other Syrian Christians; Catholic priests; touchable and untouchable Hindus (for the laws of untouchability infiltrate Syrian Christian social relations as well); and politicians like the Communist Party leader, Comrade Pillai. Through these characters, the family's history dovetails into that of the region and the nation, in a collection of myths, local stories, gossip, and political history.

The family's affairs, incidents of domestic violence, jealousies, fears, and betrayals further circle into a larger canvas of journeys, betrayals, losses, and power games:

Still, to say it all began when Sophie Mol came to Ayemenem is only one way of looking at it.

Equally, it could be argued that it actually began thousands of years ago. Long before the Marxists came. Before the British took Malabar, before the Dutch Ascendency, before Vasco da Gama arrived, before Zamorin's conquest of Calicut. Before three purple-robed Syrian Bishops murdered by the Portuguese were found floating in the sea, with coiled sea serpents riding on their chests and oysters knotted in their tangled beards. It could be argued that it began long before Christianity arrived in a boat and seeped into Kerala like tea from a teabag. (33)

Such observations are followed in later chapters by "several competing theories" on the relationship between Syrian Christians, Marxists, and Hindus offered tongue in cheek (66–67).

The Ammu and Velutha love affair ties the political argument of the novel with its philosophical universe. Of course, as the dalit character, Velutha is mythified as the dark love-god Krishna, who brings Ammu to ecstasy on the riverbed. But his godlikeness is seen from Ammu's lovelorn eyes. For the children, Velutha is a playmate; for Ammu, he is the "God of Loss," the "God of Small Things," the "God of Goose Bumps and Sudden Smiles" (330). Velutha represents for Ammu the pleasures and insights into human life shorn of political and social constraints, devoid of history: "Ammu saw that he saw. She looked away. He did too. History's fiends returned to claim them. To rewrap them in its old, scarred pelt and drag them back to where they really lived. Where Love Laws laid down who should be loved. And how. And how much" (177). The reference to rewrapping evokes the bare-bodied splendor of the last few pages of lovemaking that close the text—a flashback that remains the abiding image of union when one puts the book down. Thus the Ammu-Velutha coupling, both characters destroyed within the scope of the story, remains immortalized as eternal ecstasy that transcends the orderly progression of historical events.

For we are told that Ammu and Velutha are destroyed by history or the social perception of the human story, as the twins point out in witnessing the Touchable policemen beating up Velutha: "What Estappen and Rahel witnessed that morning, though they did not know it then, was a clinical demonstration in controlled conditions (this was not war after all, or genocide) of human nature's pursuit of ascendancy. Structure. Order. Complete monopoly. It was human history, masquerading as God's Purpose, revealing herself to an under-age audience" (309). Ammu and Velutha transgress caste barriers, those divides distorted and presented as "God's Purpose." They break the "laws," which are human social contracts set down from ancient times, "before the Marxists," "before the Christians," "before the Indian nation" (33). The adult Rahel and Esta, in their incestuous coupling, also break incest taboos that regulate human societies: "Only that once again they broke the Love Laws. That lay down who should be loved. And how much" (328). In that moment of perfect union, the stranger in Rahel's eyes disappears: "except no watcher watched through Rahel's eyes" (328).

This transgressiveness, transmitted as it were from mother to children, refutes historical laws, mythic laws, religious laws, and the laws of social contract and of family. The "Big God" is a peculiarly South Asian shorthand for the naturalized and authoritative status of manmade boundaries that seek to regulate, discipline, and divide human relationships. Roy presents an account of these Love Laws embedded in collective memory through the Karna-Kunti episode, staged by a traveling *kathakali* troupe that comes to Ayemenem.[22] The analogical relation of Karna (the bastard son) to Velutha (the low-born lover) is unmistakable; both are betrayed and forsaken within the requirements of the Love Laws, the social strictures of the Big God. Thus Ammu and Velutha find momentary happiness in sticking to small things: "Even later, on thirteen nights that followed this one, instinctively they stuck to Small Things. The Big Things ever lurked inside. They knew there was nowhere for them to go. They had nothing. No future. So they stuck to small things. They laughed at ant-bites on each other's bottoms. At clumsy caterpillars sliding off the ends of leaves, at overturned beetles that couldn't right themselves" (338).

Roy demonstrates how larger historical concerns more often than not engulf minute detail and pleasure in the world, and the narrating of the world's little stories. "Small things" become adrift and inconsequential in the onslaught of the big:

> That Big God howled like a hot wind, and demanded obeisance. Then Small God (cosy and contained, private and limited) came away cauterized, laughing numbly at his own temerity. Inured by the confirmation of his own inconsequence, he became resilient and truly indifferent. Nothing mattered much. Nothing much mattered. And the less it mattered, the less it mattered. It was never important enough. Because Worse Things had happened. (19)

The phrase "nothing mattered," repeated several times here and then later when the twins witness Velutha's beating, warns of emptiness, loss, and lack of responsibility in a world abandoned by the God of Small Things; hence the God of Small Things is always on the verge of becoming the God of Loss. Of course, Rahel and Esta, the two small things in the novel, find no benevolence in the Big God of human systems and history; they would rather inhabit a polytheistic world governed by small gods, *veluthas*, elephants, and beetles. Small things can also be dangerous, for seemingly small acts such as Velutha and Ammu's lovemaking can have large consequences in death, exile, and social ostracism. It is ultimately a matter of perspective, the significance of things to the individual being: "They would grow up grappling with ways of living with what happened.

They would try to tell themselves that in terms of geological time it was an insignificant event. Just a blink of the earth Woman's eye" (55). Here the philosophy of the whole and its parts enters the level of narratability, because it is in the act of telling a story that one imparts meaning to an event: "Little things, ordinary things, smashed and reconstituted. Imbued with new meaning. Suddenly they become the bleached bones of a story" (32–33). In the twins' story "ordinary India" gets maximum narrative space: The details of a traffic jam, for instance, occupy some twenty-seven pages of the novel (60–87).[23]

Like so many of its counterparts in the cosmopolitical novels, here too the philosophical premises of the novel inform its use of language, for it is a tale told in the vocabulary of small things, the children. Indeed part of the linguistic idiosyncrasy and innovation in *The God of Small Things* can be attributed to Roy's creation of the children's consciousness: "Children feel textures as combinations because they do not understand what is being combined. Thus Roy, thinking on behalf of her twins, flourishes "oldfood smell," "one mint" (for "one minute"), "ofcourseofcourseofcourse," "bestfriend," "train-rumble," and so on" (Wood 1997, 34). In general I would agree with James Wood's highlighting of children's speech as the reason for Roy's verbal innovation. For children who are in the process of language acquisition, the boundaries between languages are often permeable and muddy. Sometimes Roy's extensive use of capital letters signals small things of great significance to children. For instance, the Orangedrink Lemondrink man assumes stature because of his impact on Estha after he molests the boy at the *Sound of Music* screening, while questions such as, "Chacko do you love Sophie Mol *Most* in the *World*?" highlight certain words that vibrate with childish anxiety (1997b, 119; my emphasis).

But Wood misses the rhythm of Malayalam in the run-on English that the twins deploy to describe their small world. The combination words of phrases that deviate from hyphenated standard English words capture the polysyllabic verbal structure of Malayalam, and not simply the odd language of children. Here the children's innovative English represents a specific bilingual community. The Syrian Christian and Hindu communities of Kottayam and Ayemenem both use Malayalam and English, with some variations in bilingual speech patterns. Roy juxtaposes English, untranslated Malayalam, and bilingual spoken variants alongside each other, and the politics of those languages are thematically investigated in the youthful narrators' self-conscious preoccupation with language acquisition.

Because the twins are extremely self-reflexive in their use and adoption of Western cultural terms, language, icons, and images, their narration becomes a labored linguistic experiment. Much time is spent on their Anglicized education by Chacko and Baby Kochamma, particularly the latter, the aunt who levies fines for speaking Malayalam. Baby Kochamma makes the twins write, "I will always speak in English" a hundred times. She then insists on correct pronunciation (parodied by the twins): "They had to form the words properly, and be particularly careful about their pronunciation. Prer NUN sea ayshun" (36). Another half a chapter is spent on Ammu's toil in teaching them to write and spell English. Initially the twins imbibe English literary referents and use them imitatively: Rahel "wasn't sure what she suffered from" but would pull a sad face in the mirror and fashion herself after "Sydney Carton being Charles Darnay," exclaiming 'It is a far, far better thing that I do, than I have ever done'" (61). As they grow older the references become increasingly ironic, sometimes because of the ways in which Western cultural material is decoded in this local context. We see this in Esta's logical listing of the images from the *Sound of Music* standard "My Favorite Things" that takes the magical fantasy out of the song:

> The clean white children, even the big ones, were scared of the thunder. To comfort them, Julie Andrews put them all in her clean bed, and sang them a clean song about a few of her favourite things. These were a few of her favourite things:
>
> (1) Girls in white dresses with blue satin sashes.
> (2) Wild geese that flew with the moon on their wings.
> (3) Bright copper kettles.
> (4) Doorbells and sleighbells and schnitzel with noodles.
> (5) Etc. (105–106)

The fantasy is lost, and Estha overemphasizes "clean" because it is on the *Sound of Music* trip, the quintessential innocent childhood adventure, that Esta is molested by the Orangedrink Lemondrink man. The antiseptic sterility of the musical's attempted cheerfulness now becomes a mechanical and meaningless list in Esta's mind.

While Western popular culture may appear simply incongruous in Ayemenem, strictly colonial English as an abstract language has little valence in the twins' world; in fact they gradually begin to perceive the language as illogical and idiosyncratic. Rahel always refers to afternoon siestas as "gnaps" (198), parodying Latinate spelling that has little meaning to her, and the twins often defamiliarize words to test their imaginative flexibility: "*Boot* was a lovely word. A much better word, at any rate, than *sturdy*. *Sturdy* was a terrible word. Like a dwarf's name. *Sturdy Koshy Oommen*—a pleasant, middle-class, God-fearing dwarf with low knees and a side parting" (46). These perceptions tell us that in their act of memory the twins have also embarked on a linguistic search for the perfect language. Central to their project is the materiality of words, and the sounds that words make. We first begin to intuit the twins' material approach to language when on several occasions the twins try out words for sound, combining them with other Malayalam words (such as the untranslated "koshy oommen") to create an oral-visual representation. This experiment defines the English vernacular that dominates their narration.

Roy gives the reader clues for apprehending the twins' predilection for linguistic innovation quite early in the novel. From the first they seem fed up with the lack of logic in the English language in its most abstract and erudite forms, delighting in the very few logical terms in the language: "'to link cuffs together,' Ammu told them—they were thrilled by this morsel of logic in what had so far seemed an illogical language. Cuff + link = Cuff-link. This, to them, rivaled the precision and logic of mathematics" (51). But they are soon bored with verbal logistics and challenge their teachers by constantly reading texts backward:

> They showed Miss Mitten how it was possible to read both *Malayalam* and *Madam I'm Adam* backwards as well as forwards. She wasn't amused and it turned out that she didn't even know what Malayalam was. They told her it was the language everyone spoke in Kerala. . . . Estha, who had by then taken an active dislike to Miss Mitten, told her that as far as he was concerned it was a Highly Stupid Impression.
>
> Miss Mitten complained to Baby Kochamma about Estha's rudeness, and about their reading backwards. She told Baby Kochamma that she had seen Satan in their eyes. *nataS in their seye.* (60)

At one level, the delicious freedom of moving backward and forward in a language demonstrates the twins' actual mastery of the language and the willingness to explore all its contours. But in Miss Mitten there is one more proof of the disconnection of the colonial education system from the twins' lived contexts. The second backward read on "Satan" reveals the twins' deconstruction of correct English by reducing it to nonsense. Still later this proficiency for reading backward is used against the police. The children reverse the virtues listed at the police station (politeness, obedience, loyalty, and so forth) after they witness Velutha's murder by a police platoon (313). Here the linguistic deconstruction implies the egregiousness of police behavior. Through these language games, we assemble a portrait of protagonists who are deeply involved in actively crafting a world through language.

How then to present a richly textured world through a bilingual consciousness, this world of small things the twins strive to bring to our notice? The key here is the twins' musical ear, especially for Estha, silent to the world but unable to resist music. In fact he gets into trouble at the movies because he is pushed

out of the movie theater for singing all the lyrics (101). The twins display an ear
for phonetics, and for the relationship of words to objects rather than the more
abstract relationship of signifier-signified. There is a hilarious recounting of
Latha, Pillai's daughter, reciting Sir Walter Scott's "Lochinvar":

> "O, young Lochin varhas scum out of the vest,
> Through wall the vide Border his teed was the bes;
> Tand savissgood broadsod heweapon sadnun,
> Nhe rod unarmed, and he rod all lalone."
>
> (271)

Notice the preference for the pronounced word (what the twins hear) over the
correctly spelt word. And young Lenin, Pillai's son, brays: "I cometoberry Cae-
sar, not to praise him" (275). These accents may be simply parodies of the
accented Malayalam English but, given the bathetic Miss Mitten, the memo-
rization of poems not understood for their meaning is another symptom of the
deadness of colonial literary English in this cultural landscape. Of course, there
is the related irony that it is Comrade Pillai's children who are most invested in
colonial education, contradicting his search for "authentic" Indian folk traditions
in Pillai's self-fashioning as Marxist revolutionary. But more interesting are
the particularities of this Indian accent, the tendency to run English monosyl-
labic words together in rolling polysyllabic intonations specific to the Malayalam
language.

In all these examples, we have further proof of the twin's predilection for
sound over sense. Repeatedly in their games, the twins experiment with sound:

> *Nictitating membrane*, she remembered she and Estha once spent a whole day
> saying. She and Estha and Sophie Mol.

> *Nictitating*
> *ictitating*
> *titating*
> *itating*
> *tating*
> *ating*
> *ting*
> *ing*
> (189)

The manner in which the phrase is broken up displays an experiment with
combinations of consonants and vowels, and a logical breakdown of the syllabic
structure. Both these endeavors depend on the ability to hear the music in a lan-

guage, and they reflect a desire to play with syllables, intonations, and linguistic rhythms for auditory effect. On many occasions desired musical effects are created by the willy-nilly blending of languages: "Oh Esthapappychachen Kuttappen Peter Mon? / Where, oh where have you gon?" (182).

If one were to embark on a Saussurian analysis of the sign here, it is the "sound" part of the sound-image combination (the signifier) that dominates the children's new language. The overwhelming dominance of hyphenated, run-on, and combined words, always polysyllabic, seems to suggest the memory of Malayalam intonations in English. This is not the same as Chatterjee's relexified English, where actual syntactical structures (of everyday idioms and phrases) of Bengali are introduced into English. In Roy's insistence on the ontological basis of language, Malayalam accents and linguistic rhythms are deployed to create new sound images (signifiers) for a lushly verdant world that escapes the most florid of English constructions. Of course, Roy makes ample use of standard English hyphenated words: Kochu Maria, the midget cook, is described as "vinegar-hearted" and "short-tempered" (15), while the children's father is a small, "well-built," "pleasant-looking" man with "old-fashioned" spectacles (39). As these examples show, when Roy uses standard polysyllabic constructions, she overuses them, making logically consistent the more daring and extended combinations:

> Heaven opened and the water hammered down, reviving the reluctant old well, greenmossing the pigless pigsty, carpet bombing still, tea-coloured puddles the way memory bombs still, tea-coloured minds. The grass looked wetgreen and pleased. Happy earthworms frolicked purple in the slush. Green nettles nodded. Trees bent.
>
> Further away, in the wind and rain, on the banks of the river, in the sudden thunderdarkness of the day, Estha was walking. He was wearing a crushed-strawberry-pink T-shirt, drenched darker now, and he knew Rahel had come. (10)

This passage describes Rahel's return to Ayemenem and the memories evoked by that act in the joint consciousness of the twins. The torrents of memory and rain are rhythmically depicted in polysyllables piled upon polysyllables, the regular constructions like "T-shirt" and "strawberry-pink" mingling with the more evocative "tea-coloured puddles" and "tea-coloured minds." The overabundance of natural forces and greenery is further represented by the tumescence of "wetgreen," greenmossing," and "thunderdarkness." The sensual aspect of the children's milieu—rain, creepers, mud, river, and dank houses—takes precedence over logical linguistic extensions. For instance, we are informed of the Ayemenem house's relationship to the river in alliterative sentences that simulate the roll of water in their sound: "like a sea-shell always has a sea-sense, the Ayemenem house still had a river-sense. A rushing, rolling, fish-swimming sense" (30). At other points, a similar tone of overabundance is created by repetitions, such as the "brooding storm-coming sky" and the "eerie, storm-coming light" (195), or the "driftless driftwood" in the river; by hyphenated phrases, like the "green-for-the-day" that seeped in from the trees (187), or "bronze-winged lily-trotters . . . splay-footed" (124); and sometimes brief combined words and phrases for impressionistic evocations such as "[t]he Meenachal. Greygreen. With fish in it" (203). A wonderful example of such prose, now deployed to capture mounting emotions, occurs in the scene where Estha and Rahel see the policemen approach the History House: "The Kottayam police. A cartoonplatoon. New-Age princes in funny pointed helmets. Cardboard lined with cotton. Hairoil stained. Their shabby khakhi crowns. Dark of Heart. Deadlypurposed" (304). The long beat of "deadlypurposed" becomes rhythmic, as the polysyllabic constructions begin to pile up in the lines that follow: "dewdamp leghair," "steel-tipped," "legskin raw," and "crisscrossed with cuts" (304–305). The children's fascination with sound and rhythm in language above its lexical or syntactical purity invokes a certain ontological relation to the language. Engaged in privileging sound over sense, the children deploy a felt idiom that describes their visceral encounter with this locale.

We are always reminded that this language is made possible by the fact that the *children* imagine this language, a part of the usual childlike gymnastics with newly acquired vocabularies. Polysyllabic word use is further rationalized as a medium of expression for the children's hyperbolic sense of (overwhelming) moments. For instance, Estha's need to throw up is rather childishly put as a "greenwavy, thick-watery, lumpy seaweedy, bottomless-bottomful feeling" (107). And the bustle, antiseptic smoothness, and industrial drone of an airport is perceived by Rahel as "red-mouthed roos with ruby smiles moved cemently across the airport floor" (139). Yet while childhood lends credibility to linguistic innovations, the over-the-top choice of combinations, polysyllables, hyphens, and run-on words, along with a clearly identifiable rhythm that resonates with Malayalam, indicates a specific experiment with vernacularizing English.

These instances occur at the level of new signifiers that keep intact the basic grammars and syntactical structures of English. More radical is Roy's introduction of untranslated Malayalam words, most often in conversations. The whisper "Chacko *saar vannu*" (171) combines an accented English word in a Indian accent, *saar* (sir), with an untranslated Malayalam word, *vannu* (has come). The spoken English vernacular and Malayalam form this particular hybrid phrase. Koch Maria's exclamation, "She's very beautiful" is repeated in untranslated

Malayalam, *"Sundarikutty"* (179), while other interspersed Malayalam words (*oower, orkunnilley, kushumbi*) and Malayalam-accented English (Amayrica) in other conversations portray a bilingual community equally at ease with both languages. Local terms for food (*idi appams, kanji, meen*), fish (*pallathi, karimeen, paral, koori*), family relationships ("deaf *ammoomas,*" "cantankerous arthiritic *appoopans*"), and ethnic distinctions ("not a *Pelaya,* or a Pulaya, or a Paravan") are simply added to the English register of words. Songs and rhymes in Malayalam are translated only when the meaning is absolutely necessary for narrative progression. The Onam boat-race song is translated into English in brackets while Estha stirs or "rows" the sticky red jam at the factory, because the song reflects Estha's entrapment in the family, the factory, and the memory of abuse; his frantic rowing reflects a displaced desire to escape with Rahel to the river, the twins' site of fantasy. On other occasions, untranslated verse, such as the poem about the train that runs through Velutha's mind as he leaves the Ayemenem house with the sinking realization of his own doom, represents a deliberate withdrawal of the subject into silence, confusion, and fear (285).

Like Rushdie's prose, Roy's linguistic experiments demands locale-specific knowledge for fully understanding the text, an invitation to supplementarity for readers and a marking of linguistic limits. A moment built into the narrative that invites the reader to migrate between languages, then blocks entry, occurs when Comrade Pillai (in his inimitable English vernacular) tells Chacko that his wife understands English: "'Of course inside the house she is Boss.' He turned to her with an affectionate, naughty smile. '*Allay edi*, Kalyani?'" (278). Although his entire point is about Kalyani's ability to understand English, Pillai's intimate address to his wife in untranslated Malayalam draws a linguistic screen between the reader who does not understand Malayalam and the bilingually proficient members of this community.

A Performative Localism

The multivalent address of the English vernaculars in these novels certainly extends an invitation to readers to be borne across to local cultural worlds in different ways. All readers are required to perform a ritual at the border: the act of translation in the name of supplementarity demanded by these cosmopolitical writers' exhaustive linguistic experiments. In other words, these novels are exciting because they do not read easily. Gone is the historical, perhaps restful, opposition between an "Indian" English and its colonial other. Now readers are asked to perform different acts of translation on a case-by-case basis, to migrate between cultural and linguistic worlds whose boundaries are not rigorously defined as East-West or postcolonial-colonial, and which habitually collide and create subjective discordance.

Hence one cannot produce the kind of "translatese" that Spivak warns against, a practice conducive to producing surplus value for "multicultural objects" in the global marketplace: "In the act of wholesale translation into English there can be a betrayal of the democratic ideal to the law of the strongest. This happens when all of the literature of the Third World gets translated into a sort of with-it translatese, so that the literature by a woman in Palestine begins to resemble, in the feel of its prose, something by a man in Taiwan. The rhetoricity of Chinese and Arabic!" (Spivak 1993b, 182). Asking the (feminist) translator to remember her position as an agent between the original and the shadow, Spivak demands awareness of the "rhetoricity of the original": "The politics of translation from a non-European woman's text too often suppresses this possibility because the translator cannot engage with, or cares insufficiently for, the rhetoricity of the original" (181). Like the most nonexpert of readers, the cultural critic/translator hears the "fraying of language" and in the intimacy of reading, she too "surrenders" to the irreducible linguistic alterity of the text. Yet the bilingual critic bears the added burden of conveying the difficulties of being borne across to vernacular registers. Such ethical translation inheres, Spivak surmises, precisely in the recognition of maximal alterity in language while one engages in turning "the other into something like the self" (183).

While Spivak is addressing translators hungrily devouring texts written by non-European women, her cautionary tale may be extended to our acts of reading these cosmopolitical texts. Readers and critics can easily produce readings of "hybridized English" that too quickly fall into the historical oppositions of English versus the vernaculars, or "Indian English" versus some universally understood "standard English." Instead of producing such critical "translatese," if we pay attention to the rhetoricity of the text, then we embark on everyday acts of performative translation that move toward context-specific linguistic learning.[24] This performative localism of reading resists any fetishistic claims on local cultural space.

Four

The Body of the Other

Narrating Violence, Community, History

Three of the riders were dressed in police khaki. The fourth, riding pillion, was eight-armed, outlandish in a Durga mask and a tight-multicoloured jacket from which protruded six stuffed limbs. He carried what looked like a very real AK-47.

The bikes stopped before the gates of the hostel, apparently waiting for the steel-grey Contessa saloon that was emerging from the compound to precede them. As the car inched forward into the muddle, the motorcyclists got off and went up to it. One figure in khaki tapped on the rear window, and a second—a woman, with a scar across her cheek—climbed, in two feline leaps, from the back on to the roof of the car. Squatting and leaning over, she, with an iron rod, shattered wide open its rear windshield. Even as she jumped off, the other three opened fire.

—*Upamanyu Chatterjee*, Mammaries of the Welfare State

So unfold the climactic events of Upamanyu Chatterjee's third major novel, *Mammaries of the Welfare State* (2000), a virtually unreadable satire of the welfare state's bureaucratic machinery. Spewing state officialese—memos, letters, short histories, diaries, essays, catalogs—in Dickensian proportions, the narration grinds to a halt under the weight of rhetorical garbage. We scarcely notice the return of our mutual friend, Agastya Sen from *English, August*, to the plague-struck town of Madna. In this Indian interior, things have hardly changed: Only the effects of bureaucratic excess are deadlier, and the subaltern emerges as the politicized terrorist ever present at the heart of the modern nation. Indeed, if cinema is any index of the national popular, especially in India, we know that the embattled figure of the terrorist as the splinter at the heart of the imagined community is a fairly recursive one in recent Bollywood and independent South Asian films.[1]

With continuing violence from insurgents and the state in Kashmir, comprehending the ethical dimensions of terrorism has gained new salience in the subcontinent. Now an abiding if troubling presence in the national imaginary, the terrorist insurgent (against the nation-state), displaced from indigenous habitats and beyond reach of political community, is the "outsider" who is also a new national subject of narration. As the hideous progeny of the postcolonial liberal state's violence against its subalterns, this "other" implodes the body of the imagined community. In Pheng Cheah's elaboration of the "vitalist ontology" of nations who have undergone revolutionary decolonization, an account to which I will return later in this chapter, the territorial and capitalist drives of the nation-state and of national elites impose "stasis" on the dynamism of a people still in the process of becoming a political community (1999, 235). Seen in such a frame, and translated in official nationalist discourse, the terrorist appears as a hidebound angel of death. But in popular narration, the monstrous visage of the terrorist mirrors the state's own violent propensities—those mushroom clouds and life-threatening dams that signal the global military and economic aspirations of the contemporary Hindu Right.

While in *English, August*, the violent subaltern is an unknown tribal other from the Jompana forests, in *Mammaries*, the "integrated tribal" has specific location, history, and centrality in the narrative. The female "bandit," physically scarred by the upper-caste Mafia, quite blatantly draws from the popular memory of India's folk hero Phoolan Devi (popularly remembered as "the bandit queen").[2] Early in the novel we encounter Chamundi (named after the mother goddess who embodies power), the boy victim of the welfare state's Integrated Tribal Development Plan. Displaced from the forests of Jompana, Chamundi is servant and sex slave (officially, "personal assistant") to the grotesque Commissioner Raghupati. Sodomized and murdered by Raghupati, all under the auspices of the welfare state, the terrorized Chamundi disappears quickly from the story. Yet this dismembered body of the other haunts this story of effete bureaucrats, as Chatterjee speckles the novel with the many members of Chamundi's "enormous tribal clan." In the town's popular memory, Chamundi's grandfather had been one of the "beneficiaries" of a government plan to integrate the Other Backward Classes, the postindependence institutional category for historically disenfranchised lower castes and indigenous "tribal" peoples. The benefits of the government's plan had filtered down to Chamundi, who was soon integrated into the nation through government employment. His sister—the woman with the scar—had started service at the International Hotel, while his brother, Dambha, had become an auto-rickshaw driver complete with a Durga costume (a garb treated earlier in the novel with both condescension and curiosity by the middle-class protagonists). A stray bullet from the legendary vicious Mafia leader Makhmal Bagai's gun etches a livid scar on Chamundi's sister, who subsequently loses her job at the International Hotel because of her loss of sexual allure. We patch together these fragments mostly from rumor, hearsay, and deduction, after the cinematic moment of terrorist infraction.

Chatterjee's narration of the subaltern who exposes the sham of "democratic self-rule" dramatizes the ethical propositions of South Asian cosmopolitical writing. I am hardly suggesting that in underlining the disenfranchisement of the terrorist, Chatterjee (or anyone else, for that matter) provides a political rationale for terrorism—quite the contrary. In cosmopolitical writing, there is often a dual critique: a political polemic against state violence (sometimes directly referenced, as we see in Arundhati Roy's literary depiction of police brutality), and an ethical inquiry into those "in-human" capacities of the other that surface when communities violently dismember each other. I characterize such engagement as a cosmopolitan activism on the part of our writers who translate subaltern lives, subjects, and struggles for global audiences, often with the aim of forging translocal solidarities. We shall see this most distinctly in the relations between Roy's activism (in the Narmada Bachchao Andolan) and her philosophy of "small things" that frames *The God of Small Things*. Cosmopolitical novels make visible those other worlds in global and national blind spots where displaced and disenfranchised subjects (both unwilling migrants and fourth-world peoples who remain in stasis while their habitats disintegrate around them) find depiction.

In Other Worlds

Here I chalk the intellectual context for the translations of subaltern subjects and lives in the furious reworkings of the national-global dialectic in South Asia from the mideighties. Most anxieties focus on the interpenetration of the national by the global, as commentators anticipate the opening of a cultural Pandora's box in the wake of globalization: "Let the cultural policy-makers, if they will, consider the excesses of the market in the cultural field. But the odds are against them. For, the forces being released by reckless urbanization, new electronic media, imported ideas and ideologues and scores of groups looking frantically for new cultural identities have a way of getting out of control" (Lal 1992). This characterization typifies the growing consternation (from the Right and the Left) over the loosened hyphen between the nation and the nation state, the fallout from the emergent consensus "to globalize." Cosmopolitical critics of globalism worry over the lack of protection afforded the rural poor and indigenous people, famously labeled "people who have not moved" in Spivak's critique of globalizing theoryspeak (Spivak 1997). Often turned "migrant" by the influx of transnational capital (like the Enron power project in Maharashtra discussed later) and by national "development" (like the Narmada dam-building project), these are the subaltern communities whose resources the welfare state should hold "in trust": "Earth, forest, water, air. These are assets that the state holds in trust for the people that it represents. . . . To snatch these away and sell them as stock to private companies is a process of barbaric dispossession on a scale that has no parallel in history" (Roy 2001, 43).

But while making subaltern struggles globally communicable is plainly one of the projects of cosmopolitical writing, so is a sustained interrogation of these strains of virulent nationalism that shatter the social imaginary of democratic self-rule. The cosmopolitical writers engage quite self-consciously in unraveling forms of reactionary cultural nationalism, the corollary to globalism. Here the violently emplacing grammars of nationalism—the deliberations of identity in staged culture wars—come under fire in the disjunctive narration of these novels. Where official nationalism homogenizes history, the cosmopolitical writers pose the vicissitudes of unreliable memory and the discontinuities, ruptures, and silences of history writing. In this gesture, the writers mark their solidarity with scholars in other disciplines more directly employed in historiographic projects. My later discussion of an electronic exchange between Amitav Ghosh and Dipesh Chakrabarty, following their respective publications of *The Glass Palace* (2001) and *Provincializing Europe* (2000), will demonstrate my contention of a shared political commitment. Of course historians, like those in the Subaltern Studies Collective and revisionist feminists (such as Urvashi Butalia and Ritu Menon), have been at the front lines of reconstructing historical silences and showcasing the problems intrinsic to such projects. In the larger intellectual thoroughfare where this history writing takes shape, lodged in an erased heterogeneous past, the subaltern has emerged as the political trope for the disenfranchised national and global subject. Since progressive scholars are more often than not precisely troubled about their acts of transforming the subaltern into a malleable trope, they remain attentive to *unworking* their abstractions. In the case of the cosmopolitical writers, this generates a series of textual strategies that I describe as "uncanny narration." Here the "uncanny" serves as a figure for the incommensurability of the other's idiom when harnessed in modern (novelistic) discourse.

These cosmopolitical narrations are peopled by a variety of posthuman subjects who emerge, I shall argue, as one kind of register for present and past violences—with specters commanding the lion's share of attention. As unreal presences who force the ground of literary realism and who bring genres into

crisis, specters open seams between different times, spaces, and human subjects. In this regard, they inhabit these novels in a Derridean modality, the register of another sort of accounting that rational discourses of reparation or debt
cannot entertain. Invested in such a dialogue about political costs, debts, and
justice, not to mention a will to postfoundationalist history, the cosmopolitical
writers attack violent emplacing (nationalist) inscriptions by trafficking in
specters. Subsequently, their ethical spectrology reflexively unearths the spectrality of the postcolonial nation in the full flush of capitalist development.

Given the sustained questioning of nation from the mideighties, we find an
obsession with ghosts across South Asian popular media in the "return," for
instance, of national icons like Naturam Godse or Netaji Subhas Chandra Bose
to public discourse. Yet these ghosts are somewhat different from the specters
of the cosmopolitical novel. The Bengali regional attachment to Netaji and the
Hindu right-wing lionization of Godse are, for one, nostalgic reaches toward
political and cultural hegemony—they speak of the "lost" promises of regional
and micronationalist aspiration. In this sense, these fetishized embodied
specters or "ghosts" are very much within the "organic birth" etymologies of
political community to which spectrality is opposed. They hardly bespeak those
critical engagements with spectrality that I designate as "ethical spectrology."
Yet, as we shall see in Ruchir Joshi's return to the Netaji myth in the next chapter, even the historically fetishized ghost can be turned against the emplacing
capacities of historical narration. Specters, then, are always ambivalent; but
even in the cosmopolitical novels, they slip into the service of fetishistic localism now and then.

I peruse the various specters in cosmopolitical novels in much greater depth
in the next chapter. But before turning to consideration of the national intellectual discursive terrain of the cosmopolitical novels, one final point on their
"uncanny" narration. If the dislodging of emplacing narratives comprises one of
the discernible political agendas of these novels, showcasing epistemological
différance is its logical corollary. In bringing subaltern subjects, lives, and
worlds into the purview of modern discourse, the cosmopolitical writers draw
our attention to the global hierarchies of knowledge production. Their struggle
over the production of locality inheres in translating those recessive knowledges that are under cultural erasure in our time. Sometimes these are vernacular literary traditions, as in the case of Amitav Ghosh; at other times,
another mode of historical narration, as we see in Vikram Chandra. The fissures
between the different epistemologies of the postcolonial cosmopolitical novel
are highlighted in these texts through a process that I name "grafting." These
cultural grafts—the embedding of a Tagore short story in an Indian novel in
English, for instance—demand migrations into (vernacular) traditions less

known to nonexpert global reading publics. It is the task of the cultural critic to translate, with all the difficulties incumbent in that act, those traditions not in global circulation.

The Cosmopolitan Activist

We find a striking example of cosmopolitan activism in a modulated critique of official postcolonial nationalist agendas in Palagummi Sainath's internationally acclaimed *Everyone Loves a Good Drought: Stories from India's Poorest Districts*, published in 1997. As we know, Palagummi Sainath was one of the featured writers in the NPR celebration of India at fifty. Written over the two years that the Mumbai-based journalist spent living among the poorest communities in the world, the book comprises a series of reports (eighty-four, published in the *Times of India*) on the marginalized rural poor: dalits, adivasis, small farmers, and agricultural laborers. Even in its first circulation, *Everyone Loves a Good Drought* accrued weighty currency, winning thirteen international and national awards. After translation into several regional Indian and other languages, it was in its eighth printing by 1998. Its national critique notwithstanding, the text was immediately adopted in seventy Indian universities, and trainees in the Indian Administrative Service (part of the Indian bureaucracy that Palagummi Sainath blames for the chaos among the rural poor) were made to read the reports as preparation for their jobs in the rural hinterland. Palagummi Sainath was soon recognized, nationally and globally, as the conscience of the nation.

I invoke this incident because it illustrates the rather complex and ongoing reconsiderations of the national-global dialectic that are a salient aspect of globalization everywhere. Celebrating fifty years of national sovereignty in 1997 obviously merited pitched performances of nationhood on the global stage. But the jubilee also provided cosmopolitan activists like P. Sanaith and Arundhati Roy an occasion to refocus the global eye on local subjects, lives, and struggles. As my pursuit of the Renaissance as commodity has shown, these two activists' international purchase called national attention to sites of local struggle. Roy's performance of a situated cosmopolitics in both her fiction and her activisms on the behalf of dalits was honored by the Kerela Dalit Sahitya Akademi, who held a reception for her applauding Roy's decision to use the royalties accruing to the Malayalam translations of her *God of Small Things* to advance Dalit literature.

Many of the cosmopolitical novels discussed in this book engage in a situated literary activism. From a man trained as a bureaucrat, Upamanyu Chatterjee's *English, August* (1988) still stands as one of the most searing exposés of fossilized megaprojects, of those "costs of living" and "national development" that

Roy so eloquently criticizes in her nonfiction. In *English, August*, and with increasing sharpness in *Mammaries*, Chatterjee bears witness to the bureaucracy's violence on those excluded peoples of globalization, the adivasis of the Indian interior. Like Roy, Chatterjee rarely writes of "nation" as an imaginative project to which he returns, but insists on the necessary political restructuring of the state. Remember, he cautions in one interview, that the notion of a "confederation" is the only recourse for "a vast country, a varied people, a geography fashioned to cushion one region from the anxieties of another" (1997, 174). The threats he perceives to the India polity are national and global elites: the effete national bureaucrat whose counterpart is the transnational technocrat who would "de-government the nation" armed with "How-To ideas" (174). Both Roy's and Chatterjee's fundamental concerns are with the Indian democracy as the arena for political action, despite Roy's troping of herself as a country without borders. Global activism, like Roy's invocation to "globalize dissent" (2002b, 20), for instance, involves the cosmopolitical pursuit of human rights, a connection Walter Mignolo (2002) underlines in the *Public Culture* discussion on cosmopolitanism.

But here their similarity ends. On the surface, Chatterjee's stylish self-locations are introspective and sarcastic, an altogether different rhetorical vein than Roy's more earnest self-fashioning as activist. This is also indicative of their very different styles of cosmopolitanism. Chatterjee faces those interior other worlds eclipsed from national and global design, but these locales receive rather thin description in *English, August* and *Mammaries*. Bourgeois cosmopolitan migrants like Agastya or Jamun people Chatterjee's novels, but the milieus of his texts deliberately impart a suffocating provinciality. Thematically a localist, Chatterjee nevertheless renders these subjects communicable to global audiences. His novels are cosmopolitan in their modes of address rather than in their vision of global mutualities.

In contrast, Roy's small-town milieu is immensely cosmopolitan because of India's rich history of migration and settlement: For Roy, the world comes to roost at home, a cosmopolitanism that she shares with Vikram Chandra. Like Rushdie, Chandra challenges the reservation of the term "cosmopolitan" for diasporic writers, using it instead as a vector of metropolitan identity. In his view urbanites of all classes are cosmopolitan in sensibility, irrespective of subaltern status: "A woman born and bred in Dharavi, in the heart of the city, is a cosmopolitan because she lives and works in this city of many nationalities and languages, this city that has become a *vatan* or homeland for people who have traveled very far from their *vatans*" (Chandra 2000, 8). Chandra claims he is a "cosmopolitan" in the same way as are "security guards from Bihar" or the "maids from the Konkan coast" or a "painter from Nasik" living and working in

Bombay (18). He goes on to authenticate his belonging in the milieu of his birth, Mumbai, by describing his visit with a Mafia don, an "insider" link to an underworld difficult to encounter for most bourgeois Indians living in India.

This cosmopolitanism of the home is at variance with the emphasis on migration that we see in both Salman Rushdie and Amitav Ghosh, albeit in varying degree. For Rushdie it is the migrant's perspective that forecloses chauvinistic nationalism, and that makes the local visible. This is clear in Rushdie's critique of the rhetoric of residence as a performance of nationalism. In "The Fantasy That Is India," he argues that it is the Indian diaspora that is the most interesting feature of India in the latter decades of the twentieth century, one that "Indians—Indian Indians—find very difficult to understand." And Rushdie insists: "The thing that interested me the most was that there are now many, many ways of being something that you can legitimately call Indian. Being Indian Indian is just one of those ways" (1997d, 58). A notable departure from Upamanyu Chatterjee's essay on the Indian jubilee that appeared in the same issue of *India Today* magazine, 18 August 1997, where Chatterjee claims *national* citizenship as definitive of Indian cultural identity: "An Indian is one who is born one and doesn't wish to change his citizenship. It should be a valid enough definition to instill in us a lasting sense of identity, to provide for the future a sort of harmony—even better that it's low key" (1997, 174). In writing on the diaspora in Indian culture, Ghosh too underlines the centrality of migrancy to the Indian perspective: "Just as the spaces of India travel with the migrant, India too has no vocabulary for separating the migrant from India," he asserts with some vehemence (Ghosh 2002a, 249). Hence it is impossible to be "imperfectly Indian," a direct repudiation of the essentialized national subject we see in the "global-Indian consumer subject.

To substantiate the salience of the migrant's perspective for India, in their fiction Ghosh and Rushdie actively pursue alternative genealogies of cosmopolitanism. This is one of the epistemological projects earmarked urgent in the *Public Culture* introduction to contemporary cosmopolitanisms. Exhorting us to "think outside the box of European intellectual history," the editors underline the investigation of non-European cosmopolitical genealogies in the cumulative effort toward a minoritarian modernity. Amitav Ghosh's tracking of the Indian diaspora, with special emphasis on the labor diaspora (for example, the India-Myanmar thoroughfare in *The Glass Palace*), offers one vision of a "contrapuntal" modernity. Such new imaginative spatiality is also the subject of Rushdie's *Moor's Last Sigh*, in the overlapping allegories of Nehruvian India and Moorish Spain—both diverse, pluralist, and cosmopolitan cultures, in Rushdie's view.

Criticizing his old enemy religious fundamentalism in his golden-jubilee essay, Rushdie carefully accentuates the power of collective fantasy, not its promise. His changed view of nation is evident in his big project on India after *Midnight's Children*, *The Moor's Last Sigh*, where his principal disagreements are the elephantine megaprojects and majoritarian rule. As his tenure as migrant increases, Rushdie's own "mega" projects become less ambitious and he moves to the etching of Indian fragments—the biographies of a few "minority" ethnic communities. In the piece titled "There Is a Kind of Buzz about Indian Writing in English," he firmly places himself on the margins of dominant national communities: "I come from an Indian minority. I no doubt have a minority perspective" (1997e, 89).[3] In other interviews and in his nonfiction, Rushdie speaks hyperbolically of his "exile" from Bombay as the feeling of a "disgruntled lover" (2000a, 109). He remains self-reflexive about the nostalgic nature of his fantasy, acknowledging it as the psychic fallout of enforced exile. In his "Letter from India," published in the *New Yorker* in 2000, Rushdie describes his return to India with his twenty-one-year-old son, Zafar, in the following way: "Since then the characters in my fiction have frequently flown west from India, but in novel after novel their author's imagination has returned to it. This, perhaps, is what it means to love a country: that its shape is also yours, the shape of the way you think and feel and dream" (2000a, 108).

Global cosmopolitanisms are posed as a different mutuality than that of hegemonic global culture (in the singular) or global designs (evoking the cartographic hubris of colonialism). We have already seen this in Chatterjee's criticism of the corporate global culture (of the "How-To ideas"), a polemic that finds different articulation in Amitav Ghosh's nonfiction in wider global circulation (through mainstream venues such as the *Wilson Quarterly* and the *New Yorker*, as well as scholarly journals such as *Cultural Anthropology*). Born in Bangladesh and then crossing to India, Ghosh found his life even as an Indian citizen of the Nehruvian era marked by the act of migration. From these nonfiction pieces we glean Ghosh's well-calibrated opposition to globalism and nationalism. In "The Global Reservation," Ghosh writes of a U.N. peacekeeping mission in Cambodia whose presence enabled countrywide elections in May 1993. His casual encounters with some of the members of this mission soon brought home the necessity of embarking on "an ethnography of international peacekeeping" (1994, 413). Ghosh records the paradoxical role that the United Nations, with its international egalitarianism, plays in the countries where it "peace-keeps" (see Ghosh 1999).[4] UN Transitions Authority in Cambodia (UNITAC) personnel are marked as foreigners by their cars and flags. They promote political models of order and governance, but remain singularly disconnected from local and ethnic understandings of order and disorder. This "problem in the organizational culture" of the United Nations and the corporate loyalty of its personnel, remarks Ghosh, once more entrenches global hegemonies and nation-state borders. With keen insight, Ghosh remarks that despite the fact that this political third culture seems to suggest, once again, the permeability of nation-state boundaries in the age of globalization, the effect is quixotic. As a totality of its member states, the United Nations indeed embodies the presence of the world within Cambodia. By curious inversion, the UNITAC personnel privately complained to Ghosh that regardless of their country of origin, the Cambodian population sees them as just homogenized UNITAC people. This is because, Ghosh explains, wherever these peacekeepers go they recreate the locale in "their own image" of political governance, reinforcing the hierarchical global system of nation-states. This political thrust of globalization will culminate, argues Ghosh, in a two-tier system of nation-states: blurred boundaries between regional conglomerates (like the European Union) at one level, but increasingly rigid hierarchies at another, for maintenance of the new world order (420). In turn, these reconfigurations of global power generate chauvinistic nationalism on the part of industrializing nations disadvantaged by the new political equation. We see this quite clearly, for example, in India's drive for nuclear weapons.

The spectrality of virulent nationalist chauvinism manifest in India's nuclear policy is emphatically censured by all the cosmopolitical writers, with striking instantiation in Ghosh's and Roy's essays written right after India's nuclear tests in Pokhran in 1997. In "Countdown," where Ghosh recounts his visit to the Indian nuclear test site, he interprets the reactionary support for the nuclear program as born of political uncertainty: "I am convinced that support for India's nuclear program is occasioned by a fear of the future," writes Ghosh, and the testing in Pokhran is the "moral equivalent to civil war: the targets the rulers have in mind are, in the end, their own people" (1998, 197). For Roy, the nuclear shadow is spectral in its inhumanity, radically negating all sociality, including the act of writing: "What kind of book should I write?" she asks in a short polemic in the *Observer*. "For now, just for now, just for a while, pointlessness is my biggest enemy. That's what nuclear bombs do, whether they're used or not. They violate everything that is humane, they alter the meaning of life" (2002a).

Ghosh's catalog of the horrors experienced by the inhabitants of Pokhran is more restrained in tenor than Arundhati Roy's attacks on the nation-state, starting with her anguished declaration of personal independence from that state (Roy 1998). Ghosh reserves the most approbation for contemporary religious mobilizations that harness sacral authority for political gain. Writing in solidarity with persecuted cosmopolitan writers like Salman Rushdie and Naguib Mahfouz, in his essay on religious fundamentalism Ghosh categorically shows how religious mobilizations of our age are "retreats" from the modern world that are also the "means of laying claim to it" (2000c, 270). And along the way, literature and art as the "ultimate repository of value" must be "excoriated," censured, and governed; no surprise that their destruction has become such an article of "bad faith" in contemporary global politics. Even worse, these politicized modern religious discourses borrow from the modern grammar of rationalist academic discourses to make their case: For instance, the production of archaeological claims on such and such a group that has a "right" to be "there" are "entirely profane" discourses pitched to territorial control and "entirely devoid of faith" (273).[5] True to his commitment to recessive literary traditions, in the same essay Ghosh embarks on reading (and culturally translating) Taslima Nasrin's *Lajja*, a Bengali novel for which the Bangladesh writer fled a fatwa and was consequently nicknamed "a female Rushdie" (see B. Ghosh 2000).

But it is really Roy's long engagement with the Narmada Bachchao Andolan that exemplifies sustained local activism. For several years, the Indian government's Sardar Sarovar Project (SSP), a plan to build 30 large, 135 medium, and 3,000 small dams to harness the waters of the Narmada and its tributaries to provide water and electricity, has met with popular resistance in the movement known as the Narmada Bachchao Andolan (NBA).[6] These opponents of the project have long argued that the dams would merely displace large numbers of peoples, mostly dalits and adivasis, destroying ecosystems and the modes of living centered on the river. The NBA had garnered national support for many years from progressives, intellectuals, and grassroots activists mostly from the Left. International support has emerged in recent years, illustrating the transnational advocacy networks also made possible by globalization. For instance, in August 1999, hundreds of grassroots activists in Europe, Latin America, and North America who had mobilized against the Seattle World Trade Organization meeting appealed to the president of India to intervene in the Narmada situation when water levels had started to rise with the dam construction; most of these activists had met in India that month for the People's Global Action against WTO and Free Trade.

Given that from the Nehruvian era through the Manmohan Singh era of liberalization, the Indian government has always embarked on megaprojects as a part of the trajectory of nation building, the NBA has been labeled "antinational" by politicians, police, officials, and bureaucrats. The Hindu Right, with technological hubris manifest in the bravado of the nuclear blasts, has avidly embarked on the dam project, raising a slogan similar to that for building the Ram temple—"We swear by Narmada, we shall build a dam here" (my translation). Writing against such megaprojects, Sanjay Sangvai shows how the slogan effectively mobilizes religious symbols and populist sentiment against the secular anti-dam movement. The Gujarati BJP even formed the Sardar Senas (imitating the infamous Shiv Senas of Maharashtra) to highlight Gujarat's "dharma" against these antinational locals backed by "foreign powers." Sangvai points out that the SSP project has received such Hindu elite regional support because it serves only to enrich an already resource-rich central Gujarat, not the drought-prone areas of the Kutch, Saurashtra, and north Gujarat (1994, 539). Such regional and national elitism targets subaltern communities as antinational, erasing any alternative visions in the elite nationalist rush toward technological and economic development.[7] The Gujarat government filed a case with the Supreme Court against the NBA that resulted in a lifting of their stay order for dam building. In October 2000, Roy used her global celebrity to raise consciousness and money for this cause—we know that she donated the entire sum of her Booker prize to the movement and was jailed for a day, 7 March 2002. In *The Cost of Living*, published in 1999 after *The God of Small Things*, Roy reiterated her abhorrence of megaprojects or the economy of the "big" in this way:

> It is possible that as a nation we've exhausted our quota of heroes for this century, but while we wait for shiny new ones to come along, we have to limit the damage. We have to support our small heroes. (Of these we have many. Many.) We have to fight specific wars in specific ways. Who knows, perhaps that's what the 21st century has in store for us. The dismantling of the Big. Big bombs, big dams, big ideologies, big contradictions, big countries, big wars, big heroes, big mistakes. Perhaps it will be the Century of the Small. Perhaps right now, this very minute, there is a small god in heaven readying herself for us. (1999, 23)

These political recitations by the cosmopolitical writers are in part self-fashionings pitched at arbitrating their own refracted images in circulation. Whatever their differences, they share common ground: a cosmopolitics aimed at dislodging violent inscription of nationalism and globalism. Given such commitment, they join in the interrogation of emplacing cultural grammars that has been undertaken by progressive historians preoccupied with the present abuses of history that further aggrandizes political self-interest.

Emplacing Grammars

One of the most sustained attacks on violently emplacing cultural grammars has come from the subaltern studies scholars. While not discounting the impact of the colonial policy of divide and rule, Dipesh Chakrabarty and Sudipto Kaviraj demonstrate how communal self-consciousness must be comprehended in terms of a larger modern reconstitution of identities. Political scientist Kaviraj argues that, before the introduction of colonial education, the complex and absorbent hierarchies within Hindu and Muslim societies allowed for a different "grammar" of cultural identity. For instance, Hindus often treated Muslims who specialized in particular trades as "quasi-castes," a "fuzziness" of religious borders that circumvented easy majority-minority divisions. A Hindu society could thus contain several minorities who could overlap and identify with Muslims in geopolitical or class terms; hence political conflicts were less intense, because ethnic and social identities were themselves fairly indeterminate. Kaviraj notes: "It was not as if people were not Muslim before, but they were not Muslim in the same way; or rather, the significance of their being Muslim was not the same, precisely because it was a social world which lacked this accent on being something. That world admitted a great deal of cognitive and philosophical reflexivity; but this kind of political being or reflexivity is a new thing" (1995, 307).[8]

The introduction of Western education fragmented the traditional worlds of both Hindus and Muslims, creating a split between social and political worlds. Kaviraj goes on to argue that the divide was also a linguistic one in that English dominated the world of politics, while the vernaculars pervaded one's social relations. This spawned two different "grammars" of identity, two divergent senses of communal belonging that made for a different modality in performances of religious identity. The political sphere was soon peopled by "enumerated" communities, mapped and counted by censuses and the politics of representation.[9] Dipesh Chakrabarty's analysis of the 1851 census, which required subjects of the empire to identify themselves as socio-religious groups, goes some way in explaining the evolution of these modern cultural grammars (1995a, 3373).

In such a landscape, communal grammars of identity are manifested in chauvinistic drives to reterritorialize global space. In a rather differently inflected analysis from those of Kaviraj and Chakrabarty, Thomas Blom Hansen, too, recognizes the "vernacularisation" of the "dynamics of global modernity" by postcolonial nations that desire access to modern forms of organization, and simultaneously to achieve global recognition (1996, 603). Thus the colonies adopted the postenlightenment idea of a "long suppressed" natural community coming into its own.[10] Hansen notes that communalism can be perceived as a legacy of modern Indian nationalism and, like Pandey, he marks a shift in nationalist politics following Gandhi's entry into the fray. Hansen further reads the contemporary Sangh Parivar's (the "family of parties" that comprise the contemporary Hindu Right) dreams of a Hindu nation as a recurrence of this earlier desire to place the nation-state in a position of primacy among a global system of nation-states, after years of Nehruvian economic protectionism and isolation. Hence the seemingly "radical" dream of Hindu nationalism is actually performed for global consumption.

In this scenario, while Hindutva initially gained momentum from electoral strength drawn from a growing urban middle class disillusioned with the state and the political establishment, global dreams were never far off. For one, global capital provided a whole new technology of communication, cheaper means of transport, satellite television, fax machines, and videos that strengthened flows of information, money, and people. In the short history of the Sangh Parivar *Khaki Shorts and Saffron Flags,* we learn of this Hindu Right conglomerate's use of new technologies in organizing around an idea of the Hindu nation (Basu et al. 1994). A striking example is the remastering of spectacular *maidan* speeches to create immediacy and affect for those who could not be present at a particular rally in order to disseminate and keep alive the sense of a new Hindu dawn.[11] Of course as I have noted earlier, India's deregulation of the protectionist economy since 1991, and the simultaneous privatization of television, made it possible for these cultural transactions to take shape. In an essay published before *Politics after Television,* Arvind Rajagopal had cataloged these consumer logics of Hindutva (the mobilization around Hindu rule), demarcating the work of markets and the media in creating the discursive contexts for these political communities. Hindu symbols such as Ram, as well as the name "Hindu" itself, were explicitly sold as a brand by the BJP (Bharatiya Janata Party) on the eve of the Babri Masjid debacle, argued Rajagopal (1999), while advertisers used the popular aesthetics of Hindu militant iconography to sell goods to small-town and village populations.

In the era of faster and cheaper global communications, Hindutva has become a reterritorialized global cultural space with strong links to diasporic Hindu conservatives.[12] Hindu fundamentalists court NRI funds, as was evident in BJP leader L. K. Advani's 1995 visit to Britain right before the general election. Advani was given a warm reception by Asian businesspeople and politicians on his inauguration of the biggest Hindu temple outside of India, the Swaminarayan Mission, a highly evangelical and affluent wing of the Hindu religion. It is clear by now that the Hindu Right buys into the economic rationality of global capitalism, inviting foreign investment and cultivating NRI contacts. This has led to a series of treaties and acts that ease the political boundaries between India and the United States, given the political instrumentality of flexible capital.[13] The Shiv Sena's "selling out" to U.S. multinationals (specifically, the now-infamous Enron) in Maharashtra, a step that went against its previous claims of *swadeshi* (self-sufficient economic nationalism), clearly signaled the flexibility of the Hindu-run state's economic ventures.[14] These global mobilizations enable us to understand a variant of the "global Indian," fervently nationalist *and* a full participant in economic globalism. The image is promoted in pitched performances of reactionary nationalism perfected by the Hindu Right. These etch national boundaries around the idea of the cultural citizen who "belongs" to India, a reified internalization of national tradition into the transnational subject. Belonging is properly understood through a perception of otherness: The Muslim becomes the "operational other," metonymically representative of subaltern religious, sexual, and ethnic communities outside the Hindu fold.[15] We see this in the staging of anti-Muslim culture wars on the subcontinent, best illustrated in the Maqbool Fida Husain controversies of the midnineties. In 1996 and 1997, the Hindu Right alleged that Husain had insulted Hindu womanhood by sketching a nude Saraswati (the Hindu goddess of learning); the issue was revived in May 1998, now targeting Husain's nude painting of Sita, Lord Ram's consort in the *Ramayana*.[16] M. F. Husain is widely perceived as part of the progressive artist intelligentsia (in the postindependence years he was an active member of the avant garde Progressive Artists Group) and known for his elaborate and unconventional projects. On 8 October 1997, the VHP had filed a complaint with the Mumbai police against the artist on grounds of "public indecency" and the "violation of public sentiments" (Bavadam 1996, 5). And on 11 October, the militant Bajrang Dal stormed the Herwitz gallery in Ahmedabad, ripping paintings and tapestries. The 1996–1997 furor over the naked Saraswati clearly revealed the Hindu Right's manufacturing of controversies for electoral gain, since Husain had done the Saraswati sketch in the 1970s (it was reproduced in a book by Dyaneswar Nadkarni in 1996). Similarly, the May 1998 ransacking of Husain's house and studio had little to do with the "insult" in question. Rather, the Hindu Right orchestrated the event to stimulate public interest in the Hindu agenda, right before by-elections in Maharashtra, Gujarat, and Madhya Pradesh.

The details of the events that followed are less interesting than the Hindu Right's characterization of this as a cultural crime. Husain is a member of the "westernized" national elite who, the Hindu militants argue, have strayed from Hindu cultural norms. But Husain is also a Muslim and therefore "capable" of visually violating Hindu-Indian womanhood. Hence, in Husain the Hindu Right found a composite of the Muslim, the internal other, and the cosmopolitan Indian, the contaminated "outsider." The Sangh Parivar complained that Husain gave precedence to German news crews before he turned to the Indian media, and Bal Thackeray pointedly marked him as an outsider to the nation of Hindus: "If Husain can step into Hindusthan, what is wrong if we step into his house?" (Swami 1998).

In fact Husain was stranded in London for a few days while this drama played itself out, as the progressive artistic and film communities (old enemies of right-wing cultural organizers) registered a case against the state government on Husain's behalf. On both occasions, there were widespread demonstrations in support of Husain in Banglalore, Mumbai, Delhi, Bhopal, Ahmedabad, and Kolkata, joined by playwrights, artists, film directors, and writers in vernaculars and in English (Gieve Patel, Ved Mehta, Amitav Ghosh, and Mulk Raj Anand, to name a notable few), leading Husain to claim that "the entire intelligentsia is with me."[17] Husain's case exemplifies the Hindu Right's demonization of the English-speaking elites in general, and of the South Asian writers in English slotted in that category.[18] In fact Rajendra Singh of the RSS, mentioning the Husain affair in his Vijyadashami (festival) address, promised to visit the fate of Rushdie on Husain should he continue his artistic transgressions (Muralkidharan 1997, 13).[19] The Husain affairs became several of the many staged cultural events pitched to garner consensus on the Hindu nation: The disruption of Indo-Pakistani cricket matches; the Shiv Sena's storming of the Pakistani *ghazal* singer Ghulam Ali's concert at the Hotel Juhu Centaur, Mumbai; and their disruption of the Savage Garden concert (labeled a display of Western decadence) are other memorable occasions of this new marking of cultural territory.

Such performances of political subjectivity have provoked discussions of cultural citizenship among theorists of transnationality (Joseph 1999; Ong 1999; García Canclini 2001; Shapiro 2000).[20] What we see in the South Asian context finds echo in other struggles over producing and stabilizing localities in the face of increasing global motility and velocity of flows. Michael Shapiro, for example, examines global emergences of emplacing cultural grammars in his evocation of the "spatio-temporal assemblages" of the nation state, official constructs that provide stable social bonds. Specifically interested in temporalities, Shapiro focuses on official documents, histories and journalistic writings in which temporal schemata define the citizen (2000, 80). Yet these emplacing articulations of national times, spaces, and subjects are anachronistic, Shapiro contends, unsustainable after decolonization, immigration, and new flexibilities of capital and labor. Illegal immigrants, refugees, migrant laborers with no state rights, and other transient peoples bear the violence of exclusion from communities based on commonalities; and even within diverse legal populations in the nation-states of the global North, the older cohesions of official spatio-temporality no longer have adequate political valence.

In the South Asian context, such an argument on the exclusion and elision of the "migrant" subject has placed the lion's share of blame on the spatio-temporal assemblages of historical narration. In what follows we shall trace some of the debates on the emplacing capacities of history, especially at junctures when violence dismembers the body of the imagined community, creating new temporal rhizomes.

Rupturing History

Amid commemorative jubilee discourses, the memory of violence remained luminously present at the heart of nation making. The two dominant moments recurrently cited as watershed points in this collective recognition were the Emergency of 1975–1977 and the Babri Masjid riots of 1992. The period of the Emergency, when all civil rights and privileges were suspended for more than a year, led to a massive backlash against the Congress Party that had virtually dominated the Indian political scene since independence. But the political debacle was not the only aftershock. Indeed the real casualty of the dark Emergency days, so evocatively envisioned by Rushdie as the drained promise of midnight's children, was the abiding sense of national failure, at least of the Nehruvian project. The Babri Masjid destruction and the riots of 1992 represented a second jolt to Indians' sense of a unified national community, already troubled since the anti-Sikh riots of 1984. When organized militant Hindu forces mobilized to destroy the Babri Masjid on 6 December 1992, riots, widespread assaults, rapes, and killings swept the subcontinent. A censure of Nehruvian secularism, a central tenet of the decolonized nation so far, followed in the wake of the mosque's destruction. The newly sharpened lines of majority-minority populations seemed to bring to the fore old divisive (separatist) wounds, and with them the ever-present foreboding of fragmentation.

Identifying these national traumas accounted for much of the introspective note in the fifty-year celebrations. Interviewees, interviewers, writers, and commentators all seemed to be scrambling to deal with disappointment, perhaps best exampled in a front-page article in the 15 August 1997 *Statesman,* "Is India Suited for Democracy?": "Fifty years removed from the yoke of colonial imperialism," many senior citizens continue "to wonder whether the pre-15 August 1947 wasn't better."[21] *India Today* brought out a golden jubilee issue on 18 August, titled *Indian August,* for which the newsgroup invited a series of prominent writers, artists, politicians, and industrialists to reflect on the proudest and saddest moments in the last fifty years. While the proudest moments ranged from gaining independence from British rule, to legislation on women's rights, to India's refusal to sign the Comprehensive Nuclear Test Ban Treaty, the Emergency and the destruction of the Babri Masjid were the overwhelming choices for the saddest moment for a range of interviewees, such as the actress and film director Aparna Sen; feminist activist and editor of *Manushi* Madhu Kishwar; stage veteran Saoli Mitra; and novelist Shashi Deshpande ("What It Means" 1997).

Both Amitav Ghosh and Upamanyu Chatterjee have participated in this general accounting of national violence in their nonfiction, speaking to the repression of popular memory in official statist accounts. In 1997 Amitav Ghosh wrote an essay on the forgotten history of the Indian National Army.[22] A militant mobilization led by Subhas Chandra Bose against the British and repressed within official statist historical narrations of the nonviolent freedom struggle, the INA story is a fiercely remembered regional (eastern Indian) struggle that Ghosh consciously reconstructs in his commemoration of India at fifty. Ghosh contextualizes his own interest in the INA with reference to his father's growing conviction that had Subhas Bose not mobilized an Indian military, had the British not been faced with prospects of large-scale mutiny, they would have never left India; yet the lion's share of credit for independence has always gone to the Gandhian nonviolent revolution. Ghosh's 1997 recounting of those glory days becomes a political intervention of sorts into the national struggle over history at the present time. In another commentary, this time on Indira Gandhi's assassination and the Hindu-Sikh riots that followed, Ghosh performs as a national, rather than a regional, citizen: "He knew how to respond as a citizen; he is still learning how to respond as a writer," Ghosh writes, a telling distinction that invites us to ask where the "writer" is placed, if not as a citizen (1995a, 41). The year 1984, among other life-altering episodes of social violence, remained the jangling nerve for Ghosh; it is a moment to which he returns often, as we see in his recent essay on the Godhra carnage.[23] And Upamanyu Chatterjee undercuts the jubilee celebration also by remembering 1984: "How come, did you ask, that you experienced your first moments of reckoning only when you were 25, in 1984? Didn't the Emergency, for example, wake you up?" (1997, 172).

Given the censure of the nation, across media in 1997 we see a proliferation of discourses on local communities historically repressed in the colonial and nationalist projects. For example, Mani Rathnam, the director of the popular historical film romance *Bombay* (1995), chose to make a rather politically radical film in 1997. *Dil Se* features a female terrorist as one of the protagonists, a displaced subaltern migrant who plans to blow up the Republic Day parade in Delhi (the nation's capital) with her bomb-strapped body. The male protagonist, on the other hand, is portrayed as a befuddled middle-class reporter from All-India radio enthusiastically undertaking a journey to a mountainous region in northeast India. Though unlocalized in the film, the region is immediately recognizable as a part of the country splintered by separatist movements (with different allegiances in land distribution issues, language, ethnicities) and in a constant state of guerilla war. With all good democratic intentions, the reporter asks the locals: "What does India mean to you? What does freedom mean to you?" To his shock, he is told unequivocally that freedom means freedom from the Indian government. No surprise, *Dil Se* proved an expensive flop. In her analysis of the "terrorist" as the center of these new narrations of nation, viscerally fragmenting the body politic, Sumita Chakravarty (2000), a film critic who wrote one of the first monographic studies of Bollywood idioms, traces the slow emergence of this figure in Rathnam's oeuvre. While in the 1992 *Roja* the terrorist-kidnapper is the threatening other, by *Dil Se*, the terrorist has become protagonist. More recently, we find an empathetic portrait of a male terrorist, scarred by his early brush with violent insurgency, in Vidhu Vinod Chopra's *Mission Khasmir* (2000), based on journalistic reports on the human costs in Kashmir in the last decades; similarly, a sympathetically sketched female Tamil terrorist is the chief character in Santosh Sivan's acclaimed low-budget independent feature *The Terrorist* (2000). In 2003 Mani Rathnam followed up his two films on terrorism (*Roja* and *Dil Se*) with the sentimental *A Peck on the Cheek*, also an exploration of Tamil insurgency in Sri Lanka, this time from the perspective of an abandoned child.

Echoes of Rathnam's stylized representation of national disintegration are found in the press, as well. In *India Today*'s feature "What It Means to Be an Indian," a mix of ordinary and famous Indians are asked similar questions about India and the meaning of freedom. Mahasweta Devi, the Bengali writer and activist for tribal rights, is presented on the same page as an unknown Ngami tribal man, Ibethoi, from Manipur, who has this to say of the fifty-year moment: "What does the Indian map look like? You'll have to ask the children. I know that I am in Manipur. They tell me that I am in India. Here, it is enough to call yourself Meitei, that gives you an identity. I don't know if I am an Indian. I'm not educated, so I really can't say" (1997, 162).

In the revision of the Indian national-global dialectic, the Subaltern Studies Collective has framed this will to difference as the search for a heterogeneous past, a quest for the partly irretrievable "subaltern" (Lingis 1994; Agamben 1993; Nancy 1991). The weight of their scholarship on progressive discourse has been considerable, engendering what I characterize as the "subaltern effect"—that is, the deployment of the "subaltern" as a common term for grouping variously situated struggles on the part of the politically disenfranchised—always visible at moments of violent rupture, and always the cathexis of the elites who invoke this figure (see Beverly 1999, 100). It is because of this legacy, not to mention the cosmopolitical writers' deliberate invocations of subalterneity, that I briefly pause on the subaltern studies oeuvre before turning to literary cosmopolitics.

The subaltern studies oeuvre of the last two decades, then, offers substantial commentary on repressed narratives of communities, those histories placed under erasure by the larger official discourses of Indian nationhood. As a starting point, Ranajit Guha demonstrated how subaltern communities such as peasant insurgents also took on the colonial state, but to very different ends; they did not necessarily see themselves as fighting for the liberation of India. And in his exploration of communalism in colonial India, Gyanendra Pandey reasons that the abstract horizontal secular imagined community was a product of the second phase of nationalism, when nationalism came to be seen in direct opposition to communalism. The first phase of national self-consciousness, however, was dominated by various "narratives of community," of which cultural nationalisms of the Tilak or Vivekananda variety were most prevalent.[24] In this temporal schema, after the post-Emergency disillusion with nation, when unambiguous loyalties to the horizontal imagined community came under severe scrutiny, these older suppressed community ties moved to the forefront of national debates.

These conversations on subalterneity are significant to our literary cosmopolitics because these cosmopolitical writers quite directly allude to the subaltern studies project, particularly the "problem" of narrating the subaltern subject. We often see the deliberate staging of this critical discourse, for instance, in Vikram Chandra's depiction of Queen Janvi in *Red Earth*. Janvi is a fictional allusion to Spivak's subaltern queen, the Rani of Sirmur, so profoundly absent in the colonial and Brahmanical record of her *sati* (Spivak 1985a). Chandra's Queen Janvi is an amalgam of the Rani of Jhansi, the warrior hero of the first war of independence (commonly known as the Sepoy Mutiny), who died protecting her kingdom from the British, and the Rajput queen, Padmini of Chittor, who immerses herself in fire—this time in the practice of *jauhar*, a self-immolating practice among Rajputs aimed at preserving women's honor from oncoming foreign invaders. The narrator of *Red Earth* self-consciously retains the oral tales of Janvi's heroic resistance and mourns their print circulation, where Janvi has become a statistic: "All these deaths were widely written about in newspapers in India and Europe. They became the focal point of many sermons and editorials, and the campaign to allow missionaries into Indian gained momentum" (Chandra 1995, 247).

Unruly Fragments

Quite starkly in 1997 we see a powerful acknowledgment of disruptions in the official national biography. Writing amid celebrations of India at fifty, art historian Tapati Guhathakurta (1998) examines how certain "events" are manufactured via cultural rituals as singular moments in a nation's historical memory. Her example is the staging of a large and spectacular exhibition of the "masterpieces of Indian art" at the Government House, New Delhi, in 1948, an event that inscribed 1947 as a new beginning (though nothing astoundingly new happens in Indian art at this point) and narrated the nation's cultural heritage.[25] Sudipto Kaviraj, too, sees national history as cultural performance, thus insisting on subjecting nationalist discourse to critical tests:

The major question about politics of course refers to the social relations between Hindus and Muslims as religious communities. It is essential to examine this closely for two reasons. The first stems from our hypothesis that modernity not only makes new identities possible, it does not leave older ones alone. Indeed, identities that existed in a different mode earlier undergo a crucial though often undeclared transformation, becoming identities of a new type. It is essential to ask if people's ways of being Hindu and Muslim have changed. The second reason for examining this question has to do with the dominance of nationalist habits of thinking in our social science discussions. Some basic premises of nationalist thinking are so widely influential that they make us forget that these are representations of an historical reality, and thus subject to critical tests. (1995, 300)

Kaviraj's privileging of nationalist history as defining cultural identity was widely echoed amid jubilee commentary in the popular press, with historians appearing as the architects of community. On 15 August 1997, in a section called "The Road Ahead," the *Statesman* chose to reprint D. D. Kosambi's critique of Nehru. Kosambi, a Marxist historian, is well known for his methodologies of history-from-below.[26] In this reprinted text, "Behind the White Khaddar" (1997), Kosambi draws our attention to the flaws in Nehru's famous historical narrative *The Discovery of India* (1945), explaining that these flaws arise from a man who never questioned which class had benefited from a change (decolonization) at a certain period of history.[27] The Kosambi reprint on the anniversary, then, is evidence of the popular suspicion of the received national story and its myth-makers.

But reflections in 1997 are the tip of the iceberg—a revitalized recognition of an ongoing battle over the "problem" of history in the late eighties and the nineties. That struggles over national times are managed through museums, state-sponsored festivals, national archives, heritage industries, or, sometimes, just plain history textbooks has long been recognized by historians of all persuasions in this period.[28] The renowned scholar Bipan Chandra has illustrated how "history is the main ideology of the RSS," for it was through the rewiring of national histories that right-wing historians "proved" the existence of a temple under the Babri Masjid (S. Ghosh 1992).[29] Commentators in the news media continued to catalog the "war on historians" by the right-wing Sangh Parivar in the years preceding the Babri Masjid destruction. They cite instances such as the disruption of the ICHR (Indian Council for Historical Research) meetings at Ujjain in 1991, or the VHP and Bajrang Dal attack on Eklavya, an NGO in Madhya Pradesh, for publishing textbooks that did not conform to the Sangh's version of Indian history. Striking examples of rewiring history by right-wing historians are found in texts like *Itihas Ga Raha Hai*, widely disseminated in Uttar Pradesh: The words "invaders came with sword in one hand and the Qu'ran in the other," for instance, deliberately evoke and revise a commonplace about the coming of the British—"They came with gun in one hand and Bible in the other."

If official history seemed ever at the service of political manipulation, writers, scholars, and filmmakers turned to the heterogeneous fragment in their collaborative projects of narrating the subaltern local. In the face of a crumbling national biography, the historical fragment now claimed spectral revenge: If certain stories were repressed to make way for the big national story, then the violence of that occlusion gave these fragments ethical charge at a time when the larger narrative appeared an orchestrated deception. The reemergence of the fragment is possibly most notable in the case of "partition discourse" in the nineties, an event eclipsed in the celebratory nationalist accounts of 1947. Looking back at the partition amnesia, Peter van der Veer notes how narratives constructed around a unitary political subject memorized violent events as fragments of a greater story in which the imagined community achieves maturity. When this greater story falters, and the goal seems uncertain or unattainable, these fragments receive renewed attention as integral, indeed formative, parts of the story (Van der Veer 1996). The revisions in nationalist historiography that I have explicated here—the attention to the many repressed narratives of community erased in official national biographies—as well as in recent investigations of the partition are analyses of forgotten fragments. A particularly spectacular example of the uncanny fragment is found in a visual history of the Bombay riots of 1992–1993 in Anant Patwardhan's documentary, *Pitri, Putra, Dharmayuddh (Father, Son and Holy War, 1994)*. At one point a tearful female voice-over recounting the death of parents during partition is aligned to the visual image of a tear-stained Punjabi woman nursing her riot-ravaged husband at Bombay's J. J. Hospital in 1993. The woman in the camera frame does not speak, yet the viewer in manipulated into correlating the visual image of 1993 with the audio memory trace of 1947. Such acknowledgments of 1992 as a repeat of 1947 underline the inescapable iterability of what was not fully explained, accounted for, understood, and put to rest.

This focus on amnesia and violent repression as structuring principles of narrative performance locates the subaltern as a recuperable but fraught historical fragment.[30] The problems of restorative memory work are profoundly dramatized in the emerging feminist scholarship on Partition, exemplified in Urvashi Butalia and Ritu Menon's acclaimed oral history of women's experiences of it (1998). These oral histories deconstruct the promised citizenship of 1947, for women were not allowed to choose their country of allegiance; millions were raped, abducted, or killed, or found themselves refugees within the "decolonized" space of the Indian nation-state. Butalia and Menon insist on the necessity of remembering these stories, while remaining cognizant of the difficulties of narration. This duality is found in the cosmopolitical writers' commitment to subaltern politics and their simultaneous attention to a paucity of discursive resources.

But the will to remember and narrate has not remained only in the domain of scholarship. As I noted earlier, in the popular media other national erasures exert the force of repression. Quite literally, forgotten ghosts such as Subhas Chandra Bose or icons such as Nathuram Godse return to public view to "displace" conventional heroes like Gandhi and Nehru. The casting of past heroes as unrestful ghosts was especially resonant in what became known as the "Godse affair"—the furor over Pradeep Dalvi's play *Mee Nathuram Gose Boltoy* (I am Naturam Godse speaking), which features Godse's testimony and appeals to the court in 1948 before he was hung. Most South Asians of the Nehruvian era know Naturam Godse as Gandhi's assassin, RSS trained and a figure of national shame. Written in 1984, Pradeep Dalvi's play valorizes Godse as a spirited intellectual who passionately criticized what he saw as Gandhi's effete communal politics. The play had to wait fourteen years before the Stage Performances Scrutiny board in the Shiv Sena–BJP-run state of Maharashtra approved it, as *India Today* reported on 3 August 1998 in "Godse on Trial" (22). Undoubtedly it was the official ascendancy of the Hindu micronationalists to state government that made the resurgence of this historical ghost possible. For Hindu micronationalists, Godse's vision of an unpartitioned India is the specter that haunts the national deification of Gandhi. When the play opened in Mumbai, Godse's emotionally charged call for an undivided India met with jubilation from an audience reveling in revisionist history—some for ideological reasons, and others out of mere curiosity. Said one spectator interviewed by the conservative *Mid-day*, an English daily in Pune (the city that houses the Shiv Sena headquarters): "We have heard about Gandhi for 50 years. Now it's time we get a chance to hear Godse's views. Stopping the play is a denial of history" (Rahatekar 1998). In fact the *India Today* article spoke of the national public reception of Godse, and his dismissal in history textbooks, in the following way: "Yet his [Godse's] *ghost* refuses to go away. Every now and then it emerges from the recesses of the past to haunt a nation that is still unsure of how to cope with its history" (21; my emphasis). The article goes on to say that on at least three occasions, the Chitpavan Brahmin has been "put to the dock posthumously." Calculated to take the Marathi stage by storm, Pradeep Dalvi's play is only the most recent occurrence of this ghostly presence in Indian history.

Quite apart from this simplified spectrology, we now turn to the cosmopolitical writers' reconstitution of this traffic in ghosts as an efficacious ethics. I close our discussion of cosmopolitical commitments to local struggles with an account an ethical of spectrology—a practice that forecloses any fetishistic localism while speaking of subaltern subjects and their pasts.

Ethical Spectrology

As Cheah notes in his exegesis on Derrida's spectrality, the exclusionary postcolonial nationalizing drives today have "become an exemplary figure for death" (1999, 225). What is presupposed here is something common to the nations that experience revolutionary decolonization. Caught in an incomplete modernity, these nations imagine a community through a "vitalist ontology," producing those etymologies of birth and organicity, "nativity" and "natality" unique to nationalist discourses in general. The surplus desires of the postcolonial utopian promise of nation, however, create heavy reliance on those ontological metaphors that "subordinate the dead to the living" (253). Therefore the concrete actuality of capital's divisive drives underpinning global economic and military aspirations take on a spectral cast. Cheah writes: "The thematic opposition between the spontaneous dynamism of resisting people and their institutional capture by the *techne* of class and state apparatuses informs almost all theories of postcolonial nationalism" (225). Reading these grounding metaphors of the postcolonial revolutionary impetus across texts (from Franz Fanon to Partha Chatterjee), Cheah theorizes a particular historical loss of *heim* for the newborn decolonized nation. For Homi Bhabha, of course, the *unheimlich*—that unaccountable and terrifying double—lurks at the margins of all modern nations, a generalized condition exacerbated by the growing "gatherings" at "borders," "frontiers," "edges," and "ghettos" (Bhabha 1990, 291). In his *Specters of Marx* (1994), Derrida turns this psychic affect to an ethical conjecture: What if these "unaccountable" accretions command a different mode of accounting? Can those who commune with ghosts effect an ethical spectrology?

I would argue that Derrida's ethical stipulation is of particular relevance to the South Asian cosmopolitical grappling with social violence and postfoundationalist history writing within the imaginary of democratic self-rule. Derrida's concern with the discourses of wrongs, reparation, and debt that occlude the affective histories of trauma and loss makes tarrying with specters inimical to these situations. Wendy Brown highlights this angle in her remarks on Benjamin's angel of history and Derrida's specters. These "poignant signifiers" of the postfoundationalist predicament propel Brown to ask: "What kind of historical consciousness is possible and appropriate for contemporary political critique and analysis, and how can agency be derived to make a more just, emancipatory, or felicitous future order?" (2000, 139–140). Specters present new possibilities in undoing the opposition between life and death, presence and absence; by implication, they collapse the boundedness of present, past, and future. Specters are also redemptive, Brown argues, intangible sites for imagining a future beyond discredited modernist narratives of progress and a violent exclusionary metaphysics of presence. Spectrology, in this sense, is postprogressive history relocating historical meaning to "other space and idiom" (144). It imagines political justice in a world that is "contingent," "unpredictable," and "not fully knowable" (145).

Brown's commentary on Derrida brings to the fore the contemporary traffic in ghosts as witnesses to erasures in the present, now commonplace to the enormous literature on mourning and memory work of the last decades. A majority of scholars recognize literature as the domain where these specters of embodied loss roam. For instance, in *Ghostly Matters*, Avery Gordon reads that now-famous ghost in Toni Morrison's *Beloved* as the "seething presence of the absent." For Gordon, ghosts are entirely necessary to grasp the complexities of our social world, for they speak eloquently of "invisibilities" and "exclusions" (1997, 23). Derrida pushes us further, pitching ghosts as specters of futurity:

> If I am getting ready to speak of ghosts, which is to say about certain *others* who are not present, nor presently living, either to us, in us, or outside of us, it is in the name of *justice*. Of justice where it is not yet, not yet *there*, where it is no longer, let us understand where it is no longer *present*, and where it will never be, no more than a law, reducible to laws or Rights. It is necessary to speak *of the* ghost, indeed *to the* ghost, and *with it*, from the moment that no ethics, no politics, whether revolutionary or not, seems possible and thinkable and *just* that does not recognize in principle the respect for others who are no longer or for those who are not yet *there*, presently living, whether they are already dead or not yet born. (1994, 10)

He reminds us of Marx's well-known sighting of communism as a "specter that haunts Europe," a "phantomic" possibility of a future *socius*. Focusing on Marx's injunction, Derrida insists that the specter here is not just in the domain of ideas ("spirit") but is already materially *there* in the "living present." All forces of the law—the church, the family, the state in nineteenth-century Europe—girded themselves against this specter in a willful denial of those certain others whose promise preoccupies Marx; for him, the counterrevolutionaries of 1848 thus erase that strangely familiar body but continue to be haunted by its recursions. In fact it is this disappeared body of the ghost—this someone who looks at you—that gives these forces of the law their strength and organization. Marx is therefore critical of spectralization, its evacuation of the concrete; the ethical task at hand is to bring back the body proper of the ghost. The gesture toward a future/past veiled by the injunction to order, emplace, and divide—the undead Derridean thing that is there in the living present but not yet of the human world—catches the postcolonial orientation toward the future. With regard to postcoloniality, both Derrida's ethical exhortation to justice and the subsequent turn to a recessed archive beyond the shadow of the specter are compelling propositions. The figure of the invisible "subaltern" other, as an other cathected by the progressive intellectual, calls to the bar a corpus of indigenous and vernacular knowledge. In the ghostly postcolonial corpus, fragments and splinters of erased or lost knowing trouble established truths—they render rational modern discourse "out of joint."

Yet cosmopolitical thinkers are sharply attuned to their own psychic production of such recessive knowledges, those subaltern life-worlds that command translation. Hence we have the emergence of "the uncanny" as a figure for incommunicability in Dipesh Chakrabarty's *Provincializing Europe*, in which he deploys the logics of specters to the South Asian projects of historical revision. Chakrabarty continually posits the limits of modern historicism, whose language is constantly punctured by that (subaltern) other of whom the historian speaks. Subaltern life-worlds, the Derridean "non-contemporaneity" within the "living present," registers as the "shock of the uncanny" in modern historical consciousness. Chakrabarty further points to the literary imagination as an imaginative recourse in acts of cultural translation. In fact he illustrates the postcolonial *differénd* through literary example, alluding to Rushdie's writing of an encounter between the "religious" and the "modern": the evocative face-off between the increasingly fossilized Reverend Mother and the increasingly alienated Adam Aziz in Salman Rushdie's *Midnight's Children*.[31] In Adam Aziz's hyper-rational gaze, religion is a tradition that stands in the way of one's being a citizen of a modern nation. It is a pedagogical will to history that Chakrabarty explains in the following way:

> Because, however non-coercive the conversation between the Kantian subject (i.e. the transcendental academic observer, the knowing, judging, and willing subject of modernity) and the subaltern who enters into the field of historical dialogue with the former from a non-Enlightenment position, this dialogue takes place within a field of possibilities that is already structured from the very beginning in favour of certain outcomes. To put this in terms of Gyan Prakash's book on *"kamiauti"* (bonded, in bad translation) labour in the Indian district of Bihar, if the peasant has until now understood the world of power in terms of ghosts and spirit-cults, surely the intended result of this communication between the position of the modern subject and that of the

peasant would be entirely predictable: that the peasant would learn to see his world structured by the (re-moveable) inequalities of class, gender and ethnicity [Prakash 1990]. The reverse, that the peasant might convince the modern, political 'commentator' of the existence of ghosts and spirits, would be an unimaginable (therefore disallowed) consequence of this process of communication. (In the limiting case of the problem, all peasants would be educated out of their peasantness.) (1995b, 757)

But imagine, argues Chakrabarty, another subaltern history where we stay away from "the dream of the whole called a state" in a "fragmentary and episodic" structure of democratic dialogue. This would mean that the historian enters a dialogue punctured by the other and listens to the "radical polysemy of languages and practices" which testifies to the incommensurability of the multiple worlds that "we" (presumably, Chakrabarty, speaking of the secular subject) inhabit.[32]

The modality of Chakrabarty's spectrology is everywhere in the cosmopolitical writers' embedding of fragmentary local and vernacular knowledge in their novels. I characterize this textual practice as "grafting" to highlight their self-reflexive incorporation of the tropological logic of the specter in all the varying valences described here. The graft implies a historical fissure palpable on the textual body that makes for epistemological différance and insists on the fragmenting of recessive knowledges so they cannot be fetishized as traditions. The presence of grafting is often intimated by literary puzzles, logical knots in narration, or other perplexing schemata that point to the "secrets" of the archive—counterknowledges whose scattered traces lead us to local and eclipsed worlds.

But the idea of the graft is further relevant to the ontology of the *body* implicit in spectrology, and certainly to our perusal of the many dismembered and violated bodies that demand redress in the cosmopolitical novels. We have seen how Upamanyu Chatterjee's indictment of the postcolonial liberal state, in both *English, August* and *Mammaries*, poses the body as a register of violence and a space for the possibilities of language. Many of the other cosmopolitical novels that I examine, too, elaborate the connections between social and political violence and the ontology of the postcolonial subject's body through narrative situations (sometimes the individual body, and on other occasions the body as allegory for the community). Arundhati Roy presents a chilling scene of police brutality on Velutha, with excruciating emphasis on the slow breaking of the subaltern's body: "They [the two-egg twins] heard the thud of wood on flesh. Boots on bone. On teeth. A muffled grunt when a stomach is kicked in. The muted crunch of a skull on cement. The gurgle of blood on a man's breath when his lung is torn by the jagged end of a broken rib" (1997b, 308). The incident occurs on the verandah of the haunted History House, no less, as a malignant repository of past colonial violence, a point to which I will later return. Vikram Chandra, too, references colonial violence through his rendition of a Victorian gothic in *Red Earth*. When Sanjay follows Reverend Sarthey to London, he surmises that Sarthey is possibly a Jack the Ripper–like serial killer whose internal violence is played out on the body of the other. And in *Moor's Last Sigh*, Rushdie sketches the Moor's surreal experience in "the worst post-independence made-in-India institution," the jail. Rushdie strenuously underscores the monstrous visage of the Bombay state government run by the Hindu right-wing Shiv Sena in the Moor's hallucination of an elephant-headed jailor: "I narrowed my eyes and peered—the head of a bearded elephant, who held in his hand an iron crescent dripping with keys. Rats scurried respectfully around his feet. 'To this place we are bringing godless men like you,' said the elephant man. 'Here you will suffer for your sins. We will humiliate you in fashions of which you have not even been able to dream.' . . . Something—a defilement—had begun" (1995, 286). Bombay's beloved Ganesh is now the embodiment of death, complete with scythe; he is god turned spectral in the victory of the "power principle" embodied in the Moor's father, Abraham Zogoiby. The terrorist who blows up Rushdie's beloved city by the close of the novel, Sammy Hazaré, is an employee of both Zogoiby and the legitimate doyen of state politics—the "Mumbai-axis" honcho, Raman Fielding (the Bal Thackeray figure).

These connections between terrorism, the violent nation-state, and subalterns projected through the vitalist ontologies find many other contemporary treatments that I cannot discuss at length here. Yet not all excursions into the logic of specters necessarily engage in the sort of ethical spectrology related to political accountability that I have theorized in the cosmopolitical novel. For example, both Manil Suri's *Death of Vishnu* and Michael Ondaatje's *Anil's Ghost* deploy the tropology of the specter, but to very different ends. Ostensibly unusual in dramatizing the perspective of the indigent homeless Vishnu on the brink of death, in *The Death of Vishnu* Suri etches that in-between space at the moment of life and death as one where the subaltern rises to godlike proportion. This deification harnesses an unfragmented cosmic universe drawn from Hindu mythology, whose modern idiom is found in Bollywood cinema (*Death of Vishnu* doubles as the title of a mythological flick playing at a nearby theater). Only the sentient can fathom Vishnu's cosmic transformation, as we see in the case of the Muslim character Mr. Jalal, who turns to an unfamiliar "other" cosmology in the face of familial dissension over his son's affair with a Hindu girl. In Jalal's delusional role as messiah, Suri obviously writes a utopian Hindu-Muslim unity. Yet it is *Hindu* mythology that provides recompense against modern political and social divisions, as Vishnu soars to encompass the world: "He starts radiating brilliance himself. Brilliance that illuminates each row of empty seats, brilliance that paints each wall a blinding white, brilliance that turns the curtains into sheets of light. As Vishnu watches, the entire theater becomes incandescent. He looks down at himself, but he can longer tell where the light ends and his body begins" (2001, 279–280).

Ondaatje's text is quite another matter. Set in the continual emergency in Sri Lanka's post-1983 period, *Anil's Ghost* takes on the government's terrorism executed by the illegal death squads against separatist guerillas in the North and insurgents in the South. The central protagonist is the U.S.-returned Anil, a forensic expert sent by the United Nations to document human rights violations: "The disposal of bodies by fire. The disposal of bodies in rivers or the sea. The hiding and reburial of corpses" (2000, 43). A "new" body bearing marks of torture, found buried in an ancient burial site, offers Anil, the migrant intellectual, mute testimony. The body of the other assumes spectral proportion in the trail of other bodies, kidnappings, murders, mass graves, drug addiction, and shootings that become the subject of the tale.

While political accountability is then the theme of this novel, Ondaatje links this newly urgent ethical stipulation to the larger traumas of modernity—to the violences of colonialism and nationalism. The larger cataclysmic dismemberment of older forms of community before guns, money, and territorial ambition staked their claim on the body of Sri Lanka is figured in the scattering of the Buddhist rock art throughout museums and archeological exhibits in the West. Ondaatje casts this desecration in a global frame, alluding to similar Japanese imperial excavations in China: "This was a place of complete crime. Heads separated from bodies. Hands broken off. None of the bodies remained—all the statuary had been removed in the few years following its [the Buddhist cave temples of the Shanxi province] discovery by Japanese archaeologists in 1918, the Boddhisattvas quickly bought up by museums in the West" (2000, 12).

Epistemological cannibalism here parallels social and political violence. Into this critique, Ondaatje introduces the memorable Palipana, an epigraphist who had been engaged for a number of years wresting "archaeological authority" away from the Europeans (2000, 79). Like Anil, deciphering traces was once his job. When we encounter him, Palipana is in his seventies, living as an ascetic in the hills and slowly going blind. But it is his gnostic capabilities—his ability to read inscriptions on soil, rock, and flesh through touch—that inspire Anil to exert her imaginative capacities, to truly know her corpse, and to present that knowing as legal evidence of state violence. We will encounter such articulation between counterscientific knowledge, subalterneity, and violence in Amitav Ghosh's *Calcutta Chromosome*, where the violently displaced subalterns

Mangala and her assistant/disciple Lakhaan are the repositories of (fictionalized) folk medical practices. In the next chapter, I will follow the epistemological trails of this text to open up the practices of ethical spectrology and epistemological excavation—"ghosting" and "grafting"—that I have described above. There we will closely analyze the literary effects of the political and ethical commitments that underwrite cosmopolitical writing.

To complete my discussion of the shared intellectual ground of cosmopolitical thinking, I pause on a recent electronic exchange between Amitav Ghosh and Dipesh Chakrabarty, later published in *Radical History*, in which they debate questions of translation, historical evidence, and epistemologies (Chakrabarty and Ghosh 2002).[33] Chakrabarty is clearly preoccupied with the "uncanny" as an effect of incommensurability: Of concern are the condition of disjunctive historical discourses and the implications of loss (those subaltern life-worlds only partially accessible to the rational historian). Ghosh sees, in the same loss, the imperative for recovery—an imaginative project that mobilizes literary resources for its purposes. In raising the issue of race, Ghosh cautions against psychic forms of "forgetting" facilitated by the current global hierarchies of knowledge. Underlining the "silence" on race in South Asian critical discourse, Ghosh argues that this "silence" is perhaps born of an "epistemological perplexity" that engenders psychosocial "misrecognition," and he cites his father's shame over a racial slur that came only as an addendum to his father's account of military service under the British. Ghosh then proceeds to link this epistemological recognition to "our" (Ghosh, Chakrabarty, and progressive postcolonial scholars and writers in the Anglo-American academy by extension) failure to keep alive other "critical traditions" as important resources for living in a postcolonial time (160). In what ensues, it becomes clear that these "other" critical traditions are often written texts in the Indian vernacular languages: Chakrabarty cites philosophical and commentarial treatises, and Ghosh evokes literary and religious sources. These vernacular texts acquire the status of an "other" archive because of their current global invisibility, especially in view of the enormous cultural capital of the South Asian novel in English in the post–*Midnight's Children* years. Bereft of this vernacular writing, we lose entire "epistemologies" that raise crucial ethical questions about the past.

Among our five writers, Amitav Ghosh has been the most direct spectrologist in the mainstream print media. The other cosmopolitical writers embark on different phrasings of the uncanny, staging its epistemological effects in their novels. We will turn to these in greater detail in the next chapter. Here I close with Ghosh's spectrology in his nonfiction, where the concerns with violence, memory, and the dismembered political community are present in a personalized vein. I have already mentioned Ghosh's resurrection of Netaji Subhas Chandra Bose in his *New Yorker* essay commemorating the golden jubilee, because of his family's history in Myanmar; more recently, Ghosh has fictionalized the popular memory of the INA in the historical epic *The Glass Palace* (2001). Ghosh continues to investigate histories of trauma in his short essays, *Dancing in Cambodia, At Large in Burma* (1998), only this time in Cambodia, in the aftermath of the Pol Pot regime. He recounts the psychic effects of that trauma in the stories people tell him: "Some of her most vivid memories of that period are of volcanic outbursts of speech that erupted everywhere at unexpected moments. Friends and acquaintances would suddenly begin to describe what they had lived through and seen, what had happened to them and their families and how they managed to survive" (15).

But Ghosh most directly relates violence to spectrality in his essay on the Delhi riots that followed the assassination of Indira Gandhi, "The Ghosts of Mrs. Gandhi," where he addresses the ethical significance of remembering violence. In this essay published in 1995, the year following the publication of Derrida's *Specters of Marx*, Ghosh enacts many interrupted returns to the past, jettisoning chronological narration—he further describes these jolting returns *as* haunting. Ghosh's memory of the 1984 riots, during which he was working for the daily *Indian Express*, impels him to consider 1947 again. He starts writing *The Shadow Lines* (1988) soon after the Delhi riots, explaining that this was "a book that led me backward in time, to earlier memories of riots, ones witnessed in childhood. It became a book not about any one event but about the meaning of such events and their effects on individuals who live through them" (40). Further along in the essay, Ghosh's account of the pamphlet "Who Are the Guilty?"—a tract in which the citizens of Delhi question possible state participation in violence—propels him to consider another violent scene, the Bombay riots of 1992–1993. Moments of violence, ruptures in the unitary national polity, foreground those "certain others" who remain invisible and excluded from national consciousness. Each event of riot (1947, 1984, 1992–1993) jolts the memory of another specter, another sighting of unrestful spirits. Ghosh's looping narrative in this essay suggests that the cost of a unified nation has always accrued to those who do not count in our "living present."

Five

Of Ghosts and Grafts

Uncanny Narration in
Cosmopolitical Novels

> *There were two lamps, one for each desk, and a high-*
> *wattage bulb that hung from the ceiling with an Oriental*
> *shade. Despite all the light, Kalidas had to search the*
> *room to find the old man. He saw him when the armchair*
> *developed a piece of padding that seemed to move by*
> *itself. Kalidas was, at this point, twenty-five years old,*
> *which meant he had been seven when the war ended in*
> *1945. It didn't matter that the face in the photographs*
> *and paintings that had pervaded Calcutta since then was*
> *frozen from a likeness before or around 1944. It didn't*
> *matter that the death had been a famous and well-*
> *documented one, as ingrained in public consciousness*
> *as life itself. None of this came in the way of recognition.*
>
> *It took Kalidas more than a minute to get over the*
> *impossibility of it. It took him a terrifying further five*
> *minutes to control the shock on his face. Luckily for him,*
> *they were all looking at the old man and no one noticed.*
> *(R. Joshi 2001, 120)*

In this riveting scene, Kalidasbabu recounts his shock at encountering
the renowned freedom fighter Netaji Subhas Chandra Bose imprisoned in the
Russian Gulag. As a recursive specter in (Bengali) regional popular memory
("the face in the photographs and paintings"), Netaji exerts a strange fascination on Paresh Bhatt, the narrator of Ruchir Joshi's debut novel, *The Last Jet-
Engine Laugh*. Kalidasbabu, the narrator's father's friend who was arrested as
a Naxalite in 1975, is Paresh's conduit to history. Kalidasbabu paints a poignant
portrait of the great man muttering in Bengali and speaking of Panditji (Nehru)
to his uncomprehending guards, in an incident whose "reality" remains suspect,

in part because it is in Kalidasbabu's memory, and in part because of his penchant for accenting stories with heroism.

Kalidasbabu's story, challenged and dismissed by many over tea and *adda*, typifies the ongoing debate on Netaji's disappearance in 1945 among Bengalis.[1] Every so often Kolkata newspapers report another Netaji sighting. Kalidasbabu's historic meeting with Netaji, then, is hardly an anomaly. It speaks of a Bengali mourning of their lost visibility in nationalist politics, always expressed as a yearning for the lost promise of independence (If Netaji only had lived!). Joshi's return to the Netaji figure, in a novel of crisscrossing time lines and journeys, opens a seam into an alternate history of the nation, albeit from a regional perspective. In this he exemplifies the cosmopolitical novel's participation in national spectrology, a cultural phenomenon that arises from the ruptures of official histories. In such deliberative incorporation of a fragmented popular memory, whose local resonances require translation for global audiences, Joshi practices the kind of textual grafting that we see in most cosmopolitical novels.

The political imperative to vernacular restoration that such grafting implies has recently been voiced by Amitav Ghosh in a letter that explains his withdrawal of *The Glass Palace* from the Commonwealth Writers Prize Best Book nomination in 2001. Ghosh writes: "As a literary or cultural grouping however, it seems to me that 'the Commonwealth' can only be a misnomer so long as it *excludes the many languages* that sustain the cultural and literary lives of these countries" (2001a; my emphasis). His abrogation of the cultural currency of English in the postcolonial world, and his consequent focus on the vernaculars of that world, is not surprising for a writer whose fundamental concern has been the erasure of vernacular knowledges in postcoloniality. Few writers in English confident of their purchase in an expanding global market for non-Western, multicultural, or Anglophone literatures gnaw at their own participation in glamorizing the colonial tongue at the cost of vernacular literature. I will pursue Ghosh's championing of this "other" cultural archive through the example of *The Calcutta Chromosome,* because this novel, above others, dramatizes ethical spectrology as a postcolonial imperative. On the way, we shall consider other instances of uncanny discourse in some of the more radically experimental cosmopolitical novels.

Haunting is central to *The Calcutta Chromosome*'s interrogation of a specific colonial truth—Ronald Ross's discovery of the cure for malaria. Versed in medical journalism, in *The Calcutta Chromosome* Ghosh embarks on an arduous explanation of chromosomes and their functions. In this breakneck romp through medical discoveries, folk rituals, murders, hallucinations, transmigrating souls, and panoptical computers owned by megacorporations, we encounter a syphilitic migrant subaltern, Mangala. An untrained genius in pursuit of the little-known scientific discovery that the malaria bug could be used to regenerate decaying brain tissue in the last stages of syphilis, Mangala stumbles upon a DNA conglomerate that she cannot name: the "calcutta chromosome." A chromosome only by analogy, this genetic bundle, we are told with grave objectivity, is a "biological correlate" to the "human soul" (1996, 206). Residing only in nonregenerative human tissue, the "chromosome" survives only through incessant mutations, recombining the traits that designate the uniqueness of each individual. But the ability to cut and splice DNA is precisely one of the pernicious features of the malaria bug, as Mangala accidentally discovers; and in the process of cutting and splicing human DNA, the malaria bug can actually digest (and thus retain) this otherwise untransmittable genetic blueprint. An infected person's brain can thus be rewired to fit an original mold. Material souls, in this novel, migrate not through possession, but through the transmission of disease. In fact Murugan, the detective, mockingly tells us that this "scientific" soul switching is what "primitive people" thought was "spirit-possession." Hence the scientific discovery in this novel is the truth about transmigratory souls; it is a ghost story foisted upon the reader of a medical thriller that won the prestigious Arthur C. Clarke prize in 1996.[2]

The Calcutta Chromosome presents us with a template for understanding the narrative modes operative in Ghosh's work, and indeed in many experimental cosmopolitical novels. The DNA analogy of grafting allegorizes the archival search that constitutes detection in the novel. Murugan's suspicion that Ross's analysis of the Anopheles mosquito was rigged leads him to the real architects of the discovery—a group of folk medicine practitioners with immortality on their minds and no interest in the cure for malaria. But this new knowledge comes about through a continuous fragmenting and grafting of hypotheses and speculations. Each narrative about Ross's discovery is haunted by the probability of an "other" truth that confounds its credibility. As we shall see, these twin processes of *ghosting* (the spectral presence of an other) and *grafting* (the cutting, splicing, recombining of otherness) dominate the other novels discussed here. These are Salman Rushdie's *Moor's Last Sigh*, Vikram Chandra's *Red Earth and Pouring Rain*, and to a lesser extent, Arundhati Roy's *God of Small Things*. While ghosts jolt realist narration, grafts suggest the healing of an epistemological loss. Heterogeneous vernacular cultural material becomes not just the dangerous supplement, but sometimes the literary scaffolding for these novels in English.

Ghosting and grafting function metatextually, as Ghosh deliberately muddies the perimeters of literary genres and traditions. *The Calcutta Chromosome* is first a medical thriller, but also a ghost story, a murder mystery, a philosophical rumination, and a historiographic project. Further, Ghosh grafts a larger ver-

nacular tradition of ghost fiction onto this novel in English in the novel's fragmented Lakhaan stories. This vernacular fiction is written in the Indian languages standardized under colonial rule; hence it is a fiction that had
"indigenized" modern cultural forms like the short story, the novel, and the
essay (P. Joshi 2002). The Lakhaan stories are based on two Hindi and Bengali
ghost stories, and they appear three times in *The Calcutta Chromosome,* as
events experienced by Grigson (a linguist), Farley (a missionary who is killed
by the boy ghost), and Phulboni (a writer who narrowly escapes the ghost). The
details of these Lakhaan "fragments" densely encrypt specific vernacular ghost
fiction, a "ghosted" literary corpus that—by his own admission—haunted
Ghosh while writing *The Calcutta Chromosome.* In a recent conversation, Ghosh
confessed to being in the thrall of Rabindranath Tagore's "Kshudhita Pashaan"
("The Hunger of the Stones"), a short story that he had translated for *Civil
Lines 2* in 1995, before embarking on *The Calcutta Chromosome* a year later.[3]

In his exchange with Dipesh Chakrabarty, Ghosh further explains why this
story in particular remains fascinating to him. Disagreeing with Chakrabarty on
the valence of Tagore's colonial inscription, Ghosh reads Tagore as a man in
"crisis"—the Bengali cosmopolitan cognizant of his Enlightenment legacies, yet
also "anguished" over his imbrication as colonial subject. For Ghosh, Tagore's
angst eviscerates the smoothness of his prose on occasion, with particular
instantiation in "Kshudhita Pashaan" when the protagonist repeatedly cries
out: "It's all a lie." In Ghosh's reading of the tale, these recursions comprise the
colonial subject's glimpse into his own alienation. Tagore tropes this divided
subject in this story, argues Ghosh, in the furious and obsessive changing of
clothes (the *sola-topee*-clad Tax Collector's donning of the loose *salwar,* silk
achkhan, and a red Muslim fez) that signals performing difference (Tagore
[1895] 1995, 162). In my view, Ghosh encrypts the Tagorean trope in *The Calcutta Chromosome* in the many switched bodies, clothes, names, and identities
in the novel.

Speaking to the diverse transformative effects of colonialism, Ghosh criticizes Chakrabarty's emphases on the "discursive and persuasive" aspects of
colonialism. He insists that the postcolonial intellectual give equal weight to the
record of "coercion": of racial violence, of population transfers, and of massive
upheavals in the rural areas.[4] Hence, in his own writing of *The Calcutta Chromosome,* he includes both ends of the spectrum: Murugan is the cosmopolitan
from the metropolis who develops an ethics of representation, while the homeless Mangala and the rural migrant, Lakhaan, are Ghosh's colonial/postcolonial
subaltern subjects, who are literally uprooted as the transformative effects of
colonialism permeate rural India. In such a formulation, the inclusion of Tagore
(the "father" of the literary Bengali postcolonial middle-class subject) is

obviously not enough. So Ghosh encrypts another ghost story, "Smells of a Primeval Night" ([1967] 1986), this time from an interlocutor of the *decolonized* nation-state—the Hindi writer Phaniswarnath Renu. Known for his literary depictions of some of the most economically decimated landscapes of post-colonial India, Renu gave up the Padmashree (a high national award for cultural achievement) in 1975 to protest what he saw as the dictatorship of the post-colonial state. We know that Tagore used his literary stature in a similar fashion, renouncing his knighthood in 1919 to protest the violence of the *colonial* state in the infamous Jallianwalla Bagh massacare. Both Tagore and Renu saw their literary projects as crucial to the formation of a national ethics beyond the narrow concerns of territorial governance and sovereignty. But while Renu focused primarily on rural subjects, Tagore's protagonists often inhabit a colonial metropolitan milieu. No wonder Ghosh is attracted to these two literary stalwarts in his writing of the postcolonial diasporic subject's struggle to represent the subaltern "other" (note that both Antar and Murugan in *The Calcutta Chromosome* work for Life Watch, a megacorporation).

I will argue that these cultural grafts are one kind of epistemological "cure" for postcolonial writing in English. This becomes evident when one considers the many clashing epistemologies (elaborately staged) in *The Calcutta Chromosome* between received medical history and alternative medical innovation, between European medicine and "folk" medical practices, and between Brahmanical Hinduism and tantra. We find a similar invocation of epistemological différance in most of the cosmopolitical novels, but we will pursue only two relevant examples—Salman Rushdie's *Moor's Last Sigh* and Vikram Chandra's *Red Earth and Pouring Rain*—as we continue tracking cosmopolitical ethical spectrology.

Trafficking in Specters

In their fiction, almost all cosmopolitical practitioners have some degree of commerce with specters: The human subjects in these texts inevitably share their novelistic world with ghosts, gods, demons, and other spectral presences. Some of these ghosts are undoubtedly embodiments of forgotten voices returning ferociously to assert their claim on the living present. We remember the ghost of the Englishman malignantly clinging to the History House in *The God of Small Things*, making sure the violence of colonialism continues on the body of the dalit; or the child ghost, Soli, in Chandra's first story in *Love and Longing in Bombay*, who has a personal stake in lingering in the closed-up Mumbai mansion. In that story Soli's ghost is an unrestful spirit demanding recompense from his guilty traumatized brother, the major general Jago Antia, for the former's untimely death. But the ghost is also drawn from a larger cultural presence in Chandra's imagination: As Chandra explained in an interview, the inspiration for *Love and Longing in Bombay* came from the fund of ghost stories "told about empty mansions in Bombay" (3).

Alongside these spectral characters, we encounter an excess of subject formation in the cosmopolitical writers' repeated engagement with deification. Representing the hyperbolic overflow of collective sentiments, deification is properly the index of changing cultural and political needs of the imagined community. Arundhati Roy's Velutha, the dalit subaltern-turned-god character in *The God of Small Things*, is a case in point. Velutha is a faultless godlike character deified by the children and their mother. In their eyes he is "the god of small things," but also the dark-skinned love-god of the Hindu pantheon whose erotic antics by the riverbank are a staple of Hindu *bhakti* literature. Ammu sees him as elemental, attuned to the lush landscape and out of place on the historical canvas: "As he rose from the dark river and walked up the stone steps he saw that the world they stood in was his. That he belonged to it. That it belonged to him. The water. The mud. The trees. The fish. The stars. He moved so easily through it" (1997b, 333–334). The erotic close of the novel seems to move into a lyrical mode that resists the psychological realism of memory work, previously the dominant discursive mode. Ammu and Velutha, despite the tragic end to their love in the realist narrative, remain in eternal union in the reader's gaze as the novel closes with Ammu walking away, promising to come again "*naaley*" (tomorrow). The stillness of the temporal here belongs to the scope of myth rather than to teleological narration.

Salman Rushdie's pursuit of deification/demonization is rather different. In *The Ground beneath Her Feet* (2000), he presents a political analysis of celebrity, and the kind of denuding reification that turning into a celebrity entails. This follows on the heels of his biting satire of a glamour-obsessed paparazzi and public (embodied in a phallic snapping camera) who in part orchestrate Lady Diana's tragic accident in an essay titled "Crash." Here Rushdie identifies the advantages of fame—prestige, glamour, riches—as ultimately death dealing for the human subject.[5] In *The Satanic Verses* (1988), he extensively explores the psychosis of the deified subject in the delusional Gibreel, the mega–film star who has played one too many religious roles and now dreams that he was once the archangel Gabriel. Gibreel's fellow postcolonial migrant Saladin Chamcha's half-animal/half-human state is an allegory, an astute political criticism of the demonized British Muslim immigrant in Britain's own postcolonial "island of Dr. Moreau." Chamcha's state transcribes Gayatri Spivak's critique of European "soul-making" (in her analysis of the prowling, caged Bertha Mason) into literary form (Spivak 1985b). In Rushdie, the dominance of the allegorical mode keeps palpable spectrality more or less within the folds of rational discourse. Yet in repeatedly depicting radical subjective transformations whereby the one is borne across to *becoming* the almost unrecognizable other, he repeatedly draws attention to (what Kaviraj had described as) the premodern "fuzziness" of all social identities and the possibility of passing for someone else—curiously resembling Rushdie's own identity under the fatwa. In the other novels, as well, this unfixing of identity through radical transformations creates fuzziness in characters that are not posthuman in any obvious way—not gods, demons, ghosts, or hybrids. For instance, in Chandra's *Red Earth* we witness the mystical transformation of George Thomas when the Irishman metamorphoses into Jahaj Jung. "Reborn" or culturally translated into the mythic Jahaj Jung, George Thomas learns the secret mystery of origins and is therefore able to beget a new generation of Indians who are hybrid in origin.[6]

On a comparative scale, Rushdie remains more conservative than Chandra and Ghosh in his commerce with specters. Chandra insists we simply accept the realistic presence of Yama (the god of death), Ganesh (the scribe of the *Mahabharaa*), and Hanuman (the monkey-god who is also a character in the *Ramayana*) *alongside* Saira, Abhay, Mrinalini, and other realistic characters in the narrative frame of *Red Earth*. Indeed when we get to the point in the story where Sanjay goes to London to rescue another "suspended Englishman," Reverend Sarthey, we can no longer simply relegate these mythic beings to another supernatural world with different rules: They *are* the novelistic world that we inhabit. Hence I would argue that these posthuman beings affirm the uncanny presence of "other" subjectivities and their submerged histories in the cosmopolitical novels, requiring us to function in a cognitive mode apposite to post-Enlightenment rationality.

If *Red Earth* unabashedly asserts the presence of a reincarnated typing monkey, *Calcutta Chromosome* is even more radical in its demands. The physical mutations of "natural laws" in this medical thriller can only be explained if we believe in the religio-philosophical premise of transmigration. For instance, Lakhaan's or Lutchman's deformed hand physically migrates to Romen Haldar, providing empirical evidence of Mangala genetic transfers through transmigration, her practice of *corporeal* immortality. The reality of transmigration assumes centrality as the protagonist Antar becomes the John Malkovichian body, the porthole for grafting other characters in the novel. Antar's final experience of transmigration is further posited as logically commensurable with his (and our) present-day experiences of living multiple and virtual cyberlives. The close of Ghosh's novel suggests the ghostly stirrings of a collectivity in Antar: "There were voices everywhere now, in his room, in his head, it was as though a crowd of people were in the room with him. They were saying: 'We're with you; you're not alone; we'll help you across'" (Ghosh 1996, 256).

Not surprisingly, almost every character in *Calcutta Chromosome* experiences haunting in some form. A virtual ghost, flashing on Antar's screen, demands his investigation of Murugan (who has disappeared from Life Watch), and propels the mystery forward. Antar is the twenty-first-century protagonist who is also employed by Life Watch, a dystopic Kafkaesque panoptical megacorporation with headquarters in New York but "no office in Calcutta." Antar learns that it is Murugan's advocacy of an epistemological challenge—the wild chase for Mangala and her associates—that led to the latter's "ostracism" from the "scholarly community," and "estrangement from several of his friends and associates" (31). Much later in the narrative, we realize that it is not just Antar's official assignment or curiosity that keeps him engaged in the search, but his fascination with Murugan's renegade status in Life Watch. A glimpse into Antar's pre–Life Watch existence in a small village by the banks of the Nile (shades of the narrator of Ghosh's 1992 *In An Antique Land*) clues us in to Antar's sense of loss and nostalgia for a simple life, a forgotten way that haunts Antar. This explains Antar's consequent desire to "disappear" from the Life Watch panopticon, just as Murugan had done.

But Antar's haunting is not an anomaly. Each major character in the novel is haunted by a secret that links him or her to the vital calcutta chromosome mystery: Mangala and Murugan are syphilitics with personal investments in malarial research; the glamorous Sonali is in search of her natural father; Phulboni stumbles upon corporeal immortality and craves it to compensate for the more insubstantial immortality of authorship; and so on. These investments turn the larger postcolonial epistemological ventures into tales of personal sustenance. The familiar other beckons the detective, the journalist, the writer, and the missionary to a larger ethical quest. Each character is not haunted just by a ghost but by *someone else* who is besieged by ghosts: Antar is fascinated by Murugan's fascination with Ronald Ross; Urmila by Sonali's pursuit of Phulboni; Murugan by D. D. Cunnigham, Grigson, and Farley's pursuit of the shady Lakhaan. Soon we have that "specular circle" that Derrida perceives in Marx's engrossment with Stirner's immersion in ghosts: "One chases after in order to chase away, one pursues, sets off in pursuit of someone to make him flee, but one makes him flee, distances him, expulses him so as to go after him again and remain in pursuit" (1994, 140). Derrida's description exactly elucidates the spectral theater of *The Calcutta Chromosome*, where those who seek ghosts exorcise them only to hold them closer.

Postcolonial Corpus

Derrida's notes on the ghostly body proper finds fictive resonance in *The Calcutta Chromosome*, a novel about bodies in the present, past, and future.

Marx, in Derrida's view, posits the process of ghosting as the de-materialization of the body—the red specter that "was conjured (away) by the counter-revolutionaries" (1994, 117). This violent exclusion or disincarnation of the ghost does not mean that the material conditions of the specter have disappeared; it is the work of demystification to restore the body proper to the ghost. Derrida insists on the strange corporeality of the ghost shuttling between the nonhuman (a thing) and the human (someone) in the world. In the recurrence of disappeared bodies in *The Calcutta Chromosome* we inhabit this uncanny place, where only by partially abandoning the proportions of scientific rationalism can we recognize certain others.

D. D. Cunningham, Countess Pongracz, and Murugan, among other characters, are, medically speaking, dead, or they have disappeared into obscurity. But they continue to trouble our pseudo-medical rationality by constantly reappearing (reincarnated) as other characters. The novel insists that the philosophical premise of transmigration be accorded the same empirical credibility that we willingly give (even the most esoteric) medical discourse. Such epistemological leaps are necessary to speak to ghosts in our living present. In fact Ghosh restores the corporeal materiality of these ghosts by explaining the transmigration of souls in biological terms: in the lingo of chromosomes, DNA, retroviruses, and mutations well known to contemporary global cosmopolitan readers. For in Mangala's popular religious medical practice, the transfer of the human soul is effected through the transmission of malaria-infected blood—a medical experiment conducted by Mangala's visceral use of the bodies of pigeons as agar-plates. This drama of corporeal restoration in the story is homologous to Ghosh's self-consciously fictionalized restoration of Mangala's corpus of indigenous knowledge, the subaltern migrant's doctrine of corporeal immortality that troubles the colonial medical gaze. Scientists, administrators, doctors, missionaries, and computer analysts fall prey to the spectral knowledge that makes their discourse on health and cures possible but remains inadmissible in rational discourse. There are some converts to the doctrine of corporeal immortality, as we see in D. D. Cunningham, Ross's predecessor, who stonewalls Ross's search for the malaria bug for almost a year before disappearing into the steamy underground of soul switchers.

The novel's subtitle, "A Novel of Fevers, Delirium, and Discovery," invokes memories of imperial transmissions: of both disease and knowledge. An unknown corpus exerts pressure on the privileged colonial narrative of discovery, for the official narrative of Ronald Ross's romance with the Anopheles mosquito violently occludes an alternative history of medicine. Murugan finds that Mangala had stumbled on a process that won the medical visionary, Julius Wagner-Jauregg, the Nobel Prize in 1927—the process of curing syphilis with the malaria bug. Not only is Ghosh interested in unearthing these parallel histories, but also he sees the colonial narrative of discovery as an exercise of power. Thus a mediocre Englishman enters the annals of history, even though the last, and arguably the most crucial, stages of his research on the Anopheles were orchestrated by Mangala and her associates. Murugan hypothesizes that these folk medical practitioners needed specific mutations of the malaria bug to stabilize the transfer of the "biological soul," but they lacked the resources to produce those mutations in a controlled laboratory setting; hence their manipulation of Ronald Ross.

The names of Murugan's articles on his hypotheses recall old-style colonial scientific artifacts. He revises "Certain Systematic Discrepancies . . ." to "An Alternative Interpretation of Late Nineteenth-Century Malaria Research: Is There a Secret History?" So does the name of the institution with the power to ratify his theories, the History of Science Society. Clearly, Ghosh is playing with the enormous production of classificatory colonial knowledge, and the hubris of "discovery" narratives, by initially setting up his detective as a modern employee at the new center of imperialism (the global North–based Life Watch) and hungry for recognition there. Indeed, by giving us a list of (European) scientists whose research Ross basically filches, Ghosh exposes the "discoverer" as a charlatan, and the act of scientific discovery as a collaborative and cumulative enterprise often indebted to those on the radical edge of science. The postcolonial version of this scientific underground, the spectral corpus, is even more radical in touching upon a matter troubling to our contemporary moment—biological cloning (Ghosh 1996, 207).

Ghosh is not content to offer Hindu philosophical "truth," the doctrine of transmigration, as the alternative to Western discourses of the body. We enter seamy underground gatherings of spooky syphilitics in forest clearings and Spiritualist séances (the European counterpart to accessing multiple souls, scorned by scientists). We are in the domain not only of religion, but of *popular* religion. The nature of the performances described in the novel—rituals with punchy charge—refers us to Tantra, that other of Brahmanical Hinduism. Always seen as a counterreligion, Tantra works against the Brahamanical imperative to control and prohibit desire in order to attain *moksha,* freedom from the cycle of reincarnation. Tantric cults deploy desire, and therefore the body, as a means to freeing the soul. The ecstatic antics of Mangala's followers, their ease with violence and the worship of sexualized female deities, echo the tantric rites exalting the goddess Kali—a malignant (and sexualized) manifestation of the mother-goddess widely venerated above male gods in Bengal.[7]

The Calcutta Chromosome attenuates Ghosh's inclination toward the uncanny in almost all of his oeuvre. The travel/quest novel, *In an Antique Land,* is possibly his most overt restorative project. A thinly veiled autobiographical narrator's obsessive search for a slave's story, one that would have otherwise remained a "footnote in history," fuels the excavation of the forgotten histories of the Jews, Muslims, and Hindus who traversed Egypt and India. The narrator consolidates these histories from the "forgotten" archives of the Geniza in an Egyptian synagogue, first coming across a passing allusion to the slave, Bomma, in a letter written by a merchant in Aden to his friend Abraham Ben Yiju in Mangalore (see Ghosh 2002g). The narrator becomes intrigued by the second appearance of the slave in a letter from S. D. Gottein's collection of letters in the Bodleian Library. Curious about this recurrent trace, and convinced that only "the wazirs and the sultans, the chroniclers and the priests had the power to physically inscribe themselves upon time," Ghosh deploys the imagination to gnostically recreate Bomma's presence and life-world (1992, 917). The narrator marks his uncanny affinity and fascination with the premodern other, noting that Bomma "had given me the right to be there, a sense of entitlement" (19). Luxuriating in Bomma's boisterous laughter that he imagines he hears over the voice on a research tape, the narrator ruminates, "I could have been walking with ghosts" (324).[8]

We are invited to a somewhat different kind of haunting—and thus a different kind of excavation—in Rushdie's *Moor's Last Sigh*, from our early encounter with the possibly prophetic blue ceramic tiles that decorate the floor of the synagogue. We are told that if one gazes for a while at these tiles, visual pictures "emerge" in which one recognizes the past or future, according to one's desires. Thus the grim future-oriented crook Flory Zogoiby sees a country near China eaten by a giant mushroom, while her fatherless son, Moraes Zogoiby, finds the spectral shape of his absent father inscribed in the floor. These visions constitute gnostic acts of reading, speaking to and of presences beyond surface graphics. Invisible knowledges remain secret until "read" in the imagination, as the boy Abraham learns. The scene provides a major *mise-en-abyme* for reading the cultural layers of *The Moor's Last Sigh*, where Rushdie's major aesthetic of the uncanny is best characterized as "palimpsestine," a term that he uses to describe Mooristan/Bombay. The visual architecture of the palimpsest determines every painting described in the novel, for we find "secrets" and "puzzles" encrypted in many paintings. Some of these are citations of local cultural events. Like the fading erasures of the palimpsest, not every layer can be "known" to every gazer. Given that our gaze on each painting is dramatically prolonged, one is caught in uncanny discordance—sensing a citation not fully recuperable without active investigations of the textual fragment. We see this, for instance, in the four-page description of the "early Moors" (1995, 224–227), or in the two-page exegesis on a single painting, *Mother-Naked Watches Chimène's Arrival*

(246–248). We find a particularly densely encrypted example of palimpsestine citation in Aurora's *The Kissing Abbas Ali Baig*, where our full viewing requires considerable context-specific knowledge. The work depicts a historic kiss from a starlet bestowed on the stylish cricketer Abbas Ali Baig at the Brabourne stadium in Mumbai. Recording this real event in the nation's history, the painting further grafts this earlier historical moment with the more recent Shiv Sena–instigated culture wars: the disruption of India-Pakistan cricket matches, the sudden characterization of M. F. Husain as a "Muslim" artist, and the storming of the Savage Garden concert that featured a kiss. A political cartoonist ridicules the painting, in Rushdie's thinly disguised portrait of Bal Thackeray (who started his career as a cartoonist), and Aurora is suddenly "a *Christian* artist" in the wake of this cricket controversy. Rushdie further dramatizes the idea of palimpsest in the two *Moor's Last Sigh* paintings, both lost or stolen in the unfolding of the plot. Aurora's painting of Sultan Boadbil and Axya prophesizes Aurora's death, and it is stolen from a public gallery. The other painting of the same name is Vasco Miranda's loving rendition of an erotic Aurora, quickly painted over with a lachrymose kitsch image of Boadbil leaving Granada (at Aurora's jealous husband's behest). To really "see" the first painting requires an excursion into prophecy, faith, and belief, while the second testifies to art's subversive power to register naked erotic truth now sold out to a defunct commercialized kitsch. Together the two paintings insist on a search for different and lost forms of knowing, newly erased in the Hindu micronationalist commodifications of culture.

If the spatial and the visual mark Rushdie's disjunctive narration, Vikram Chandra engages with temporal schemata as his primary project. As with Ghosh, a personal haunting engenders Chandra's first novel, *Red Earth and Pouring Rain*: his fixation with Captain James Skinner's biography, which gives rise to a colossal trail of quests, adventures, and discoveries. Chandra was captivated by the interpretive license of the biography's translators who rendered the original Urdu text into English, the mutations of an original acting as the narrative motor (see Chandra 1998b). When it appeared in 1995, *Red Earth* was a departure from earlier South Asian modes of writing Indian stories, and different in its mythographies of India than Rushdie's groundbreaking *Midnight's Children*. Chandra went on to win the Commonwealth Writers Prize for Best First Fiction.

Most obviously, in *Red Earth* the decolonized nation is not the primary object of interest. In his focus on the time just preceding the consolidation of British rule, Chandra poses the birth of India as nation as the occasion for, but not the subject of, the tale. *Red Earth* explodes the category of the "precolonial" by transcribing colonial India as a short episode that followed a more complex and tumultuous time between 1750 and 1900. This is a period when there is a paradigm shift between the Islamic and Christian civilizations. Those years see the "fall" of the Mughal Empire implicit in the era of Maratha wars, the spectacle of Western powers battling each other for control on the subcontinent, and the first war of independence/Sepoy Mutiny of 1857. The monkey narrator, Sanjay, recounts the events of 1750–1900 in the presence of Abhay, our diasporic South Asian narrator who has "returned" home. Chandra juxtaposes this early period against the contemporary "civilizational encounter" between India and North America. Conventional national histories that explain the "rise" of British power are now seen appositely as describing the "fall" of the Mughal Empire. The modern story of nation making (1900 through Nehruvian India), more often than not the temporal arc of Indian novels in English, is nowhere to be found. Chandra wrests the popular time line of Indian novels in English to a different scheme, the temporal graft of the "precolonial" jostling the calmer chronologies of Abhay's immigrant stories.

Yet the postcolonial as a *critical* gesture informs our perception of the events recounted in this novel. For instance, from the present postcolonial perspective nested in the "now" sections of the novel, the orientalist dreamer is perceived to be a mythic figure whose life of often-destructive dream-making and dream-seeking is a modern parable at best—his fantasies are delirious and magical but always at a disconnect from reality. We see this in Chandra's memorable depiction of the adventurer and hero Benoit de Boigne. When Benoit de Boigne of Chiria Fauj fame in India returns to France, his fantasy self and memories prove psychologically destructive. He degenerates, becoming restless and speaking in alien tongues that nobody understands. Orientalism turns out to be finally most destructive to the orientalist dreamer. The visionary power of orientalist fantasy is after all, Chandra suggests, only a passing moment in Indian history. In fact Chandra offers a rather interesting take on orientalism, first by featuring a Frenchman, rather than a Britisher (usually the orientalist figure in the South Asian imagination); and then by implying that such dreamers are simply absorbed into India's luscious heroic landscape, where they are embalmed alongside other mythic figures.[9] And paradoxically, like those heroes, these orientalists may even have been seers or visionaries of some kind, made ill by their fevered and overworked imaginations. Sanjay recounts how, upon his return to France, when "he [Benoit de Boigne] whispered in alien tongues, some thought he was asking for forgiveness, and others that he was giving it" (1995, 37). Of course, the fact that Benoit de Boigne (1751–1830), the German Walter Reinhardt (1720–1778), and the Irishman George Thomas, alias Jahaj Jung (1756–1802), were actual historical figures makes their mythic reincarnation in Sanjay's tale a deliberate postcolonial remaking of history proper. History proper is always seen as intrusion, worthy only of summary dismissal. The paragraph-long chapter titled "What Really Happened," for instance, ends with this terse sentence on a historical event—"Then the English came." But mythic events stretch lyrically over several pages.

As is true for Rushdie and Ghosh, a part of Chandra's epistemological critique inheres in his condemnation of hegemonic print culture and the dominance of English. Consider the memorable story about the Shakespeare-obsessed Bengali who supervises a printing press. Sanjay swallows English type and his throat, Shiva-like, turns blue until he bleeds and bleeds and writes a single Hindi sentence into the Stratfordian's book—"This book destroys completely, this book is the true murderer" (299). Of course, Markline, the British press owner, thinks of the sentence as a "code," since he has not bothered to learn Hindi despite living in India for most of his life. On other occasions, it is commodification in both print and visual registers that poses danger to human subjects. We have seen how Chandra self-consciously registers the turning of the hero, Janvi, into commodity and statistic. We see a similar move in Chandra's depiction of Kyrie, the sex worker and U.S. subaltern, who is consumed on screen and in the flesh. Only in Abhay's story we do hear her "confessions," and she is given more psychological depth than any other female figure in the North American part of the story—including the female leads to Abhay's unfolding drama.

It may be evident in my explorations of these restorative projects that Rushdie, Chandra, and Ghosh are deeply critical not only of colonial "truths," but also of the concomitant commodification of indigenous knowledge. These recessive practices are put to instrumental and quantifiable use in the colonial regime. Hence a knowledge of possible corporeal immortality is transformed into the cure for malaria. Looking anew at Marx's conception of the commodity fetish, Derrida notes that it is in the translation of things—their coding in systems of exchange—that they acquire a *ghost-effect*. The table, he argues, continuing with Marx's famous example, is after all an "ordinary, sensuous thing" that has use value; it is "human at the bottom" (Derrida 1994, 151). In the Derridean landscape of specters this sensuous thing acquires the mystical properties of commodity when it enters into a chain of exchange: "The ghostly scheme now appears indispensable. The commodity is a 'thing' without phenomenon, a thing in flight that surpasses the senses (it is invisible, intangible, inaudible, and odorless); but this transcendence is not altogether spiritual, it retains the bodiless body that we have recognized as making the difference between specter and spirit. What surpasses the senses still passes before us in the silhouette of the sensuous body that it nevertheless lacks or that remains inaccessible to us" (151). Knowledge fetishized as "medical discovery," the conquest of the corporeal, is uncanny commodity in *The Calcutta Chromosome*. Mangala's insights lose their sensuousness in the transfer to Ronald Ross's lab and its incumbent colonial mystique; they become uncanny knowledge.

Elaborating on the relationship of commodity-formation and haunting, Derrida continues: "But if commodity-form is *not, presently*, use-value, and even if it is not *actually* present, it affects in advance the use-value of the wooden table. It affects and it bereaves it in advance, like the ghost it will become, but this is precisely where haunting begins" (161). The colonial chimera of scientific knowledge affects and bereaves folk and vernacular knowledges, as the story of multinational corporate bio-piracy has so powerfully brought home to us in our current phase of capitalist expansion.[10] To understand the loss of the ownership of knowledge in terms of epistemological robbery with economic implications (medical lab research sold back in the form of pharmaceuticals to the ex-colonial world) is to fully grasp the condemnation of present practices implied in Ghosh's fictionalized materialist critique. The knowledge that is Murugan's legacy from Mangala is not recognized as such, but refracted through the figure of Ronald Ross. Mangala is ghosted in this exchange. And so the "commerce in commodities" transforms "human producers into ghosts," as Derrida notes: "Men no longer recognize it [the commodity form] in the *social* character of their own labor" (155).

The use-value of finding the malaria bug's ability to cut and paste DNA remains mundane in Mangala's routine soul transfers; but for Ross the malaria bug is his ticket to fame. Hence the discovery acquires mystical value; his "cure" becomes a treasured commodity in the colonial rationale for government. Despite his critique of colonial appropriation, in his fictional medium Ghosh *can* imagine an "outside" to these systems of exchange and commodity formation. In the secrecy of Mangala's rituals, the use-value of the calcutta chromosome retains its materiality, its sensuousness, its silence. Seen from within modern epistemological hierarchies, the spiritual reaching toward the eternal is of secondary importance to the scientific hubris of rejuvenating mortal bodies. Spirituality acquires the shadiness of a "counterscience"; and the other side of mortality remains inadmissible, assuming proportion only as occult, as excess.

But these alternative medical and philosophical practices rely on secrecy, the very opposite of communication and/or discovery, for their continued transmission. "Silence is their religion," Murugan explains to a bewildered Antar (Ghosh 1996, 88), and we soon realize that silence is indeed thick discourse in this novel, transforming those who "answer" it. The writer in the novel, Phulboni, imagines silence to be a material thing, a "creature" that haunts the bowels of the city: "But here our city, where all law, natural and human, is held in capricious suspension, that which is hidden has no need of words to give it life; like a creature that lives in a perverse element, it mutates to discover sustenance precisely where it appears to be most starkly withheld—in this case, silence" (121). This is precisely Chakrabarty's idea of uncanny discourse, in which the "facts" of science, requiring communication (the narrative of discovery), are indeed "punctured" by the counterscientific will to secrecy, improbability, and inadmission. As ever, the shadow of the "uncanny" only reinforces the modern subjects' sense of the prison-house of rational knowing.

Time Bleeds

Transmigration implies a surplus of time within the living present. It seems we cannot live in thick time; anachronous presences appear spectral in our "proportional" perception of the contemporary (Derrida 1994, 7). Following this Derridean sense of the noncontemporaneous in the living present, Bliss Cua Lim (2001) elaborates on the notion "spectral times" with reference to the ghost-film genre, an analysis useful for our discussion of disjunctive generic modes in *The Calcutta Chromosome*. For Lim, ghosts compensate for a problem of time in realism: They figure a nonsynchronism that is opposed to the empty homogenous time of history proper.

The Calcutta Chromosome specializes in temporal grafts. The description of the underground folk rituals through which the calcutta chromosome is transmitted from host to host deliberately evokes the magical proto-demonic rituals of early scientific alchemy with its reliance on the secret transformative properties of metals, as well as alternative tantric processes driven underground during the British Raj.[11] The text's subtitle—"A Novel of Fevers, Delirium, and Discovery"—also self-consciously references two different historical periods similar in their radical expansions of territory, knowledge, and disease: the early modern age of fevered expansions, medical breakthroughs, and the scientific classification of other worlds, and the current times of globalization. Antar's delirious head rush is like the heady fever of imperialism, a precolonial expanding of worlds grafted onto an equally borderless twenty-first-century world of diasporic crossings and virtual heterotopias.

More importantly, ghosts as thickened time lie at the heart of *The Calcutta Chromosome*; nonsynchronism is its mantra. The philosophical premise of transmigration makes possible the coexistence of the dead with the living: Several materially present ghosts wander through the story, recursive presences luminously represented in the vengeful ghost of Lakhaan. The biological avatar of Lakhaan/Lutchman is Romen Haldar, whose deformed hand is the physical giveaway of successful genetic transfer; but this example of physical reconstitution can be multiplied in most characters of the novel. Time has texture in this novel, with ghosts depicted as porous membranes for accumulated pasts.

Only if we believe in reincarnation, the thickness of ghosts, does the uncanny and disjunctive temporality of the novel's frame sit comfortably with us as readers. The novel starts with the ID card of a disappeared man, Murugan, flashing on Antar's computer sometime in the twenty-first century; and it is in investigating Murugan's strange disappearance that we chance upon the possibility of the calcutta chromosome. This discovery leads us to believe that the characters we encounter in the story's present are mutations of those living in the 1890s. The story insists on this temporal leap, challenging our idea of rational time by a curious moment of closure. Antar realizes that at 5:25 P.M., the exact time his journey (and our story) started, someone had already begun to "load" the story he had lived *since* then onto his computer. Hence he was actually playing out a virtual script that, paradoxically, could not have come into being without his actions within it. As Antar slowly becomes a "believer," his actions become steadily more illicit, idiosyncratic, and unpredictable. Logically, then, anticipating and scripting Antar's actions beforehand would be impossible; yet the end of the novel suggests this without explanation. This scrambles the temporalities of narration: Realist time bleeds into the virtual time of cyberlives and the philosophical time of the soul, a noncontemporaneity the puts historicism "out of joint."

Such "time bleeds" are commonplace in the cosmopolitical novels, a concept that I extend from Gyanendra Pandey's work on communal history writing. Analyzing modes of history writing in Hindu militant literature distributed through pamphlets and calendars at temple sites and pilgrimages, Gyanendra Pandey (1994) explores the Hindu Right's popular use of mythic time schemes. For example, in the new Hindu calendar, there are a series of prophesied wars with Muslims, and only tangential references to anticolonial struggles (the latter count as only two of the seventy-seven battles Hindus have fought so far). Pandey argues that here mythic time bleeds into real time, for all Hindus are urged to literally inhabit these times and places. He cites Hindu militant histories that fabulate seventy-nine battles, returns of ruptures between "us" and "them," Hindus and Muslims. The cycle of war ends with the establishment of Ram's rule. In such populist histories, linear historical time (that has a specific "goal") leaks into these cyclical accounts of violence (savage bloodletting alternates with remote, golden periods of harmony). It is no mean irony, Pandey remarks, that the ahistorical character of these narrations parallels modern orientalist histories in which "Hindus" and "Muslims" are unchanging cultural entities "fully constituted," with their animosities ever "smouldering beneath the surface" (1525). Such an entrenched Hindu-centric perspective is found in V. S.

Naipaul's argument of the historical wound that Hindus bear as a cross, the "reason" for their million mutinies in the present.

While for the modern historian such seeping of time explodes the skin of rational discourse, these bleeds may be curative for fiction writers. Most of the cosmopolitical novelists partake in the conversation on history proper, the formalized rational ordering of time and place within narratives. Ostensibly at least, Rushdie, famous for his speeded-up narrations, "chutney-fied" histories, and labored temporal inaccuracies (which he first "explained" to horrified critics in the "Errata" essay on narration in *Midnight's Children*), is the most savvy practitioner of cutting and splicing histories.[12] In *The Moor's Last Sigh* he trenchantly criticizes the spatial version of the Hindu Right's will to history, its claim over Ram's original "birthplace." The very idea of a dominant nation-space is deconstructed even as the novel commences, for we begin to read the Indian polity from the tangential position of Goan Christian political subjects, with their allegiance to Portugal and not Britain. Rushdie's uncanny spatialities stand at a reasoned distance from V. S. Naipaul's validation of Hindu roots on the subcontinent. In his commentary "A Million Mutinies," which appeared in the golden-jubilee issue of *India Today*, Naipaul offers a vigorous defense of Hindu majoritarianism as recompense for a historical wound inflicted by Muslim invaders:

> What happened from 1000 A.D. on, really, is such a wound that it is impossible to face. Certain wounds are so bad that they can't be written about. You deal with that kind of pain by hiding from it. You retreat from reality. I wrote a book about that, and people thought I meant India hasn't really a civilisation, or India can't go ahead. What I was saying is that you can't deal with a wound so big. I do not think, for example, that people like the Incas of Peru or the native people of Mexico have ever got over their defeat by the Spaniards. In both places, the head was cut off. I think the pre-British ravaging of India was as bad as that. The Muslims shouldn't be too sensitive about this. Because in the Islamic world, a similar vandalisation occurred with the mongols. Muslims all over the world still grieve about that. (1997, 37)

Naipaul's conservative logic of violated roots—to whose emotional outcomes "Muslims shouldn't be too sensitive"—rationalizes a "mutiny" that may well culminate in vicious carnage of the magnitude we witnessed in Godhra in 2002.

In terms of splicing time periods, *The Satanic Verses* is Rushdie's most ambitious project, with the psychotic angel/film star's delusional memory of the birth and migration of an "idea," the moment of the Prophet's revelation. In fact the historical period of the seventh-century birth of Islam is lyrically presented in the space of Jahilia, a corrupt and fallen state of mind rather than an actual place, representing Makkah or Mecca before Islamicization. The entire novel moves back and forth, quite symmetrically, between the period of Islam's birth and its consolidation in the holy city of Medina, and present postcolonial Bombay and London—contemporary places where the question "What kind of idea are you?" resurfaces with renewed urgency. All this mobility of time and landscape in *The SatanicVerses* is, as is mostly the case with Rushdie, overtly self-conscious. Hence I would argue, in the vein of Kumkum Sangari, that Rushdie remains a modernist in his historical endeavors, always drawing attention to the fragment in terms of the whole. His historical antics more often than not have clearly allegorical functions, the mythic or fantastic yarns figuratively representing national histories; and his excursions into radically disjointed historical periods are psychologically rationalized within the text. Hence a radical *incommensurability* of historical discourse, or disorientation from the present, is not quite as sharp in Rushdie as it is in Chandra or Ghosh. In Rushdie's text, we remain more or less in contemporaneous time.

What makes *The Moor's Last Sigh* temporally innovative, however, is the curious reversal of political desire that we see in this text—especially if we were to regard the Moor's narration as Rushdie's own Rip Van Winkle–like dream of plural renaissance worlds, since the novel ends with the Moor falling into a long sleep. Rushdie's desire for an "Indian Renaissance" is made "visible" by his grafting of Moorish Spain, the moment of an Islamic renaissance, onto the Indian landscape. But India's present fallen state allegorizes the general state of the contemporary world after virulently politicized religious mobilizations. Nehruvian India, then, is the allegory for Rushdie's desire for a cosmopolitan world of plural Islam, certainly a liberal Islam that will undo his "fate." Hence "diverse" Moorish Spain and "plural" Nehruvian India double and shift in their allegorical function, as the Moor's desire creates a slippage between two historical dreams. This analytic instability of major structuring allegories is quite rare in Rushdie's novels.

Vikram Chandra's *Red Earth* overtly retells historical episodes in epic mode, presenting a more engaged experiment with noncontemporaneity in the seeping of rational teleological time into mythic history or *itihasa*. In an effort to counter colonialist claims about the "inadequacies" of historical consciousness in classical Indian modes of historical thinking, Sheldon Pollock historicizes contemporary understandings of *itihasa*. He provides a history of how we come to our common understanding of *itihasa* as eternal stories that have sacral authority. Now genealogically fitted to Vedic discourse, Pollock explains, "the primary reference of *itihasa* . . . is the eternally repeated and no longer the contingent, the localized, the individual—that is, the historical" (see Pollock 1989, 610). It is this later version of *itihasa* as eternal truth that contemporary writers like Vikram Chandra adopt as the traditional Indian mode of history writing.

Chandra follows the larger traditional premise that *itihasa* is an important source for understanding how to live (*dharma*) or what is good (*artha*), and that all great epics are authoritative social codes for living. At the beginning of the cycle of stories in the novel, upon the advice of the god Hanuman, the typing monkey narrates his remembered account of previous lives. Thus a mythic frame creates the conditions for narrativity. A mythic character, Sandeep, in some timeless setting tells Shanker (one of the previous incarnations of our monkey narrator) of his encounter with a seer. In Sandeep's company, Shanker loses all sense of ordered teleological time, a dissolution Chandra implies as necessary for revelation: "I felt as if we had both vanished into the light and dark of the forest, melting away until we were nothing but two particles in the huge surge of life that swirled around us" (1995, 22). It is worth noting that later in the novel, for Jahaj Jung this mystical experience of dissolving time and space is the condition of knowing, and therefore for "begetting," modern India. The dissolving into the fecund chaos of noncontemporaneous existence is pitched as generative for stories, communities, and civilizations. We see this again when the woman seer of Sandeep's narration transforms the historical life of Benoit de Boigne into a story that is "always-already." It therefore acquires contemporary relevance:

> This is what she told me. Like Valmiki and Vyasa, who are our elders, incomparable and dazzling, she spoke of honour among men, and of true love long remembered, as in the stories of kings and demons that are told to children by old people—but do not think that this story is untrue because it is *itihasa*: thus it was; let this story appear among you, as it happened long ago, and it will clear your heart and cleanse your soul, but beware, for it is no story for those with weak stomachs and nervous hearts—it has in it the heights of passion and the depths of loneliness, the tender wounds of love-making and the hideously cheerful, grinning death-faces of the battlefield. Remember, the players and the play, the song and the singers are the same, there is no difference, remember and listen. Listen. (23)

Here *itihasa* is historical consciousness that transmits codes for present-day living. We are admonished, "Do not think that this story is untrue," and the stories invoke Vedic authority when they close with "thus it was" and continues to be. Localized contingent histories exist in the fallen world of rational time, colonial and national. In Chandra's text they occur as the intrusive "what actually happened" sections, which catalog the historical movement of armies, stories of war, and fortunes of the winners and losers. In the postcolonial world of burdensome history, rational knowing is once more "anti-knowledge," and history proper attaches to the nation (always the figure of a divided community in the South Asian context) and thus fractures the subject. *Red Earth* imposes civilizational scope on national and colonial modern history: Imperial (e.g., Benoit de Boigne), colonial (e.g., Markline/Sorkar), and postcolonial diasporic (Abhay in the United States) encounters are perceived as the meeting of civilizational forces (Europe, India of the Mughals and Hindus, and North America). Grafted together, they become the new epic for our times.

Finally, on occasion the cosmopolitical writers spatialize noncontemporaneity by placing time *under* the earth: The force of the forgotten, the lost, or the sacred exerts a geophysically uncanny presence. The unseen co-presence of an old city provides Vikram Chandra with an occasion for writing of ghosts in contemporary postcolonial Mumbai (Chandra 1997). Arundhati Roy's *The God of Small Things* is, of course, about remembering personal and collective traumas, and some of these are embedded geophysically in locales where the central events take shape. Both the back verandah of the History House where Velutha is beaten to death and the river bank where Sophie Mol drowns, for instance, carry unmistakable traces of the past. We are told: "Something lay buried in the ground. Under grass. Under twenty years of rain. A small forgotten thing" (1997b, 127). Here the "small things" are fragments of repressed memories, demanding geophysical excavation. Even the most cleaned-up places carry unclean histories, evident in the cycle of violence in the History House, which had been turned into a tourist resort by the time Rahel returns to Ayemenem—"Nothing worse than kebabs and caramel custard happened there now," say the two-egg twins with irony and foreboding, before they witness Velutha's death (127). Ghosh's *In An Antique Land* features a topographic haunting when the narrator recounts the fact that a canal constructed in Nashawy, Egypt, had to take a different route in order to avoid the grave of a local saint, Sidi Abu Kanaka. Traveling in Mangalore, a taxi driver tells the narrator of a similar instance when a road under construction deviates to make room for a Bhuta shrine: "In both cases, the construction work comes to a halt, when the grave turns rock without yielding to the spades of the workers or when the bulldozers are immobilized" (Belliappa 1996, 62). Marking the parallel, the narrator is clearly delighted at the force that the mystical exerts on the secular space of modernized nations such as Egypt and India.[13]

One of the cosmopolitical writers not discussed at length here, Amit Chaudhuri, achieves similar uncanny textual effects through his transcription of alternative histories. Writing about Chaudhuri's strange temporalities, Amitava Kumar (2002) notes: "In Chaudhuri's prose, history always happens elsewhere. It is like an earthquake at the heart of the earth." This is a particularly apt description indeed for the uncanny narrations that I have recounted above. Moreover, as in the case of many of the cosmopolitical writers discussed here, much of Chaudhuri's attention to alternate histories becomes political commitment after the shock of the 1992 riots following the Babri Masjid destruction. In his latest novel, *Real Time* (2002), Chaudhuri recounts how, on his return to Mumbai, he found that metal plates bearing Muslim names (on house fronts) had been erased to protect the inhabitants of the buildings. "Small, accidental sensations, too small to be called incidents told me I was now living in an altered world," writes Chaudhuri, registering this violent erasure (see Kumar 2002). Uncanny discourses in such novels, then, are a literary cosmopolitics aimed at dislodging spatio-temporal assemblages that might culturally emplace some subjects at the cost of others. In turn, these "other" times, spaces, and subjects of narration point to a restorative project: the necessity of consolidating a vernacular cultural archive, an imperative that returns us squarely to the door of cultural translation.

Cultural Grafts

In his argument on the contemporary necessities of cultural translation, Chakrabarty asks: How *does* one capture subaltern significations of supernatural and cyclical time that compel understandings of work? How does one translate not just life-worlds, but also the entire belief systems that they carry with them? Certainly historians, Chakrabarty continues, have lesser license than do literary practitioners to jump the parameters of rational narration. Historians must become ethnographers, turning to songs, idioms, poems, and festival rituals for evidence of "other times" in subaltern life-worlds. In their efforts to rewrite modern history, the cosmopolitical writers, too, embark on an ethnographic enterprise. They become collectors of quotidian cultural forms that they graft onto received novelistic genres. For example, Rushdie draws extensively on Bollywood culture—*masala* stories, star hagiographies, musical numbers, and industry trends—as his popular idiom of choice. Vikram Chandra's chosen medium is oral storytelling, a cultural practice that he perceives as global but peculiarly relevant to Indian postcolonial locales. And Amitav Ghosh is relentlessly "local," picking specific vernacular literary traditions as fuel for his novels in English. In turn, this writerly attention to the local and the vernacular leads the postcolonial cultural critic to break new ground. In these productions of locality, the cosmopolitical writers once more sharpen our sense of the costs of their own global circulation, referencing circulation in the many writers, painters, critics, readers, and listeners who people their novels.

The hankering for buried truth, the "secrets" hidden in the lost paintings, motivates the odyssey in *The Moor's Last Sigh*. Both paintings hide "authentic" truths lost in the contemporary world of politics and commodity. These personal truths are allegories for the modern national subject: Vasco Miranda's lustful depiction of the erotic mother is an allegory for the libidinal male subject-motherland erotic core of the Indian nationalist imaginary. Further, the Axya-Boadbil tales painted over both of the *Moor's Last Sigh* paintings telescope these personal allegories into a historical past: the fall of Moorish culturally diverse Spain "expelled" by the homogenizing kingdom of Catholic Isabella and Ferdinand, a story that then indexes the present expulsion of diverse Nehruvian India under the rule of Ram. The novel further establishes a Middle East–Malabar coast link, an imaginative topography of personal significance for Rushdie. For the boy from Bombay, Rushdie, named after Ibn Rushd (the Islamic intellectual of Muslim Spain who was criticized by the Islamic philosophical establishment for his "westernized" inclusion of Plato and Aristotle), the progressive, richly diverse culture of Muslim Spain was always one that he claimed as his own cultural heritage. Hence in the final scenes of the novel Rushdie allegorizes his own fate in a world of politicized art. The "authentic" Moor/narrator is imprisoned in the megalomaniac Miranda's postmodern Alhambra, a kitsch version of Aurora's pluralistic little India. Now disconnected from the living world, the Moor has for his only companion in exile the elegance of language (whose essence is embodied in the fabulous and feminine "Aeiou" character).

In *Moor* these historical and personal grafts are not just allegorical, when one unearths Rushdie's complex argument about media. To begin with, the historical forays are sometimes literal embellishments of a family saga. The Moor imagines that the da Gama wing of his family comes from Vasco da Gama's line, albeit on the wrong side of the blanket, while the Zogoibys are related in equally unsavory ways to the Sultan Boadbil. The Moor represents his mode of storytelling, his spilling of the dirty secrets of use, abuse, and murder behind his parents' Norman Rockwell love, in the following way:

> I have grave doubts about the literal truth of the story, with its somewhat over-wrought Bombay-talkie *masala* narrative, its almost desperate reaching back for a kind of authentification, for *evidence*. . . . I believe, and others have since confirmed, that simpler explanations can be offered for the transaction between Abraham Zogoiby and his mother, most particularly for what he did or did not find in an old trunk underneath the altar; I will offer one such alternative version by and by. For the moment, I present the approved, and polished, family yarn; which, being so profound a part of my parents' pictures of themselves—and so significant a part of contemporary Indian art history—has, for those reasons if no other, a power and importance I will not attempt to deny. (1995, 77–78)

Notice the Moor's abrogation of the "approved" family story and his consequent search for a more authentic story in the Bollywood vein. He draws on what "others have since confirmed" for his alternative version of the convoluted family yarn.[14] Our unreliable asthmatic narrator gossips out of habit, an extension of his family's masala-making traditions that "reach back" for authentification. Reach back where? To the myth, fabrication, and fantasy that energizes Bollywood narratives in their mythological antecedents. And in such a reach Rushdie embarks on an investigation of Bollywood masala as national fantasy, turning ethnographer in his consolidation of a heterogeneous cultural catalog of vernacular resources.

Bollywood is clearly mass culture here, but it is Bollywood's flattening of myths that preoccupies the narrator. Rushdie painstakingly places Bollywood in a larger domain of vernacular *visual* cultures. India for the most part appears in the hands of her painters. In fact one could do a history of modern Indian painters if one were to follow the painterly trail in *The Moor's Last Sigh*: from members of the Progressive Artists Group (notably Husain, but also Francis da Souza, the exile, and H. Gade) to present-day luminaries such as Bhupen Kakar (referenced in Aurora's painting *You Can't Get What you Please?*) and Nalini Malini. Aurora's "high cultural" paintings are in direct opposition to "mass cultural" Bollywood cinema. Hence Aurora's depictions of "authentic" mother-son love in its complex, challenging, and mobile exercise stand at a reasoned distance from the slushy mother-son sentimental flick *Mother India*. In a Benjaminian move, Rushdie evokes the "aura" of the original lost under its mechanized kitsch versions: Miranda's lachrymose Boadbil resembles mass-produced calendar art, while Aurora's paintings retain their artistic singularity. The Moor hybridizes his own narration when he recycles Bollywood masala into a "literary" narrative of highly connotative, allusive, and metaphorical value, albeit hilariously embellished.

Folk cultures vie for attention in these battles of high- and mass-cultural forms, as Rushdie consolidates a folk repository: nursery rhymes, like the chilling "Baby Softo"; fairytales, from Rumpelstiltskin to Rip Van Winkle; legends of talking elephants; Western myths, from *Paradise Lost* to *Treasure Island*; and epic lore from the *Mahabharata*, among others. Rushdie locates the Moor's narration within the popular, a domain where mass-, high-, and folk-cultural artifacts are recycled for a contingent moment of address. Hence the sweet "Baby Softo" becomes a complex jingle on drug trafficking; *Paradise Lost*, a modern parable about a fall from *secular* grace; and the two parts of *The Godfather* (the Vito-Michael contretemps and Michael's later transformation into a killer) assume allegorical function in the telling of the father-son and son-as-killer stories, now alluding to the current Bollywood scavenging of Hollywood staples. The story of India in the eighties and nineties becomes an ethnographic document and a treastise on media.

Vikram Chandra's recycling of the mythic to represent a culturally layered India approximates Rushdie's novels, but with an eye to privileging oral culture over other cultural forms. Chandra saw his 1995 collection of short stories, *Love and Longing in Bombay*, as "collaborating in the myth of Bombay." He was no doubt referring to Rushdie and others who have made that metropolis the testing ground for the survival of Indian democracy. In *Love and Longing in Bombay*, Chandra translates oral lore and gossip on the old "empty mansions" in Bombay into print, while in *Red Earth* the typewriter transcribes Sanjay's mythic tale into a written version. Writing imparts humanness to the monkey-narrator, as he is able to "prove" his previous existence as Sanjay, the warrior-poet, by his intelligence. Here Chandra obviously alludes to a magic realist novelistic lineage, specifically Julio Cortázar's human-turned-axolotl who can prove his intelligence only when given a pen. But if print or the written text is inevitably the test of learning in this modern world, the superior structure and modes for good storytelling, in Chandra's view, remain in the oral tradition. The linearity of classic realist novels or autobiographies is inadequate for telling "our story," but the long, accumulated, endlessly proliferating yet strangely relevant story that Ganesh demands of the monkey captivates the reader. It is the only story long enough to hold death (waiting in the form of Yama) at bay. So the sea of stories is indeed life affirming for the characters, storytellers, negotiators, organizers, and audience (who soon become the nation): "These accumulated stories became the stories of stories, the stories of a nation made up of many nations, the collective dreams of many peoples who were one people" (Chandra 1995, 253). Postcolonial India is embodied in the listeners, but the stories of love, revenge, madness, betrayals, alliances, and failures are as old as history. In its mythic mode, history as *itihasa* circles back so that the novel ends with "We shall start all over again" (617).

Hanuman, the great "dialectician," teaches Sanjay such canny storytelling and advises him:

> Straightforwardness is the curse of your age, Sanjay. Be wily, be twisty, be elaborate. Forsake grim shortness and hustle. Let us luxuriate in your curlicues. Besides, you need a frame story for its peace, its quiet. You're too involved in the tale, your audience is harried by the world. No, a calm storyteller must tell the story to an audience of educated, discriminating listeners, in a setting of sylvan beauty and silence. Thus the story is perfect in itself, complete and whole. (20)

The relevance of myths to contemporary Indians lies in distancing narrative frames, usually marked by the presence of a self-conscious storyteller within the story. The attention to contingent transmission makes each of these stories transposable, and potentially opens up an endless space for related plots, finished or unfinished.[15] This antirealist self-conscious mode, and the "double vision" of seeing both the story told and the story of the storyteller, confuses the British printing-press owner, Markline, who censures this "backward" nonlinear narrative tradition: "Plots meander, veering from grief to burlesque in a minute. Unrelated narratives entwine and break into each other. . . . Beginnings are not really beginnings, middles are unendurably long and convoluted, nothing ever ends" (335). Of such circuitous narration, one reviewer exclaims in an otherwise laudatory piece: "As the tales turn and twist like mountain roads, the audience is never quite certain where they will end up. Keep your wits about you when you read 'Red Earth and Pouring Rain' unless you want to feel like that confused child, who having heard the entire *Ramayana* in one long session, asks his grandmother 'Who was Rama?'" (Hiatt 2002).

In its content, *Red Earth* cuts, splices, and grafts several great collective narrations such as *Panchatantra*, the *Kathasagarisarita* (the "sea of stories"), and the *Thousand and One Nights* with epics, novel subgenres (the magic realist, detective, and gothic), diaries, biographies, legends, folk tales, adventure fiction, and romance traditions. These are recycled into a modern *myth* about three empires: the Mughal, European, and North American. *Red Earth* foregrounds its classical lineage as a tale about displacement by evoking an age-old question in its title, which, Chandra suggests, is peculiarly relevant to modern migrants. The title is derived from a classical Tamil poem, Chempulappeynnar's *Kuntakai*, where the speaker yearns for relocation in this world: "What could my mother be to yours? What kin is my father to you anyway?" The story of the Indian people in *Red Earth* is begun in *medias res* and in strange circumstances, but the "origin" remains shrouded in mysterious and mystical forces. The transformed Irishman Jahaj Jung is initiated into the "mythos" of India by Guha, who leaves him in a ring of fire (alluding to Christ's revelations) until Jahaj Jung properly hallucinates India. It is his transformation into a mythic figure that makes it possible for Jahaj Jung to "beget" Sanjay and Sikander and Chota Sikander, who represent the new emerging Indian civilization born in those transitional years, 1750–1858. For Chandra, such Indian myths become the vernacular register for the modern Indian novel in English.

In Rushdie and Chandra it is the audience who finally defines their popular tellings of the Indian story. There is the single unforgettable listener in *Midnight's Children*, the bodacious Padma, and in *The Moor's Last Sigh*, both the artists are the tellers, listeners, and subjects of each other's tales: Aurora's paintings of the (male) national subject, the Moor, are sought by her son who, in turn, obsessively recounts mother-son masala in his own tale of the lost motherland. In *Red Earth* the "now" sections of the novel recount the story of storytelling in the modern age, with the little girl listener, Saira, finally growing into a national audience. The first mass audience is a crowd of multilingual children who, of course, can all "understand" this familiar acculturating tale. Then the story becomes the subject of (adult) critical discussion when a fierce battle of interpretation occurs between the head of the literature department at Janakpur University and a biologist from Calcutta (the antagonists are a composite of the well-known literature department at Jadavpur University, Calcutta). This adult audience soon expands into a culture industry with a "bazaar of *thela-wallahs* selling fruits, ice cream, *kulfi*, *filmi* magazines, chaat, and kitchen appliances" (Chandra 1995, 313). Then there are translations and retellings, the mass manufacture of stories and the breaking of copyright laws (178). Television cameras and death threats that stem from "careless use of religious symbology" follow, as do reporters and photographers who make the right to story a national issue (354). And finally a tragedy occurs, when Saira is wounded in a bomb blast (Chandra's response to the Mumbai bomb blasts of 1993, following the Babri Masjid debacle). Chandra is obviously referencing the politicization of stories, wistfully noting the fall of multiple narrations, dreams, and memories to the hegemony of oneness: " There was this one new thing," he says, "this was simply that there should be only one idea, one voice, one thing, one, one, one." (518). At the close of the novel, the modern-day protagonist/storyteller, Abhay, longs for the regenerative power of myth—the "great music of that primeval sound"—that might revive Saira, the new generation, from her wounded state (520). By the time we are comfortably into the novel, the short realistic sections set in modern times begin to jar against the easeful circularity of the mythic narration, a disjuncture that highlights epistemological différance.

Such a battle recurs on a smaller palette in Roy's *God of Small Things*, staged as a conflict over cultural forms and their contemporary relevance in the Kathakali performance episode. The great mythic stories of the Kathakali tradition are well known in the South Indian town of Ayemenem. Yet that tradition is commodified into a tourist attraction, "Regional Flavour." Six-hour-long performances are now twenty-minute cameos sold as authentic "folk tradition" by the Marxist cultural arbiters of Kerela. Roy is bitingly critical of such reification, insisting on the cathartic value of long folk performances for local audiences. (We see a similar gesture in Amitav Ghosh's treatment of dance as a practice of healing trauma in *Dancing in Cambodia, At Large in Burma*). Roy chooses to make her argument through the Kathakali troupe's performance of the Karna-

Kunti scene that Rahel and Estha attend. A profound moment of revelation in the *Mahabharata*, in this episode, Kunti, the mother of the five heroes, admits to Karna, her first-born illegitimate son, that she had disowned him because he was her love child. Kunti therefore admits to the breaking of love laws, those social taboos forsaken by the children's beloved mother, Ammu, in her love for the "untouchable" Velutha; and Kunti, like Ammu, sees "Big Things" as tragically separating and dividing those mundane but concrete unions of mother and son, brother and sister, lover and beloved. Hence, for the twins, the Kathakali dance is a cathartic retelling of this elemental tragedy.[16] This earlier mythic reference finds fuller treatment at the end of the novel, when Roy ends her realistic narration on a mythic register. The tragedy of the Ammu-Velutha story ends with a lyrical moment of lovemaking on the banks of the river reminiscent of the erotic spiritualism of *bhakti* vernacular traditions, where spiritual bliss exists in the sublime union of the love-god Krishna and his beloved, Radha. When the realist work of memory and narration fails, the grafting of vernacular lyricism and mythic tradition heals the wounds of remembering.[17]

Remaining true to its own analogy of grafting, each kind of narration in Ghosh's *Calcutta Chromosome* requires the interpersing of other forms of "evidence." For instance, Murugan realizes that the Bengali writer Phulboni's ghostly Lakhaan stories contain an embedded "message" about the calcutta chromosome mystery. And Murugan wonders if Phulboni (his name an obvious reference to a reputed Bengali writer's pseudonym, Bonophul) wrote the story first and then later "heard" its folk version, or vice versa. Ghosh suggests that this confusion of folk versions, literary manifestations, and hearsay as "scientific" evidence really indicates the necessity of an expansive cultural archive, particularly one of the consolidating of oral knowledge (gossip, legend, story) threatened by erasure. The media trail in *The Calcutta Chromosome* finally ends in performance, when written and oral traces lead the investigator to hidden rituals: of illicit healing, unsavory séances, and sexual fusion between bodies. In such analyses of the relations between media, the cosmopolitical writers firmly situate literary production as public culture, prey to all the vicissitudes of consumption practices as are dance, theater, television, radio, and cinema.

But it is finally vernacular literature that provides Ghosh with a curative graft. Throughout the novel, Ghosh repeatedly dramatizes the transformative capacities of the literary as many of the characters actively translate found evidence into stories. For example, Murugan excavates a female figurine from a hole in the wall of P. G. Hospital, Calcutta. But he has no understanding of this geophysical embodiment of an occult goddess (Mangala) until Urmila *translates* the figurine into a story—an allegorical tale about a woman bather who is "saved" by this hard stone as she is about to drown in a pond. The power of a stone is reimagined—transformed—through Urmila's story. More specifically, it is Phulboni's fierce struggles over language and form that present a writerly *mise-en-abyme* for Amitav Ghosh's literary practice. As the literary visionary in the tale, Phulboni is the one most tuned to the stealth of the silent underground, and his language eddies around its possibilities. He communicates this to his fictionalized literary audience early in the novel, too early for us to take him seriously:

> The silence of the city . . . has sustained me through all my years of writing: kept me alive in the hope that it would claim me too before my ink ran dry. For more years than I can count I have wandered the darkness of these streets, searching for the unseen presence that reigns over this silence, striving to be taken in, begging to be taken across before my time runs out. The time of crossing is at hand, I know, and that is why I am here now, standing in front of you: to beg—to appeal to the mistress of this silence, that most secret of deities, to give me what she has so long denied: to herself to me. (1996, 27)

In Bengali, "the time of crossing" refers to death ("when borne across"), and Phulboni's search finally ends (as he disappears) in Mangala's promise of corporeal immortality. Phulboni's capable expressivity in the novel convinces us that Mangala's steamy underground cannot be spoken of in denotative descriptive language—its only tongue are those figures of excess that are the purview of the literary imagination.

The argument advances through Murugan's progression from a Life Watch employee, to detective, to postcolonial archivist. As the novel proceeds we are faced with a crisis in narration. The narratives of several scientists, administrators, linguists, missionaries, doctors, and Spiritualists are constantly displaced, replaced, cut, and pasted. In fact *all* major acts of detection in the novel involve deconstructing existing and discordant accounts: journal entries, diaries, logs of scientific research, oral memories, and letters from the colonial era. The main pursuers of truth in *The Calcutta Chromosome* figure out the puzzle of the counterscientific by filling in gaps, finishing log entries, or writing in indecipherable scribbles. Soon our main fact finder Murugan's epistemological frustrations give way to an oppositional subjectivity. He rejects the institutional parameters of discovery, and he begins to supplement the fissures of the colonial story with fragments of other unconventional knowledges. For new evidence he draws on unfinished fragments of records from other men who came in contact with Ross and his strange crew, Elijah Farley and D. D. Cunningham, both of whom traffic in ghosts. Finally Murugan has to turn to ghost stories published in an obscure and out-of-print vernacular magazine to understand what ghostly presences are doing in the narrative of discovery.

There are three sightings of Lakhaan's ghost in the novel's denouement.[18] In Phulboni's oeuvre, the Lakhaan stories circle around different mutations of the same character, Lakhaan, a formation that Urmila reads as a "kind of allegory" (93). Urmila, Murugan's love interest and fellow investigator, is in pursuit of the story of Phulboni's spiraling personal decline and his delirious wanderings. These she relates to the "mystery" of the Lakhaan stories. Urmila's quest, that of a journalist/literary critic, allegorizes Ghosh's "recovery" (and embedding) of vernacular antecedents to his novel in English. In its ability to figuratively gesture toward another story that remains silent in the text, literary practice edges closer to the truth of counterscience than does scientific explanation. By the end of the novel, the vernacular literary tale is the only authoritative means through which we can decode the muddled and untruthful records of scientific discovery.

In terms of postcolonial literary practice, vernacular ghost fiction presents a certain "native" version of the colonial presence, a register of its violence upon the colonized world. Scattered encryptions of vernacular ghost stories in *The Calcutta Chromosome* exert an uncanny pressure on any reader familiar with vernacular literatures. Even on my first read, I was struck by the three Lakhaan ghost stories embedded in the novel. They seemed to be a part of a corpus of writing best described by Parama Roy as the Indian "bureaucratic gothic," a genre that figurally records the trauma of modernity in the postcolonial liberal state.[19] In the case of Bengali literature, I could identify antecedents to this genre that date back to literature written under colonial rule, albeit inexpertly. It would be virtually impossible to catalog that long record of dead Englishmen (Elijah Farley, in *The Calcutta Chromosome*), of abandoned *dak* bungalows (like the one that Ross inhabits in Secunderbad), and of deserted railway stations (the remote Renupur station that is Lakhaan's birthplace). So I will simply mention two inspirational sources cited by the author himself: the Bengali litterateur Tagore's "Kshudhito Pashaan" and the Oriya writer Phaniswar Nath Renu's "Smells of a Primeval Night" (Tagore [1885] 1995, 1–15; Renu [1967] 1986).

I would further explain this personal haunting by a quick look at the subject of these two stories (metonymically, the subject of the colonial and postcolonial bureaucratic gothic). The Lakhaan story in *The Calcutta Chromosome* is a tale of vengeance, in which the boy's ghost takes revenge on the stationmaster who attempts to kill him. The boy is a poor rural migrant violently abused by the agent of empire, the stationmaster, who treats him as an outcast drifter of suspect parentage. Living in a railway station, he is caught in the transition between the village and the modern city. He becomes the recursive ghost of the postcolonial state—the specters from the hinterland that inhabit Mahasweta Devi's ghost fiction—who reminds the liberal urban postcolonial bureaucrat of an ethical failure. The rural or tribal other is that figure of excess that "free" India cannot account for and for whom there are no rights and no redress.[20]

Yet in the many reviews of the book that are in circulation, only one mentions the Tagore and Renu influences, despite these writers' cultural eminence. Most reviews cite contemporary Western sources as inspiration for *The Calcutta Chromosome*—for example, John Clute (1997) indicates Robert Irwin's *The Arabian Nightmare* (1983) as a guiding force. Katherine Hansen (1998), a scholar who has translated Renu into English, is the single exception, identifying Renu as a source in her review.

Numerous references to these tales find their way into *The Calcutta Chromosome,* creating a literary puzzle of sorts. The haunted station is explicitly named *Renu*pur, and we are told it lies somewhere between Barich and Darbhanga, Barich being the setting for the Tagore story. "Kshudhito Pashaan" commences with a ghost story told by a tax collector in the employ of the Nizam to his fellow travelers on a train; in *The Calcutta Chromosome*, Phulboni hears the story of Lakhaan's ghost also on a train—the classic Indian setting for storytelling—with the railways symbolizing the reach of the state/empire. The Tagore story is suffused with the changing and exchanging of clothes, much like the obsessive changing of bodies in *The Calcutta Chromosome*. Phulboni works for a British company when he encounters the boy ghost, and thus qualifies as a protagonist for the bureaucratic gothic; further, Phulboni chooses his pseudonym from the wild Phulboni region in the eastern state of Orissa, the place of Santhals who are Karma's (Renu's servant boy) people. One could go on. But my point here is this: In Ghosh's hands, this vernacular ghost genre becomes the genetic blueprint for the novel in English. The Lakhaan ghost fragments to which all trails return are the mutations of original vernacular literary fare, perhaps Ghosh's elaborate allegory for the primal scene of postcolonial writing in English.

New Trails for the Postcolonial Critic

Such a grafting of local and vernacular traditions onto a literary tradition that characteristically, and often problematically, references only its Anglo antecedents is a polemical refiguring for postcolonial literary practice. In all these cosmopolitical novels we have a vernacular catalog that requires sustained digging on the part of the critic. Now any postcolonial criticism on the novel in English must recuperate a vernacular archive to make good its critical promise. Derrida concludes his rumination on ghosts with the injunction not only to speak of and to ghosts, but also to let them speak to us:

> If he loves justice at least, the 'scholar' of the future, the intellectual of tomorrow, should learn it and from the ghost. He should learn to live by learning

not how to make conversation with the ghost but to talk with him, with her, how to let them speak or how to give them back speech, even if it is in one-self: they are always *there*, even if they do not exist, even if they are no longer, even if they are not yet. They give us time to rethink "there" as soon as we open our mouths, even at a colloquium and specially when one speaks there in a foreign tongue. (1994, 176)

My engagement with *The Calcutta Chromosome*, for one, has finally led me to a substantial venture of consolidating a vernacular catalog of ghost fiction featuring the colonial and modern bureaucrat. Following the Derridean injunction to speak to, of, and especially with ghosts, as cultural translator I am confronted with an archival venture of daunting proportions in the absence of an existing formal collection of Bengali ghost fiction (the well known and the obscure).

And very much in the spirit of *The Calcutta Chromosome*, it is a project that stems from a personal haunting. For there is spectral logic to the fact that I grew up around the corner from the haunted house on Robinson Street where the climactic events in *The Calcutta Chromosome* take place. My young world was full of stories of incommunicable presences much like those that Phulboni describes; and abandoned houses *always* involved dead doctors, an Englishman, some forbidden folk ritual and, inevitably, retributive ghosts. It is no wonder that this novel puts my present out of joint in the echo of tales read and heard elsewhere; a mutation, a secret fascination that leads to not just this scholarly trail, but a remembered street, a house, a story.

Epilogue

Emphasizing the historical and political significance of the migrant perspective as it unravels globalism's localisms, *When Borne Across* invites readers to perform habitual textual migrations across cultures, media, and disciplines. While underscoring this (writerly and readerly) mobility as a cultural intervention into globalism, I have further etched critical borders that distinguish a group of South Asian cosmopolitical writers from the general category of "Indian writers in English." The cosmopolitical writers, I have argued, are commercial successes who quite reflexively manipulate the terms of their own popular circulation through linguistic praxes and the staging of epistemological différance. Such aesthetic choices speak to the political and ethical agendas that they share here with historians, filmmakers, philosophers, ethnographers, and activists, among others, who aim at producing a minoritarian modernity. So in the final analysis, *When Borne Across* investigates the political potentials of the literary in our contemporary global cultural arena and in the face of the deepening crises of late capitalism.

Both Godhra and September 11—historical events that outstrip this project, jolting its temporality out of joint—are just such crises, engendered by military chauvinism, political greed, and economic cannibalism. Their aftershocks often constrain the widening gyre of cosmopolitical activity, as we have recently witnessed in the furor over a cosmopolitical writer of substantial stature—Rohinton Mistry. Mistry became the subject of controversy most recently when he canceled his U.S. book tour in the fall of 2002 on the grounds of racial profiling by officials at U.S. airports. We have encountered Mistry as an interviewee earlier in the NPR golden jubilee show, and now I close with the present celebration of him as a South Asian writer because the moment exemplifies much of my argument on the circulation and impact of cosmopolitical writing today. As a cosmopolitical writer with formidable global currency, Mistry is indeed one of the towering absences in the book. Born in Bombay but emigrating to Canada in 1975, Mistry, too, fits the profile of the internationally glamorous IWE. But he is also an active participant in South Asian cosmopolitics, sharing many of the political and ethical commitments of the writers examined here. For instance, his early novel *Such a Long Journey* (1991) is set in post-1971 Bombay after the IndoPak war that saw the emergence of Bangladesh, a historical event that Amitav Ghosh represents from a regional perspective in *The Shadow Lines* (1984). Like many of *our* cosmopolitical writers, Mistry regards the Emergency as a "watershed in Indian history"—an enactment of state violence on its heterogeneous populations. Rushdie's surreal Widow in *Midnight's Children*, Indira Gandhi, and particularly her son's infamous population-control campaign come under fire in Mistry's 1991 novel. "We have to leave accounting to one side, sacrifice our fondness for numbers, and look to the human cost," remarked Mistry, once more underscoring the urgency of an imaginative register where a different accounting can take place.[1] *Such a Long Journey* catapulted Mistry to fame, winning the Governor-General's Award and the Commonwealth Writers Prize for Best Book, among others, and Mistry made the Booker shortlist that year. Soon the book was translated into several languages and into visual media (the film *Such a Long Journey,* 2000). Mistry returned to his history-from-below in 1995 with his acclaimed *A Fine Balance,* which also ran the gamut of literary prizes: Canada's Giller Prize, the Commonwealth Writers Prize, and the 1996 Booker shortlist (this time as a finalist). And in *Family Matters,* which appeared in 2002, Mistry continues his cosmopolitical critique of micronationalist chauvinism in attacking the Shiv Sena stranglehold on Mumbai.

The point of this quick and dirty portrait (that does little justice to Mistry's writing) is to establish his growing "currency," marking the stages of that growth through a series of national and international sanctions. More importantly, Mistry's currency in *literary* circles took an abrupt turn when *A Fine Balance* was chosen by Oprah Winfrey's Book Club in December 2001, the first Canadian book read in that public arena. The 750-odd-page book was soon in reprint, with 750,000 new paperbacks in circulation. Unfazed by this popular glamour, Mistry noted somewhat dryly: "I have no qualms about that [the Oprah logo] because I'm well-acquainted with logos, having had so many on my books in the past—the Governor-General's, the Giller Prize, the Booker Prize short-list" (Jain 2001). But it was Oprah herself who unwittingly stressed the act of being borne across in literature: "After September 11, I started taking more time for myself. I read it [*A Fine Balance*] and thought, This will do, in some ways, what September 11 has done. Take us out of our own little shell. Expose us to a whole other world out there going on beyond our backyards'" (see *www.oprah.com*).

In a loosening of economic borders, the translation of the book *via* the *Oprah Winfrey Show* increased and dispersed its circulation. Sound bites from the show mediated the value of the text, its salience for our times. Most of the participants of the book club assumed the job of transcribing the unfamiliar content of the book, speaking to the relevance of *A Fine Balance* to their lives: a second-generation diasporic Indian waxed nostalgic about her grandfather's village; one of the men aligned characters in the book with "real characters" in his college experience as a member of the Social Service League; and one of the women even remarked how the book convinced her of the correctness of Dr. Phil's advice that there are no accidents in life. Against this leveling effect—guided by questions like "Who is the true villain?"—Mistry struggled to underline history, context, contingency.[2]

Yet the effects of September 11 truncated the popular circulation of *Family Matters* when Mistry canceled his U.S. book tour, much to the disappointment of the booksellers in the United States who had invited him to promote his new book.[3] Following on the heels of an uproar that forced the United States to exempt Canadians from a controversial border policy that Ottowa decried as racist (anyone born in Iran, Iraq, Libya, Syria, Sudan, Saudi Arabia, Pakistan, or Yemen was subject to fingerprinting and photographs), one suspects Mistry's withdrawal from circulation was a judicious use of his high profile in the international media. Claiming no brownie points for his move, Mistry offered little in the way of comment, leaving it to Knopf's director of publicity, Paul Bogards, to clarify in a guarded manner Mistry's reasons for his withdrawal: "This is the way of the world now, and, after a time, Rohinton Mistry became uncomfortable" ("Rohinton Mistry Cancels" 2002). In the sudden tightening of nation-state borders, Mistry's participation in a postnational public sphere was now severely crippled. Yet Mistry's withdrawal from the book tour ethically intervened into the spiraling racism of U.S. "homeland security" policies that perpetrated violence toward specific populations in the name of protection. In a November 9, 2002, article in the Canadian English-language daily the *Globe and Mail*, Heather Mallick hyperbolically valorized Mistry's stance on racial profiling: "He gave up his U.S. book tour halfway because his treatment at airports was consistently racist, rude, and ultimately unbearable. And you know what that makes him. It makes him a modern Rosa Parks. A quiet 'No' can work wonders. I don't mean on the American airport officials who take him aside for scrutiny, questions, luggage dissection and shoe examination so that passengers stare in fear and loathing. And I don't mean on an American government that announces it will zero in on Canadian citizens born in certain countries. Mr. Mistry isn't even from those countries and isn't even Muslim. He just isn't white."

Like Arundhati Roy, Mistry used his international celebrity—the very success of South Asian writing—to intervene on behalf of minorities with little access to global media. Such intervention is immediately obvious in its progressive politics. More difficult to excavate are the political imperatives at work in the cosmopolitical writers' fiction, a task I have undertaken in my elaboration of a *literary* cosmopolitics. In many of the novels I have explored, the ethical censure is unmistakable, the political diagnosis unerring.

Thus the cosmopolitical imagination offers critical resources for inhabiting these times of accelerating and deepening global crises. To highlight the significance of this imagination, I close with two texts whose political diagnoses appear—after September 11, after Godhra—as almost prophetic. In early 2002, I attended a performance of Tony Kushner's exegetical *Homebody Kabul* at the Berkeley Repertory, after the play's release in December 2000. As a fan after *Angels in America* (1993) of Kushner's leaps of imagination and faith, Kushner's new play seemed at once extraordinarily prescient and virtually outdated in 2002. Prescient, because Kushner's accentuation of the geopolitical significance of Kabul—at once the locus of self-aggrandizing imaginative forays (or escapes) and a weary bombed-out city betrayed by everyone and policed by the vicious Taliban honchos—foreshadowed the military fallout from September 11. Yet Kushner's deliberately hyperbolic registers seemed to fade into a chilling realism against the magnitude of events more incomprehensible than magic, more surreal than their most embellished representation.

For a playwright whose strengths lie in the expressive representational mode, in precisely accentuating the fantastical aspects of historical and present events, the Kabul-turned-real on stage was an unexpected disappointment. The descriptive functions of this "realism" simply reinforced the emergent recognition after September 11 that Kabul was truly that "other" alien world bereft of Western civil values. These "truths" of Kabul, in other words, outstripped Kushner's trenchant critique of the Western imaginative othering (through his main character, an Englishwoman who fantasizes becoming a "homebody" in Kabul), an orientalism that Kushner suggests is complicit with the Cold War and post–Cold War military and economic ravaging of Kabul.

Such an experience of prescience was repeated while I watched a South Asian cosmopolitical text from a documentary filmmaker, Anant Patwardhan, whose decade-long critique of Hindu fundamentalism and nationalism (*Ram Ka Nam*, 1992; *Pitri, Putra, Dharmayuddh*, 1995; and *A Narmada Diary*, 1995) shares political ground with our South Asian cosmopolitical writers. Just as news of Godhra filtered in, Anant Patwardhan's latest film, *Jang Aur Aman*

(2001), hit international screens, while still blocked at that juncture by the Indian Censor Board (which proposed twenty-one cuts that Patwardhan refused to make). Filmed over three years in Pakistan, India, Japan, and the United States, the film is an act of peace activism that attacks global militarism in its many manifestations: the Indian and Pakistani nuclear texts that have wreaked havoc on communities at the test sites and on the environment; the U.S. bombing of Hiroshima and Nagasaki, still the only aggressive use of a nuclear arsenal; and the Twin Towers tragedy of September 11. With a family history of participation in the Gandhian nonviolence movement, Patwardhan argues that there are no winners in this global nuclear war. "The US has become a role model to Third World elites and, as we enter the twenty-first century war has become perennial, enemies are re-invented, economies are inextricably tied to the production and sale of weapons," says Patwardhan, underlining the links he makes in his narrative. "And in the moral wastelands of the world, memories of Gandhi now seem like a mirage, created by our thirst for peace and our very distance from it" ("Battle Cry" 2000). The "mirage of Gandhi," in a text framed by Gandhi's murder in 1948, is indeed a poignant invocation after Godhra, when violence exploded in Gandhi's home state with the Modi administration colluding in attacks on Muslims. In establishing the links between global acts of violence, *Jang Aur Aman* was precisely a plea for global mutuality of the sort we have seen in cosmopolitical writing. Its political diagnostics were right on target and rendered more acute every day. Yet its phrasing of an Indian apocalypse *to come* was overtaken by new atrocities at Godhra.

While finishing this manuscript, whose first full draft I completed in 2000, I find in my critical narration the same strange temporality at work in the Kushner and Patwardhan texts. My own obsessive returns to dismembered bodies and the cuts of history were initially a kind of critical mourning work for 6 December 1992. But every time I began to write, new cataclysms overtook the book's contemporaneity, its attempt to foreground imaginative resources for a human accounting where political analyses falter. Failing to keep contemporaneous time, I could finally close when I let new specters (now with the invasion/occupation of Iraq funded in part by the taxes I pay) gather around the book, demanding redress.

Notes

Prologue

1. As Himachal Som, the veteran of ICCR, characterized it (D. Singh 2002).
2. Carnage on trains running between India and Pakistan in the Northwest is one of the most traumatic memories of the Partition, the bloody twin of Indian and Pakistani independence of 1947.
3. Himachal Som, speaking of his intentions (D. Singh 2002). The infamous remark appeared first in Rushdie's introductory essay on Indian writers in English, in the double issue commemorating India's fifty years of independence from the British (Rushdie 1997a).
4. "Home in the World" is also a collection brought out by Himachal Som that contains excerpts from Indian literature with their translations on the facing page. The first of its kind, the anthology offers the first Hindi translation of Arundhati Roy's *God of Small Things*. The book appeared the day before the festival commenced.
5. The phrase is from the *New Yorker* special issue, 23 and 30 June 1997, characterizing an earlier meeting of Indian writers in English for a group photo shoot in London.
6. The Sangh Parivar refers to the Hindu Right coalition comprised of a social movement, the RSS (the Rashtriya Swayamsevak Sangh), with the VHP (Vishwa Hindu Parishad) as its churchlike global network and the BJP (Bharatiya Janata Party) as its political party.
7. Pheng Cheah (1999) makes this point about vitalist ontology in his perusal of Derrida's spectrality. His formulation is of considerable importance to my deployment of Derridean spectrality, so I will return to it more substantially in that later discussion (chapter 5).

One   Sighting Circulation: A Renaissance at the Golden Jubilee

1. I make these distinctions within a global arena heuristically, as "local," "national," and "transnational" mark the specific cultures of circulation where the different values accrue to the renaissance.

2. When I treat the discourses of the golden jubilee, I retain the moniker "Indian writing in English," largely because at this juncture (and in these commentaries drawn from the Indian public sphere) "India" is the object of historical scrutiny

3. Owen Smith's *The Elephantine Prophecy*, the painting that graces the cover of the *New Yorker* for 23 and 30 June 1997, sutures the colonial past to its postcolonial legacy by coding (and incorporating) E. M. Forster's *Passage to India* and Salman Rushdie's *Midnight's Children* in the same visual space (see figure 3).

4. This entire issue is devoted to all things Indian known to the watching "world"— curry, cricket, movies (women's TV serials are featured in the media segment)— but predominantly dedicated to the renaissance writers as the premier national representatives.

5. See, for instance, Rosemary Marangoly George's discussion of Bhabha's "Dissemi-Nation," an essay in which Bhabha situates the migrant at the "margins" of the modern nation. The migrant thereby becomes a corrective to the essentialist conceptions of imagined communities (1996, 186). For these functional reasons, I would argue that in Bhabha's formulation the migrant rather quickly becomes a celebratory trope, and the material differences between migrant gatherings are substantively elided.

6. The impulse to reterritorialize on the part of this elite diaspora finds formulation in recent accounts of cultural citizenship. As one of the theorists preoccupied by border drawing in transcolonial terrain, Aihwa Ong draws our attention to acts of reterritorialization on the part of elite transnationals whose very existence paradoxically depends on the smooth functioning of global flows. Cultural practices such as John Woo movies, in Ong's view, structure cultural normativity for these mobile populations. Ong further criticizes theories of globalization that emphasize the increasing economic, political, and cultural flows over national borders, without adequate attention to the systems of governmentality that constrict—discipline, limit, channelize, and interrogate—these flows. In fact Ong takes issue with Appadurai's inattention to current cultural reentrenchments, and I take up these reservations in my emphasis on localisms (Ong 1999, 10).

7. For a fuller discussion of the differences between Guha and Spivak, see Young 2001, 354–355.

8. The "in-human" is Chakrabarty's term for the radical otherness with the self, and the fear it generates in instances of communal violence: What cannot be humanly acknowledged in the self is aggressively directed toward a politicized other (2002).

9. Given the velocity and dispersion of information flows, electronic media have commanded the lion's share of attention. In his discussion of local entries into public modernity Appadurai (1995) focuses on television, movies, billboards, architecture, and only sometimes print media (newspapers and magazines). My concern is with print media with relatively small circulation—a literary practice; but as my analyses of global "literary" circulation will demonstrate throughout the book, time is ripe for considering those translations *between* media that recompose literary value.

10. Globalization has been a hot issue variously theorized in *Public Culture* throughout the late eighties and the nineties. *Critical Inquiry* has also featured some seminal essays on the topic, the most significant of which for our purposes is Miyoshi 1993. The spring 1992 issue of the same journal, edited by Homi Bhabha and titled "Front Lines/Borderposts," devoted itself to migration. Of course, Fredric Jame-

son's early work on postmodernism (1991) prepared the ground for theorizing globalization, a project followed up in midnineties: compilations such as Wilson and Dissanayake 1996 or Shapiro and Alker 1996. Two recent anthologies of note that focus more on cultural globalization are Jameson and Miyoshi 1998 and Lowe and Lloyd 1997.

11. Yúdice (1996, 1992) examines how transnationalism affects national public spheres: As transnational relationships and networks—economic, cultural, communicational, technological, political—emerge in deterritorialized intersecting public spheres, national affiliations become secondary to dominant financial, technological, and military interests.

12. Better known for his 1995 *Hybrid Cultures*, in his latest book, *Consumers and Citizens*, Nestor García Canclini argues that the consumer options presented in global media offer new modes of staging cultural citizenship in Latin American contexts.

13. During (2000) dates critical postcolonialism as an epistemological space-clearing gesture that lasted from 1985 to 1994. It remained, in his opinion, a gesture, for it failed to institute non-Eurocentric modes of knowledge. During represents a thread of thought in postcolonial studies of the nineties that worries over the bad marriage of the postmodern and the postcolonial (see Spivak 1993a; Appiah 1991; Dirlik 1994; Mishra and Hodge 1991; Shohat 1992). I have engaged in this conversation elsewhere (see B. Ghosh 1998).

14. For instance, commentators in "Outsourcing India" in the February 2001 *Economist* foretold a massive change in India's GNP because of these increased transnational flows, with India providing a white-collar "hinterland" and workforce for U.S. businesses.

15. Note Rushdie's defense of Indian literatures in "'Commonwealth Literature' Does Not Exist": "It is worth saying that major work is being done in India in many languages other than English; yet . . . the Indo-Anglians seize all the limelight" (1991a, 69). In fact, in this earlier piece, Rushdie acknowledges the logical problems of positioning English in opposition to the vernaculars for three reasons: He points to English as a foreign tongue having resonance only for the older generation of Indo-Anglians, while the children of independent India simply use it as "an Indian language" (64); to the friction over languages in India having more to do with the debate over Hindi versus other Indian languages than with a conflict over English; and to Mulk Raj Anand and others writing from India probably having more in common with vernacular writers than with a diasporic litterateur like himself. In light of these assertions, the *New Yorker* essay (Rushdie 1997a) is quite a volte-face, perhaps the result of Rushdie's self-professed vulnerability to critics—especially postcolonial critics who had taken him to task for becoming the signifier of free speech after the *Satanic Verses* controversy. Rushdie's awareness of his critics finds voice in the latter piece: "There is a whiff of political correctness about them: the ironic proposition that India's best writing since independence may have been done in the language of the imperialists is simply too much for some folks to bear. It ought not to be true, and so must not be permitted" (54). Here Rushdie cleverly clears his critical ground, for to be up in arms about Indian vernacular literatures and their merit can now easily be shrugged off as simply chauvinistic (see Rushdie 1991, 61–70).

16. In contrast to Rushdie's perspective, V. S. Naipaul envisions an essentially Hindu India in the same issue of *India Today* in which the earlier-cited Rushdie piece

appeared: In "A Million Mutinies" (1997), Naipaul rationalizes Hindu majoritarian politics as a backlash against the Muslim conquest of India.

17. The reference to the Indiana Jones neocolonial adventure is not facetious but engendered by a personal account from a friend. Upon arriving as a foreign student on the U.S. east coast in 1984, he was asked with genuine curiosity by a delighted roommate whether his family ate monkey brains.

18. For a fuller analysis of the cannibalization of the postcolonial by the postmodern will to cultural sampling, see B. Ghosh 1998.

19. Arif Dirlik locates surplus value in the Anglo-American academy, and his critique of postcolonial studies explicitly attacks Spivak's own star status in that field. Dirlik suggests that the term "postcolonial" achieves epistemological function in the "first-world academy" and has less significance for the worlds postcolonialists' attempt to describe. He delves into the postmodernity of critical discourse itself, locating the emergence of the category "postcolonial" as a "first-world" response to the conceptual needs generated by the rapid transformations of a world capitalist order. In the changing relationships within the world market, "third-world" intellectuals "arrived" in the first-world academy and serviced that first world through their various forms of crisis management. He reminds us that the category that describes and evaluates global relations in the latter half of the twentieth century is always imbricated in those relations—a perception similar to Brennan's description of new cosmopolitans caught in the structural imbalances of the globalized world (see Dirlik 1994).

20. Spivak (1993a) argues that Marx's notion of value, a "content-less" thing without form before it is coded into an "economic system of equivalences and entailed social relations" (exchange value), best elucidates the currency of highly vaunted postcolonial objects today. The postcolony is named and coded in North-based "equivalencies of knowledge" and placed in hierarchical colonial-modern epistemologies where it commands high exchange value. Social relations that produce this material act of writing are disconnected from its circulation (205–206).

21. Bahri furnishes this example from *Forbes* magazine's triumphant article "Now We Are Our Own Masters," 23 March 1994. Postcolonial discourse—such as Bahri's critique alluded to in the text—intervenes in the bartering of simulacra by insisting on historical- and geographical-specific (re)locations of cultural artifacts (1996, 137).

22. See Leela Fernandes's (1999) discussion of the *Bandit Queen* controversy, where she elaborates on national and transcolonial dissonances. She argues that discordant national responses to perceived global flows occur more frequently in the transnational age because of the speed and mobility of cultural practices, and the "temporal simultaneity" of their interpretations (127). Fernandes notes that, although global electronic circuits provide nonlocalized spaces for information to travel, critics must embed the decodings of sound-image bites within specific discursive regimes of power.

23. Swapan Dasgupta (1997b) complicates this domain of the popular by pointing to *Border*, a 1997 film about terrorism in Kashmir, which was a national hit but also representative of an emerging popular critical cinema that repudiates its mass cultural other—the Bombay Hindi melodramas (13).

24. One representative view is Geeta Kapur's articulation of the "counter-value" of the national-modern in postcolonial contexts. Kapur maintains that the postcolonial mod-

ern, in both its national and (leftist) international impulses, has always been of "paradoxical value" to the Western project of modernity with its imperialist agenda; and while the modernist nationalist projects (with their inception under colonial rule in the nineteenth ~entury) have fallen into disrepute, the left avant-garde potential of modern teleologies has not been exhausted in the Indian context. What is important here is the recognition that while modernist political impulses and global alliances have met with progressive political censure in the North—under the aegis of late capital, nations appear as "defunct sites of social antagonism" (Jameson 1998, 59)—they may be still incomplete in the modernities of the postcolonies and, Kapur hopes, headed in a different direction (Kapur 1998; for the first version of this essay, a more polemic piece, see Kapur 1993).

25. In Chatterjee's view, civil-social institutions, those networks of modern associational life such as the print media that create "citizens" with loyalties to the legal-bureaucratic state, remained partial and unformed in postcolonial societies (1998b, 61). How then to conceptualize this "rest of society" within the nation-state? Chatterjee suggests we employ the concept of a political society, a domain of democratic institutions and activities (mass mobilizations; parties based on ethnic, class, or caste politics; women's groups) through which the population beyond the reach of postcolonial civil societies mediates its relations to the state. Chatterjee's political society models a coalitional political praxis that articulates different culturally mobilized communities with each other (1998a).

26. See also Meenakshi Mukherjee's introduction (Mukherjee 1997), and Viney Kirpel's characterization of "post-Rushdie" Indian fiction as "the postmodern Indian novel" or the "New Indian Novel" in his introduction (Kirpel 1997).

27. Afzal-Khan (1993) represents a certain strand of literary criticism on the Indian novel in English that is invested in charting literary genealogies. See, for example, one of the earliest full-length books on this tradition of writing, Meenakshi Mukherjee's *The Twice-born Fiction* (1971), now followed by Mukherjee's *Perishable Empire* (2000).

28. Leela Gandhi (1998) illustrates the "win-win" situation of the elite postcolonial critic/writer using Edward Said as an example, given Said's institutional status in the U.S. academy: Said is a "subaltern" in majority cultures, but marked by privilege in the very worlds he writes about.

29. A recent collection on a single text—*Midnight's Children*—edited by veteran critic Meenakshi Mukherjee (1997) provides a model for the kinds of questions I ask about cosmopolitical writing. These essays on Rushdie's seminal novel explore its relation to popular culture, history writing, language politics, and other media, thereby placing the novel within a shared realm of cultural practices rather than strictly within its vertical literary lineage.

30. Dingwaney and Maier 1994 is an early volume on the problems of cultural translation. Venuti 2000 is a more recent compilation of inquiries into translation, while the winter 2001 issue of *Public Culture*, "Translation on the Global Market," was also devoted to the problems of global circulation that have been the subject of my scrutiny of the renaissance sightings.

31. Two commentaries in this issue of *Public Culture* seem particularly significant for my work: Spivak's (2001) censure of a homogenizing "translatese" that discredits the rhetoricity of the original, and Brennan's (2001) attention to the ideological "conversion" entailed in acts of translation.

Two   Passages and Passports: Globalism, Language, Migration

1. The new writers' canny sense of audience is best described in Mukul Kesavan's quip, reported in "Area of Brightness" (1998) (a title that contests Naipaul's *An Area of Darkness*): "The problem is not only that of explaining India to foreigners. . . . Even if we don't want to make concessions for foreigners, refuse to put in a glossary of Indian words at the end, there is still the problem of explaining a part of India about which one is writing to other parts of India. If I use an expression like *seedha palla* saree without explaining, will people in all parts of India understand?" Kesavan's perception of national, local, and global registers reiterates my point in chapter 3 about different kinds of readerships. There I will argue that the renaissance writers precisely do not gloss their English vernaculars for political reasons that run counter to the market currency that worries Kesavan.

2. *The Intelligent Person's Guide to Liberalisation* (Bhaduri and Nayyar 1996) is an exegesis posed as a cautionary tale for ideologues on both sides of the political spectrum who are waging war over globalization: "We decided to write this book," insist the writers, "in part because the debate on economic liberalization in India sounds like a dialogue among the deaf" (xi). These writers counter the neoliberal view that globalization necessarily brings democracy and corrects entrenched political abuses within nations. See, for instance, Thomas L. Friedman's elaboration of the impact of global entrepreneurs (who want closer ties with the W.T.O., APEC, and the Asean) on Indonesia: "So what the pro-democracy pro-clean government forces are relying on is not a revolution from below, not a revolution from above, but a revolution from beyond" (1997).

3. See, for instance, Arundhati Roy's account of the call center at Gurgaon (2001, 83–84).

4. My own discomfort with Jameson's all-pervasive paranoia lies with his inability to theorize the hegemony of any mass cultural forms besides Hollywood. The dissemination of Bollywood films in India, the former republics of the Soviet Union, the Middle East, and Africa receives passing attention in Jameson's Eurocentric read of cultural imperialism, in his otherwise compelling critique of globalism (Jameson 1998, 60).

5. Sen takes her data from *Census of India*, the New Delhi office of the Registrar General of India (1995, 654).

6. One of the interesting facts Jeffrey brings to our attention—and this is of some relevance to my discussion of the Emergency in chapter 4—is the jump in newspaper circulation after Indira Gandhi's defeat in the 1977 elections. The passing of censorship in the Emergency years gave new stimulus to newspaper circulation, registering a 40 percent rise in dailies and a 34 percent rise in periodical circulation (2000, 38–39).

7. The Ramjanmabhumi movement refers to the Hindu mobilization around the Babri Masjid issue that culminated in the destruction of the sixteenth-century mosque on 6 December 1992. The Hindu Right argued that the Muslim "invader" Emperor Babar had built the mosque after demolishing a Hindu temple that supposedly marked the birthplace (*janmabhumi*) of Ram, the hero of the Hindu epic *Ramayana*, worshiped as a god across the northern Indian Hindi-speaking belt. *Janmabhumi* also connotes the land of one's birth, the territorial resonance deliberately harnessed in L. K. Advani's right-wing campaign for all Hindu pilgrims to head to Ayodhya—the

city that once housed the Babri Masjid. The 6 December 1992 event is commonly referred to simply as "Babri Masjid" or "Ayodhya," and sometimes "December 1992" (much like current allusions to "September 11").

8. Khacha Tölöyan, the editor of the U.S. journal *Diaspora*, eloquently characterizes this dynamic of the pedagogical and the performative of diasporic cultures in the following way: "*Diaspora* is concerned with the ways in which nations, real yet imagined communities, are fabulated, brought into being, made and unmade, in culture and politics, both on the land people call their own and in exile" (qtd. in Cohen 1997).

9. Such firm roots for migrant communities bespeak a part of a more general move by recent theorists of globalization to reconcretize locales in which transnational subjects interact. Sassen's (1998) critique of the discourses of globalization as they render invisible certain actors and networks, such as urban migrant female laborers, suggests that we restore notions of territory—bounded physical landscapes such as global cities where invisibilized populaces have presence, if not clout—to discussions of globalization that mostly conceptualize space as nation space.

10. An example of such a slide is to be found when Swapan Dasgupta (1997a) titles his review of Shashi Tharoor's *From Midnight to Millenium* "Imaginary Homelands." Dasgupta scornfully delegates Tharoor to an international elite signaled by Rushdie, exemplar of the deracinated transnational elite. (Tharoor is a part of the political elite, certainly, having a high-ranking job in the United Nations).

11. Hence, the writers display a hyperawareness of the currencies of critical discourse in framing acts of reading, and indeed the intellectual purchase of literatures. Certainly, it was the Rushdie affair that etched the significance of decoding deep into the psyche of postcolonial writers. In "Postcolonial Tour 93," Amitava Kumar articulates the gap between postcolonial-knowledge production by both writers and critics and its implied subjects and audiences. Referencing conversations on the Rushdie affair as it unfolded in the leading journals of transnational culture, such as *South Atlantic Quarterly, Public Culture, Cultural Critique,* and *Discourse,* Kumar notes that the controversy marked a historic moment when postcolonial literary and critical discourse came face to face with hitherto unanswered questions: "Who are readers and what are the limits of the readings we propose?" (1995, 235). This is precisely the question that haunts not just Rushdie but all of the cosmopolitical writers discussed here, as they struggle to self-consciously engage with reading practices that inevitably define the idioms of their text.

12. The initial use of English as a language of trade and revenue collection found new impetus in 1813, an impulse carried forward by Lord Bentinck's English Education Act of 1835, which created a unified educational system, curriculum, and orientation. The result was a decline in the traditional elites, some of whom (Brahmins and *kayasthas*) did find their way into the new middle-class intelligentsia. Thus began the first Anglophone writing, in the work of Henry Derozio, Raja Rammohan Roy, and Michael Madhusudhan Dutt.

13. See Rukun Advani (1992), Lola Chatterjee (1992), and Gauri Viswanathnan (1992) for a fair sample.

14. And the British were no strangers to conflict in their own ranks: Macaulay's Anglicist position, which reduced all Indian vernaculars to dialects, was strenuously debated by orientalist scholars who sought to revive the classical Indian literatures. But as the language of the colonizers, English had the currency of an international

(European) audience. Indians such as R. C. Dutt produced abridged translations of the *Ramayana* and the *Mahabharata* (four thousand lines each), while literary giants such as Tagore had to translate their own works (in his case, *Gitanjali)* to gain international acclaim. Looking back at this moment of ascendancy, linguists such as Braj Kachru have argued that English "won" the battle of the Indian languages on account of its neutrality—it did not "belong" to any one community, it was not a cultural marker for any ethnicity, religious group, or region. By the 1800s, Sanskrit was already restricted in its pan-Indian status, and the cause of Hindi as a lingua franca was not helped by the controversy between Hindi, Urdu, and Hindusthani. English became the language of administration, and soon also of political and cultural debate (Kachru 1986).

15. The self-determination of these peoples in the context of the global-local nation has found critical attention elsewhere. For instance, Majlis, a legal and cultural resource center, held a seminar titled "The Nation, the State, and Indian Identity: A Post-Ayodhya Perspective" in February 1994 that featured a session chaired by Gyanendra Pandey (best known for his work on communalism and nationalism), "The People's Movement of Self-Assertion in the Northeast and Kashmir." Pandey introduced the session with the assertion that it is easy, in the aftermath of Ayodhya, to end up "talking only about the BJP and Hindutva," and to ignore what he characterized as "long-neglected problems" of nationhood and its linguistic communities (Dutta, Agnes, and Adarkar 1996, 2–14).

16. K. C. Lalvunga captures this feeling: "Independence came not so much by our demands as by providence. We have, therefore, been overtaken by the new republic. Our aspirations have clashed in some way with that of the new nation" (1996, 15).

17. Rajeswari Sunder Rajan quotes chief minister M. Karunanidhi's warning before the language riots broke out as a characteristic perception of the English-Hindi divide in the Indian South: "If English, which protects us like a shield, is banished, the Hindi sword will cut us to pieces" (1992, 15).

18. See Angana Parekh, "New Urdu Body Plans to Modernise Language," *Indian Express,* 10 July 1995, where she quotes the aims of the national council on Urdu usage: "Functional Urdu . . . could make a significant contribution toward the integration of Muslims into the mainstream." The twenty-member council is headed by Shahid Siddiqi and features luminaries like the film director Gulzar.

19. See "The Pune Resolution on the RSS," *Statesman,* 4 May 1997. Hindi has also received global impetus, as was evidenced in the Fifth World Hindi Conference at Port-of-Spain, where there was a plea to make Hindi the language of the Indian diaspora; see "Report on the Fifth World Hindi Conference," *Economic Times,* 16 April 1996.

20. In the polemic "How to Teach a 'Culturally Different' Book," Spivak (1996a) explains how the translations of the "*devadāsi*" into English (in R. K. Narayan's 1958 novel *The Guide*) and into Hindi (in the widely popular Bollywood classic *Guide*) both enact violence on Tamil-Kannadese specificity: one by colonial inscription, and the other by translation into the national-popular Bollywood idiom.

21. For an excellent analysis of the relations between the vernacular Indian novel and the novel in English, see Padikkal 1993.

22. Rushdie portrays Desani's project as "the first great stroke of the decolonizing pen," in the London *Times,* 3 July 1982.

23. The *gurukul* is a traditional learning center (from Hindu tradition) where a teacher (the guru) imparts formal knowledge and instructs disciples in daily practices of living. Usually, such live-in centers are in remote locations where student-teacher relations can blossom devoid of distraction or interference.

24. Rushdie has been touted as the Indian postmodern, but I would argue that he is a cusp figure in the evolution of the new Indian novel. Certainly, his vision is a modernist one tied to a clear world-text divide (see Rushdie 1984) and a linguistic project. In a PBS interview, "A Conversation," on 14 August 1997, Rushdie spoke of visions: India as a fount of inspiration, the "cornucopia," the "horn of plenty" whose "inexhaustible" abundance cannot ever be absorbed by a set of narratives. Despite the always already present prospects of failure, Rushdie professes to take on "the whole damn thing." "Anyway, I'm a boy from a big country, and there's a part of me that's always hankering for a big country around me, not a small island," affirms Rushdie in "Keeping Up with Salman Rushdie" in the *New York Review*, 28 March 1991, 29. This focus on a fragment (but with a clear sense of the whole) is aptly described in Kumkum Sangari's reading of *Midnight's Children*: "Running aground on the shoals of parody and allegory, [Rushdie] scarcely uses his freedom as a professed fabulist. The totalizing potential of his chosen form cohabits uneasily with the modernist epistemology of a fragment, the specific perspectivism of the bourgeois subject" (1993, 264). It is the uneasiness of form, according to Sangari, that moves Rushdie into the realm of the postmodern.

25. On a personal note, I remember meeting Salman Rushdie on his book tour for *Midnight's Children* in 1982 at Vidya Mandir, Calcutta. As a student of literature at the local Presidency College, I had been impelled to attend by news of a cultural phenomenon on the horizon.

Three Linguistic Migrations: Experiments in English Vernaculars

1. Ganesh is the god of prosperity, but also the scribe of the Hindu epic *Mahabharata*, while Hanuman—a well-beloved storyteller—is the monkey king who joins forces with the mythic hero Ram in the latter's war against Ravana (the demon king) in the *Ramayana*. Both these venerated figures preside over Sanjay and Abhay's modern epic in Chandra's *Red Earth*.

2. The Ngugi wa' Thiongo–Chinua Achebe debate marks an inaugural moment in postcolonial studies. For an elaboration, see my discussion of Rushdie's Bombayspeak in the context of this larger authenticity-hybridity debate (B. Ghosh 1999).

3. Bombay is now called Mumbai (after a local goddess), a deliberate name change upheld by the Shiv Sena, part of the Hindu Right coalition in the state of Maharashtra. Since Rushdie attacks these right-wing militants in *Moor*, he explicitly maintains the old "secular" Bombay as his chosen term; in designating his politics, I retain his use.

4. In our global age, vernacularism and cosmopolitanism are opposed to each other, but this was not necessarily the case, insists Pollock, in past epochs. He then delineates these past epochs of cosmopolitanisms and vernacularisms, specifically as evidenced in literary cultures or "practices of attachment." The literary mode, for Pollock, is an especially sensitive "gauge of sentiment of belonging," creating texts "meant for large worlds or small places," a declaration of "affiliation with that world or place" (2002, 16).

5. Shivarama Padikkal places the emergence of modern Indian vernacular prose in an era of conflicts, between the reformists and the revivalists, the Anglicists and the orientalists. He traces the inception of the modern vernacular novel from Peary Chand Mitra's *Alaler Gharer Dulal* (Bengali, 1858), followed by its Marathi (Baba Pamanji's *Yamuna Paryatan*, 1858), Assamese (Padmanabha Barua's *Bhanumati*, 1890), Tamil (B. R. Rajam Aiyar's *Kamalampal Charittiram*, 1896), and Malayalam (T. M. Appu Nedungadi's *Kundalata*, 1887) counterparts (Niranjana et al. 1993, 220–241).

6. While in the fairytale world of *Haroun* this kind of cultural reference is deployed to evoke a lost world more fully, in politically astute texts such as *Moor* the same knowledge invites us to critical insights buried in more generalized reading. For example, the truck and bus citation in *Haroun* merely flavors Alifbay for nostalgic purposes, but the Nargis reference in *Moor* enacts a political critique of mass cultural reification that is quite significant to the novel's argument. Harveen Sachdev Mann argues that Rushdie translates most of the "Eastern" cultural signs for his Western audience (e.g., *kathaputhli* or *padyatra*) but fails to do the same in his use of Western material (e.g., Nietzsche, Red Riding Hood, Punch and Judy). Quite the contrary; there are several popular cultural signs from the East—as Vijay Mishra and Bob Hodge's elaboration of the *Shri 420* subtext of *Satanic Verses* demonstrates—that are not translated, and sometimes not even quoted or italicized. Significantly, the examples Mann seizes on are typically those classical "Eastern" terms (marked by orientalist difference) that hail the scholar of "native" cultures (see Mann 1995; Mishra and Hodge 1991).

7. The use of *sthan*, the Sanskrit word for "place," has a long Bollywood lineage. After Partition, the studio Filmistan advertised itself as an imaginative domain where the twin independent nations could come together (for an elaboration, see B. Sarkar 1999). Aurora's Mooristan is another such place of healing political fracture.

8. Sunil Dutt, who played the role of Nargis's son in *Mother India,* later married her. Nargis is Bollywood's Mother India of the Mehboob's social, *Mother India* (1962). In the Rushdie novel, Nargis is seen as a competitor to Aurora's claim on the Mother India iconography.

9. This follows the affair of the *Kissing of Abbas Ali Baig* painting that references several real culture wars waged by Maharashtra's Shiv Sena on artists, musicians, and cricket players (Rushdie fuses these incidents into one incident), and I discuss this at greater length in chapter 5.

10. The title juxtaposes Homi Bhabha's seminal essay on nation and migration, "Dissemi(nation)" (1990), and Roland Barthes's famous structural analysis in *S/Z* (1974).

11. Note that the book jacket carries a cave painting, possibly drawn from the Ajanta caves, a clue to the central subjects of the work.

12. Given Ganesh's popularity in Bombay, elephants proliferate in *Moor*, assuming threatening (elephantine majority) and vicious (the elephant-headed jailer) proportions when the sacral and popular valences of Ganesh are wrenched to narrow political self-interest (in the hands of the Shiv Sena).

13. For a discussion of the thoroughfare between Indian modern painting and cinema, see Tapati Guhathakurta's analysis of Ravi Verma (the great Indian modern painter of popular art) (1992, 186–188).

14. In an essay, "Satyajit Ray," Rushdie remarks on his own fascination (represented through Aurora in *Moor*) with Ray's vein of fantasy: "Ray came from a family of fan-

tasists, creators of nonsense verse and fabulous hybrid animals," a reference to Ray's father, Sukumar Sen, a renowned poet of nonsense rhyme (1991, 111).

15. Some clues to Rushdie's situating of Ray and art cinema can be found in his essay on Satyajit Ray, where Rushdie underscores the localism of Ray's "fabulous" films. These are, in Rushdie's view, not successful outside India perhaps because of their context specificity, failing "to attract the plaudits accorded to his more realist films" (1991, 111).

16. In the essay on Ray, Rushdie actually quotes the Nargis interview in which she complains of Ray's ambition for awards that led to his presenting (to the West) a familiar image of India—an "abject" India. When the interviewer asks her what characterizes the "modern" India that she would rather have on screen, she replies vaguely, "Dams . . ." (Rushdie 1991b, 109). This last comment is sardonically produced verbatim in an earlier reference to Nargis in *Moor*. Rushdie goes on to comment on the Nargis-Ray interchange as a clash between the old intellectual traditions of Calcutta and the brash urban mass culture of that "bitch-city," Bombay.

17. For example, S. Aravamudan's (1989) analysis of the 420 motif in *The Satanic Verses* shows how Rushdie deploys that reference to effect a critique of Islam.

18. See Amitava Kumar's (1996) discussion of Mahasweta Devi's and Upamanyu Chatterjee's respective visions of the "Indian interior."

19. For a critique of the relegation of the tribal subaltern to the (middle-class national subject's) unconscious, see Kumkum Sangari's discussion of Arun Joshi's novel *The Strange Case of Billy Biswas* (1971). Sangari demonstrates how a fetishized "unspoilt tribal culture" appears as the unconscious (an "area of anterior ascription") of a national collectivity. Agastya's journey to the Indian interior fits Sangari's typology of colonial and postcolonial quest narratives that position indigenous peoples in such a way (Sangari 2002a, 74).

20. "Non-Bengali" is a parochial term used by Bengalis to mark their regional others, erecting cultural and social divides, and it is deliberately evoked here to capture Chatterjee's depiction of middle-class Bengali family sensibilities and attitudes.

21. Claiming a lack of "inwardness" of the metaphysical kind in Roy's characters, James Wood (1997, 36) pithily sums up Roy's effort: "Roy . . . explains in her novel that India always snatches away one's inwardness, one's own beliefs, and presses her larger, epic claims on the soul. . . . The individual soul must surrender to the Big God, and the Big God is always India." Not only is the Big God not always India, and perhaps only so in the passage Wood cites (admittedly it is one of the few direct references to "God," in Roy's metaphoric use of the word), but Wood further perceives Roy's abrogation of individualism as a lack of philosophical depth. That is, the lack of individualism in the novel, a requirement for the metaphysical understanding of presence in Western philosophical and religious paradigms, is read as a disadvantage, or a "surrender," by some. In Hindu philosophy, the act of surrender to a greater whole in ecstatic union constitutes the deepest kind of self-realization ("presence") one can achieve. Roy's tumultuous ending, with Ammu and Velutha's lovemaking breaking human love laws (as do Rahel and Estha and the mythic Kunti and Karna), enacts this philosophy of spiritual bliss.

22. Kunti, in the *Mahabharata*, reveals herself as Karna's mother, who abandoned him in order to prevent him from killing her other sons, the Pandavas, in the mythic battle to come at Kurukshetra: "It was *them* Kunti sought to protect by announcing to

Karna that she was his mother. She had a promise to extract. She invoked the Love Laws" (Roy 1997b, 233). Here the Love Laws, used as an interpretive paradigm in the story, are explained as the duties and obligations that regulate love relationships. But in this instance, Kunti manipulates the love relation to divide her sons, privileging her Pandava sons over her abandoned (and unclaimed) child, Karna.

23. Roy insists that while larger paradigms separate human experiences, the small things are what we all share: "So if you actually address that question, everything is just ordinary everyday life, which is why even if you don't know about [the town] Ayemenem, you know what it's like to be caught in a traffic light, you know that society has these brutal ways of dividing itself up, you know what it's like to be a child" (see Roy 1997c).

24. Such case-by-case translation is what Chakrabarty (2000, 183) advocates in his preference of an "informal barter economy" of translation over a "general exchange of commodities." Universal "translatese," in other words, should not govern the rites of passage between languages.

Four The Body of the Other: Narrating Violence, Community, History

1. For example, Mani Rathnam's *Roja* (1992) and *Dil Se* (1997); Santosh Sivan's *The Terrorist* (2000); and Vidhu Vinod Chopra's *Mission Kashmir* (2000). See a discussion of the different terrorists in these films in Chakravarty 2000, 222–237.

2. Phoolan Devi, commonly known as India's "bandit queen," was a dalit woman who, having been violated by the Thakurs (upper-caste men) in the village of Behmai, avenged herself in the historic Behmai massacre of 1981. Surrendering to police forces in 1983, she (after her jail term) became a member of Parliament in 1996.

3. An astute political read of Rushdie's relationship to the Indian polity may be found Mufti 1999, where Mufti describes Rushdie's movement from "the politics of constituency" (in *Midnight's Children*) to the "politics of oppositionality" (in *The Satanic Verses*). Mufti's political pointers tell of Rushdie's gradual alienation from a larger (national and cultural) community of belonging, and of his current minoritarian identifications.

4. This aim results in the United Nations not having terms for international hierarchies, save colloquialisms such as the "perm five" or the "donor country" (A. Ghosh 1994).

5. Ghosh wonders what investment the Cambodian professionals, middle-class men, could have in religious fundamentalism. For he finds, in this visit to Cambodia, the same will to "supremacism" that censors writing all over the world—"supremacism" is defined by Ghosh as ensuring the continuity of a group by exerting "absolute cultural and demographic control" over territory (A. Ghosh 2002, 268–288).

6. In October 2000, a three-judge bench of the Supreme Court ruled against the NBA and in favor of the state governments in question.

7. One such alternative vision is found in Mahatma Jyotiba Phule's model of indigenous development (based on organizing peasants and preventing large-scale building or deforestation), a logical corollary to his nation of *"shudra"* and *"ati shudra"* ("backward" and "untouchable" classes). The Savarkarite Hindu Brahmanic conceptions of nation, culture, and development stand in direct opposition to this other vision of nation. It is in the vernacular regional literatures and presses (both Gujarati and Marathi) that we find the local intelligentsia's take on the "national" cause of dams

and identities—in these accounts we find very different local bindings of nation and culture, of dalits and Indians. For instance, Dattaprasad Dabholkar, in his Marathi book on the Narmada Project, exudes admiration for "the children of India" who had mastered modern technology; and the Gujarati newspapers like *Sandesh, Loksatta,* and *Gujarat Samachar* participate vigorously in labeling the adivasis and dalits "anti-nationals." Dalits are racialized in Dabholkar's constant references to the *Ramayana* as the founding narrative of the Hindu polity. They are objects of pity, the impracti-cal though well-meaning descendents of the legendary Jatayu and Vaali who were, not coincidentally, defeated by Ram, the Aryan king: "But, in the new way of life [Ramrajya or the kingdom of Ram] Vaaloi and Jatayu had no place. But, that does not mean that these people were exterminated. The new civilisation accommodates them" (539). Thus the "anti-nationals" are culturally differentiated (the nonhuman bird forms of Jatayu and Vaali) and assimilated into the idea of the Hindu nation that energizes this mode of Gujarati regional identity (see Sangvai 1994).

8. These overlaps were possible in a world of "thick" religiosity, where the individual's religious identity was spread over a wide variety of levels, "from large metaphysical beliefs about the nature of existence, to minute ritual practices in worship," and so the religious identity was determined by numerous criteria (Kaviraj 1995, 307).

9. This reading of a national fracture well before independence finds elucidation in Chakrabarty, who examines the census practices of the colonial administration that "ethnicized" social and religious groups in the colony. Invoking Foucault's investi-gation of the deep structure of eighteenth-century European governmentality and demographic measurement, Chakrabarty asserts that one of the symptoms of moder-nity is that its "techniques of government" are "very closely tied to techniques of measurement": "It is this pervasive marriage between government and measurement that I take as something that belongs to the deep structure of the imagination that is invested in modern political orders" (1995a, 3375). What remains interesting in the British practice of instrumental rationality in the governance of the colonies was that those practices differed widely from those used in Britain. Chakrabarty references the work of U.S. historian Kenneth Jones, who demonstrates the gap between cen-sus practices in Britain and in the colonies. Religion was never an important category for British census between 1801 and 1931 (only once, in 1851, were people asked about religious affiliations, and the question was optional), but the colonial popula-tions were enumerated according to socioreligious communities, for in the eigh-teenth century, British thinkers certainly perceived India as a society weakened by its divisions of religion and caste (3376). The administrative act of transforming what seemed to the British a collection of "backward communities" to universal indices conveyed three messages to the Indian populace: that political clout lay in numbers; that the social and economic progress of a community was a measurable entity; and that governments and communities could devise tests for the relative backwardness of a community (3377).

10. Nehru's speech on the midnight hour speaks of this "long-suppressed soul" of nation, abstracting "India" (a cultural idea) from the "Indian people": "Long years we made a tryst with destiny, and now the time has come when we shall redeem our pledge, not wholly or in full measure, but very substantially. / At the stroke of midnight hour, when the world sleeps, India will awake to life and freedom. A moment comes which comes but rarely in history, when we step out from the old to the new, then an age

ends, and when the soul of a nation long suppressed finds utterance. It is fitting that at this solemn moment we take the pledge of dedication to India and her people and to the still larger cause of humanity" (quoted in full in Rushdie and West 1997b, 3–4).

11. See Tanika Sarkar's long analysis of Sadhavi Rithambara's remastered 1991 speech, "Heroic Women and Mother Goddesses," in Sarkar and Butalia 1996, 187-215. *Khaki Shorts and Saffron Flags* (Basu et al. 1994) was one of the educational "Tracts for Our Times" series aimed at a general readership.

12. A 1992 publication by senior BJP functionary K. R. Malkani, full of "positive statements" about the RSS, reveals the anxiety on the part of these local intelligentsia for validation from the very people they demonize as Western and anti-Indian.

13. In the fall of 2002, Paula Chakravarty and Kamala Viseswaran, two U.S.-based academics, compiled a huge list of signatures from global North-based progressive scholars who marked their disagreements with the Hindu Right's collection of donations (on the pretext of relief work) for narrow and violent nationalist agendas. See the feature "Stop Funding Fate Campaign" against the IDRF in *India West*, December 2002, 1–2.

14. A significant illustration of this may be found in the Enron project case in Maharashtra. The Shiv Sena had grass-roots support in Maharashtra, particularly in the lower-middle-class and poorer urban sectors of Bombay, long before it came to state power. In July 1991 the Indian government had modified the Industrial Policy Resolution to remove the power sector from a list of areas limited to the public sector. The Enron $2 million Dabhol project received approval from central government and negotiated a deal with the Maharashtra State Electricity Board. The project was supposed to be an example of successful new economic policies, and the deal transpired after the BJP's election to state government. By spring 1995, it had become part of the heated debate over India's commitment to economic reform. New negotiations in November 1995 followed, with Enron receiving a new contract from the state in January 1996 that agreed to slash the project cost, a gesture staged just before the national elections.

15. The authors of one of the first historical accounts of Hindutva, *Khaki Flags and Saffron Shorts*, outline the partially repressed cultural nationalist project of the RSS founder and intellectual, V. D. Savarkar—a project derailed by Nehru's ascendancy to political power in the 1920s and through the 1930s—whose nationalism is not anticolonial, but anti-dalit and anti-Muslim (Basu et al. 1994, 5, 8).

16. The controversy originated when *Vichar Mimansa*, a recently founded Hindi monthly magazine from Bhopal, ran an article by Om Nagpal in the September issue, "Is He [Husain] an Artist or a Butcher?" 1.

17. *Frontline* interview with Husain, 15 November 1997, 13.

18. Mary John (1998) underscores the Hindu Right's general strategy of generating "moral panics" to garner consensus on a unified "national culture," and to deflect attention from pressing political issues and/or failures.

19. The parallel with Rushdie is significant because of Hindu right-wing efforts to ban *The Moor's Last Sigh* for its negative portrayal of Bal Thackeray and the Shiv Sena.

20. In the Indian postcolonial state, the categories of the scheduled castes, the scheduled tribes, and the other backward castes comprise the lowest rung of socioeconomic power. These are administrative categories set up by the welfare state to "protect" indigenous peoples and their natural resources, as well as to facilitate their institutional upward mobility.

21. The gaze of freedom fighters met with homage and acknowledgment, but also evaluation and a commitment to change. Partha Chatterjee reports that the impetus for this collective retrospective analysis of the Nehruvian era—"often remembered as the golden age of the postcolonial state in India"—came from his own concern with the disillusion of veteran freedom fighters. In a series of interviews that he had conducted for the last twenty years, Chatterjee records this older generation's sense of betrayal: "Driven by the utopian ideals of their promised dreamland, they were using impossible standards to measure the achievements of independence" (1998, 5).

22. Ghosh starts his essay by evoking popular memory—the contradictory stories about this untold war that he received from his parents, motivating his historical exploration. Many Bengalis still believe that Bose's disappearance was actually a murder covered up by the colonial British government.

23. Ghosh writes of Partition and 1971 traumas in *The Shadow Lines* (1984); of the 1984 Hindu-Sikh riots in "Ghosts of Mrs. Gandhi" (1995a); and of recent Hindu-Muslim violence in "The Gujarat Carnage" (2002d).

24. As I have argued elsewhere, it is important to note that the cultural nationalist legacy of contemporary Hindu militant nationalism is a source of contention. For some, the Hindu nationalists have rather opportunistically laid claim to a historical connection with the nineteenth-century cultural revivalisms, in order to legitimize their essentialist appropriations of certain iconographies and even heroes, such as Shivaji and Tantia Tope (now read as nationalist heroes). This presupposition of historical continuity is found in RSS literature and among scholars who sympathize with the RSS (e.g., Anderson and Damle) (B. Ghosh 2002). The civilizational argument is found again in some global North-based commentaries that support the Huntington thesis. See a critique of the civilizational hypothesis (that Huntington finally deploys to reinstate Euro-American supremacy) in Dirlik 2000.

25. Guhathakurta (1997, 89) notes that 1948 thus becomes a memorable date in the nation's art history when nothing particularly revolutionary was going on in the Indian art world; most strains and traditions of art at this time were continuing aesthetic movements.

26. A Renaissance man, Kosambi wrote extensively on philology, religion, archaeology, folk knowledges and historical reconstruction, and anthropology.

27. The article is a critique of those left out of the national equation by an elite whose will to nation making Nehru so well exemplified. The pristine white "khaddar," the homespun of Gandhi's "swadeshi" (economic nationalism), thus masks the impurities of the Nehruvian will to power. Jawaharlal Nehru wrote *The Discovery of India* in 1944 while imprisoned for the Quit India movement at Ahmadnagar. His daughter, Indira Gandhi, edited and put the volume together in the year that followed.

28. Shapiro offers an analysis of the political means for consolidating modern citizenship, or the "practical, legal, and conceptual recognition" of the political subject as a "licit presence" within a nation-state. For Shapiro, in these classic terms, the nation-state is a territorial entity inhabited by a people who share a culture or unite on the basis of common descent; the very idea of a stable and coherent "people" enables a mode of belonging for political subjects (2000, 79–80).

29. Sagarika Ghosh (1992) describes the takeover of the Indian Council of Historical Research by pro-*Ramjanmabhumi* historians three months after the BJP-led coalition came to national state power.

30. Gyanendra Pandey (1991) powerfully suggests the amnesia theory, and recent work on Partition has taken up his contention by further exploring how cultural memory works to repress this kind of national trauma.

31. Chakrabarty takes on formidable critiques of radical Left histories from more traditional Marxist critics such as Sumit Sarkar. Sarkar has most famously criticized the subaltern studies scholars for their undermining of the legacies of Enlightenment rationalism, an underscoring of rationality that celebrates all manner of the affective, the unsaid, the lived. This includes religious understandings of community, which, in the age of chauvinistic Hindutva, seem particularly dangerous to the goals of secularism. Chakrabarty defends his critical engagement with Enlightenment rationalism, which in no way entails a "wholesale rejection of the tradition of rational argumentation." Rather, his work rejects the "hyper-rationalism of the colonial modern" that would deny anything affective—"pleasures, desires, emotions"—as being of importance to the tasks of historical investigation (1995b, 752).

32. Chakrabarty's rendition of polysemic worlds is not an unusual one in postcolonial studies in general. In Mignolo's (2000) look at the implications of subaltern knowledges for Latin America, for example, Mignolo posits "gnosis" as a way of knowing that is different from the scientific knowledge of the colonial epistemology. Mignolo's idea of "gnosis," a concept that Africanists such as Valentin Mudimbe have explored in the African postcolonial context (*The Invention of Africa: Gnosis, Philosophy, and the Order of Things*), *is* the presence of subaltern knowledge that Chakrabarty recognizes in the seams of rational epistemology—in fact, Mignolo goes to lengths to distinguish "gnosis" ("to know, to recognize") from "episteme" ("to know, to acquaint") in order to resolve what he calls "Chakrabarty's dilemma," the dilemma of working within colonial epistemologies to produce subaltern knowledge without commodification. Gnosis, then, enables the recognition of a different order of things, an order easily classified within colonial systems of knowing as "traditional systems of thought," "folklore," "magic," or "mysticism," as opposed to philosophy or history. Describing what these narratives that intuit hidden presences might shape up to be, Mignolo gives as an example Cherrie Moraga's experiments with dual memories, remembering in two languages, in her latest work, *The Last Generation* (1993). More recently, Steve Blevins (2002) has underscored other mobile applications of "the *unheimlich*" for postcolonial work in his excellent essay on Tracy Moffat, where he resituates both Bhabha and Achille Mbeme's articulations of the uncanny for the purposes of exploring cinematographic space.

33. This correspondence was published in full just as I was revising this essay. I was immediately struck by the two scholars' interest in the vernacular idiom as a central resource for postcolonial historiographies, an insistence that has earned both the label "nativist."

Five   Of Ghosts and Grafts: Uncanny Narration in Cosmopolitical Novels

1. Dipesh Chakrabarty (1999) elaborates on the social practice of *adda*.

2. The uncovering of "facts" in *The Calcutta Chromosome* leads us to a series ghost stories which supposedly explain the puzzle set up in the opening pages of the mystery; these turn out to be the "Lakhaan stories" published in an obscure Bengali literary rag by a local writer, Phulboni. For many, the novel fizzles out as a medical mystery.

Said one irritated reviewer for *Under Cover Book Review*: "He [Ghosh] veers sharply from the detective mystery format some thirty pages from the end of the book in that he fails to deliver the promised solution. . . . In the end he serves to only denigrate the resourcefulness of the human mind" (Acton 1998). If we take seriously Ghosh's postcolonial unraveling of established colonial truth, then the very genre of truth telling must suffer. In fact a great deal of "resourcefulness" is required to graft onto the body of a mystery another manner of telling more capable of visionary praxis.

3. In February 2002, Amitav Ghosh presented a lecture on mourning and ethical mapping at the University of California, Riverside. I had the singular pleasure of spending an afternoon with the writer chatting about politics, his travels, and recent work; I took the opportunity to voice my uncanny feeling about *The Calcutta Chromosome*, the sense that the novel drew substantially on Bengali ghost fiction. It was at this point that Ghosh mentioned the two inspirational fragments integrated in the novel— Tagore's and Renu's ghost fiction. See also Amitav Ghosh's translation of the Tagore story (Tagore [1895] 1995) in a *Civil Lines 2* issue on "new writing from India."

4. One of Ghosh's major criticisms of *Provincializing Europe* is Chakrabarty's inattention to the question of "race," that invisible category in South Asian postcolonial explorations. Ruminating on the shame and anguish of the postcolonial subject (with a personal evocation of his father's experience of the colonial military regime), Ghosh returns to Tagore as the exemplar of the divided colonial subject, Tagore's self-reflexivity notwithstanding. Ghosh's preoccupation with race receives extended treatment in Ghosh's *Glass Palace*, the historical novel published in 2000 (U.S. edition 2001), a year after *Provincializing Europe* appeared.

5. Salman Rushdie's "Crash" appeared in the *New Yorker* after Princess Diana's death and is reprinted in Rushdie 2002f, 109–112.

6. In a conversation with Günter Grass, Rushdie elaborated on his phrase "to be borne across" in the following way: "Translation, from Latin, means 'to carry across.' Metaphor, from Greek, means 'to carry across.' So again this comes back to my preoccupation with the idea of migration. People are also carried across, you see; they are physically carried from one place to another and I formed the idea that that act of migration was to turn people somehow into things, into people who had been translated" (Rushdie 2000b, 77).

7. Tantra was most widely practiced by forest dwellers, "outlaws" who worshipped Kali and were often characterized as dacoits in common Bengali lore. The British abolition of Thugee in 1837 attempted to clean up these populations, driving them underground along with their tantric practices—no surprise, given that tantra was always perceived as popular religion by Brahmanical Hindus, the Hindu elites who parlayed in social reform with the British rulers. Even more interesting for our purposes is the fact that these bands of thugs acquire heroic proportion as freedom fighters in the fiction of the nineteenth-century novelist Bankimchandra Chattopadhyay (especially enshrined in his widely circulated *Devi Chaudurani*). Amitav Ghosh is interested in Chattopadhyay because the latter wrote the first Indian novel in English, *Rajmohun's Wife* (1864), a novel that Ghosh reads as a dress rehearsal for Chattopadhyay's more celebrated Bengali fiction (see Ghosh 2002e, 287–304, for a reprint of "The March of the Novel through History," written as a lecture in 1996).

8. The pressure of the affective that troubles rational collective narratives is also a theme in Ghosh's slim collection of essays *Dancing in Cambodia, At Large in Burma*

(1998a). There are two encounters between Cambodia and "the West"—the 1906 visit to Marseilles by a troupe of Cambodian dancers, and Ghosh's own 1993 visit to a Cambodia ravaged by the Pol Pot years, both accounts of the East from the East. The "ethnographer" king records the Marseilles visit in his diary (recounted by Ghosh); and in the second instance, Ghosh collects memories from Cambodians on the years of war and repression, accounts that differ significantly from those of the members of the UN peacekeeping force he meets when he first arrives there. Cambodian "tourist" spots such as Angkor Wat become, for the ethnographer and traveler, repositories not only of traditional stories but also of modern encounters of soldiering and shelter. Ghosh suggests that all forms of memory (dual and disjunctive memories, in this case) are folk understandings of violence and trauma.

9. But Chandra also suggests that orientalism is alive and well among Anglophile Americans. Abhay recoils from his girlfriend Amanda's father, whose conversation and cricket habits Abhay finds deeply offensive.

10. For an example of contemporary commentaries on globalization, intellectual property, and indigenous knowledges, see Shiva 1997.

11. As I have noted earlier, "tantric practices" were often practiced by bands of forest dwellers characterized as thugs by the British administration. For an elaboration of the colonial take on "Thugee," see P. Roy 1996.

12. See "'Errata': or Unreliable Narration in *Midnight's Children*" (Rushdie 1991, 22–25), in which Rushdie defends his misdating of Gandhi's death and other such mistakes as deliberate in fashioning unreliable narration.

13. The harnessing of sacred geographies as forgotten topographies is a matter of global significance: Consider Jane Jacobs's (1996) work on the aboriginal claims to sacred places in the city of Sydney, where she documents cultural mobilization around these sacred spatialities to oppose the sites of capitalist development.

14. See the discussion of Rushdie's history writing as gossip in Nair 1997.

15. Chandra privileges oral narration in its flexibility, writing at a time when the two Indian epics (the *Ramayana* and *Mahabharata*) were homogenized into televisual versions. See Mankekar 1999.

16. Dancing is also seen as panacea in Ghosh's *Dancing in Cambodia, At Large in Burma*, for not only personal, but also collective, historical trauma.

17. Cultural recycling for Roy reifies and appropriates versions of the vernacular. Global colonial literary (*The Tale of Two Cities*) and mass culture (*The Sound of Music*) are found to be an integral part of the children's postcolonial world, but also quite disconnected from their experience of that world. The sugary innocence of *The Sound of Music* becomes, for Estha, tarnished by his encounter with sexual abuse from the Orangedrink Lemondrink man. The juxtapositioning of the real and the imaginary is quite deliberate and it takes up a long segment in the book.

18. "Lakhaan" is a common name with an interesting mythological referent, for our particular ghost. Lakshman (the Sanskritized version of the eastern Indian variant, Lakhaan) is Ram's brother, who follows the former, the epic hero of the *Ramayana*, into his fourteen-year exile. Lakshman's motives are heroic loyalty and love, but it is a common Indian joke to cast aspersions on Lakhaan's motives. The name Lakhaan therefore conjures one who comes second, who follows faithfully, but who remains partially eclipsed in the narrative—a resoundingly good choice for the recursive Lakhaan/Lutchman, Mangala's assistant, in *The Calcutta Chromosome*. Mangala's

name connotes "one who brings good," in direct opposition to her perceived malignant role in the novel.

19. Parama Roy, author of *Indian Traffic*, spoke from her new work at the Cultural Analysis Colloquium at the University of California, Santa Barbara, 6 March 2002. Titled "Figures of Famine," the talk presented Mahasweta Devi's literary and journalistic "accounting" of famine, a phenomenon that troubles the postcolonial liberal state and its agents (bureaucrats). Fiction that captures the shock of this traumatic excess within the bureaucratic imaginary is what Roy pithily transcribes as "the bureaucratic gothic."

20. Parama Roy eloquently made this point about ghosts as a record of the excess inconceivable to the liberal postcolonial subject, an excess that activists like Mahasweta Devi catalog in their fiction. Phaniswarnath Renu presents an interesting parallel to Mahasweta Devi, since he is best known for his intellectual commitment to nonmetropolitan milieus and his critique of the postcolonial liberal state—especially in his celebrated novel *Maila Anchal* (*The Soiled Border*, 1954). Like Mahasweta Devi, then, he is both a chronicler of and an active interventionist in the modern violences that the nation inflicts on its own people.

Epilogue

1. See Mistry's comments on the *Oprah* show in December 2001, available on *www.oprah.com*. Of course, Rushdie has written eloquently of this particular human cost in his short story "Free Speech Radio" (1994) and in *Midnight's Children* (1981).

2. I am not sure he ultimately succeeds, since one of the closing remarks on the caste-system part of the discussion failed to catch the local resonance as Oprah asked: "So once born a laborer, you're in the laborer caste system, you can never be something else?"

3. See *news.bookweb.com*, 5 November 2002.

Selected Bibliography

"A Cannibal Time." 2002. Special issue of *Seagull Theatre Quarterly*. Calcutta: Seagull Press.

A Nation Challenged. 2002. New York: New York Times/Callaway Press.

Acton, S. M. 1998. Review of *Calcutta Chromosome,* by Amitav Ghosh. *Under Cover Book Review* 24 (September): 1.

Advani, Rukun. 1992. "Master English, Native Teacher: A Publishing Perspective on English Studies in India." In *The Lie of the Land: English Literary Studies in India*, ed. Rajeswari Sunder Rajan, 112–129. Delhi: Oxford University Press.

Afzal-Khan, Fawzia. 1993. *Cultural Imperialism and the Indo-English Novel: Genre and Ideology in R. K. Narayan, Anita Desai, Kamala Markandaya, and Salman Rushdie*. University Park: Pennsylvania State University Press.

Agamben, Giorgio. 1993. *The Coming Community*. Trans. Michael Hardt. Minneapolis: University of Minnesota Press.

Anand, Mulk Raj. 1982. "Pigeon-Indian." *World Literature Written in English* 21 (spring): 325–336.

Appadurai, Arjun. 1990. "Disjuncture and Difference in the Global Cultural Economy." *Public Culture* 2, 2: 1–24.

———. 1993. "Patriotism and Its Futures." *Public Culture* 5: 411–429.

———. 1995. Introduction to Carol Breckenbridge and Arjun Appadurai, *Consuming Modernity: Public Culture in South Asia* (Minneapolis: University of Minnesota Press).

———. 2000. "Grassroots Globalization and the Research Imagination." *Public Culture* 12, 1: 1–19.

Appiah, Anthony. 1993. *In My Father's House: Africa in Philosophy and Culture*. New York: Oxford University Press.

Apter, Emily. 2001. "Translation on the Global Market." *Public Culture* 13, 1: 1–17.

Aravamudan, S. 1989. "Salman Rushdie's *The Satanic Verses*." *Diacritics* 19, 2: 3–20.

"Area of Brightness." 1998. *The Week. www.pugmarks.com*.

Bacchetta, Paola. 1996. "Hindu Nationalist Women as Ideologists: Rashtriya Swayamse-
vak Sangh, Rashtra Sevika Samiti, and Their Respective Projects for the Hindu
Nation." In *Embodied Violence: Communalizing Women's Sexuality in South Asia,* ed.
Kumari Jayawardena and Malathi de Alwis, 126–167. New Delhi: Kali for Women.

Bahal, Aniruddha. 1995. "Literary Chemistry." *Outlook* 8 (November): 1–3.

Bahri, Deepika. 1996. "Coming to Terms with the 'Postcolonial'." In *Between the Lines:
South Asians and Postcoloniality,* ed Deepika Bahri and Mary Vasudeva, 137–164.
Philadelphia: Temple University Press.

Bahri, Deepika, and Mary Vasudeva, eds. 1996. *Between the Lines: South Asians and Postcoloniality.* Philadelphia: Temple University Press.

Barthes, Roland. 1974. *S/Z.* Trans. Richard Miller. New York: Hill and Wang.

Barucha, Rustom. 1994a. *In the Name of the Secular.* Delhi: Oxford University Press.

———. 1994b. "Somebody's Other: Disorientations in the Cultural Politics of Our Time."
Economic and Political Weekly of India 15 (January): 104–110.

Basu, Tapan, Sumit Sarkar, Pradip Datta, Tanika Sarkar, and Sambuddha Sen. 1994.
Khaki Shorts and Saffron Flags: A Critique of the Hindu Right. Delhi: Oxford University Press.

"Battle Cry against Militarism." 2000. *Sunday Times* (South Africa), 1 September.
www.suntimes.com.

Baucom, Ian. 1999. *Out of Place: Englishness, Empire, and the Locations of Identity.* Princeton: Princeton University Press.

Bavadam, Lyla. 1996. "In Defence of Freedom in Art: Against the Hindutva Attack on
M. F. Hussain." *Frontline,* 15 November, 5–13.

"Behind the White Khaddar." 1997. Reprint, *Statesman,* 15 August, 2.

"Be Indian, Write English." 1997. *India Today,* 14 July, 6.

Belliappa, K. C. 1996. "Amitav Ghosh's *In an Antique Land*: An Excursion into Time Past
and Time Present." In *The Postmodern Indian English Novel,* ed. Viney Kirpel, 59–66.
Bombay: Allied Publishers.

Benjamin, Walter. [1923] 2000. "The Task of a Translator." Translated by Harry Zohn.
Reprint, *Translation Studies Reader,* ed. Lawrence Venuti, 15–22. New York:
Routledge.

Beverly, John. 1999. *Subalterneity and Representation: Arguments in Cultural Theory.*
Durham, N.C.: Duke University Press.

Bhabha, Homi K. 1990. "Dissemi(Nation): Time, Narrative, and the Margins of the Modern Nation." In *Nation and Narration,* ed. Homi K. Bhabha, 291–322. New York:
Routledge.

———. 1997. "Editor's Introduction: Minority Maneuvers and Unsettled Negotiations."
Critical Inquiry 23, 3: 431–459.

Bhaduri, Amit, and Deepak Nayyar. 1996. *The Intelligent Person's Guide to Liberalisation.*
Delhi: Oxford University Press.

Bhadra, Gautam, Gyan Prakash, and Susie Tharu. 1999. "The Subaltern-effect: Negation
to Deconstruction Hybridity." In *Subaltern Studies: Writings on South Asian History
and Society,* ed. Gautam Bhadra, Gyan Prakash, and Susie Tharu, 1–10. Vol. 10. New
Delhi, Oxford University Press.

Bhandare, Namita. 1997. "Patriotism, Inc." *India Today,* 25 August, 46–47.

"Bibliofile." 2002. *Outlook* 8 (July), 1-2. *www.outlookindia.com.*

Blevins, Steven. 2002. "Uncanny Postcolony: Disrupting Cinematographic Space in Tracy Moffat's *Night Cries*." Paper presented at the Scholars Symposium, University of California Davis, March.

Booker, M. Keith. 1999a. "Salman Rushdie: The Development of a Literary Reputation." In *Critical Essays on Salman Rushdie*, ed. M. Keith Booker, 1–15. New York: G. K. Hall.

———, ed. 1999b. *Critical Essays on Salman Rushdie*. London: G. K. Hall.

"Books That Made a Difference." 1997. *Business India,* 11–24 August, 253–256.

Breckenbridge, Carol A., Sheldon Pollock, Homi K. Bhabha, and Dipesh Chakrabarty, eds. 2002. *Cosmopolitanism*. Durham, N.C.: Duke University Press.

Brennan, Timothy. 1989. *Salman Rushdie and the Third World: Myths of the Nation*. New York: St. Martin's Press.

———. 1997. *At Home in the World: Cosmopolitanism Now*. Cambridge: Harvard University Press.

———. 2001. "Cuts of Language: The East/West of the North/South." *Public Culture* 13, 1:39–64.

Brown, Wendy. 2000. *Politics out of History*. Princeton: Princeton University Press.

Buford, Bill. 1997. "Declarations of Independence: Why Are There Suddenly So Many Indian Novelists?" *New Yorker,* 23 and 30 June, 6–8.

Butalia, Urvashi. 1998. *The Other Side of Silence: Voices from the Indian Partition*. Delhi: Viking.

"Call for Manipuri." 1996. *Telegraph,* 13 December.

Chakrabarty, Dipesh. 1995a. "Modernity and Ethnicity: A History for the Present." *Economic and Political Weekly of India,* 30 December, 3373–3378.

———. 1995b. "Radical Histories and the Question of Enlightened Rationalism: Some Recent Critiques of Subaltern Studies." *Economic and Political Weekly of India,* 8 April, 751–759.

———. 1999. "Adda, Calcutta: Dwelling in Modernity." *Public Culture* 11, 1 (winter): 109–145.

———. 2000. *Provincializing Europe: Postcolonial Thought and Historical Difference*. Princeton: Princeton University Press.

———. 2002. "The In-Human and the Ethical in Communal Violence." In *Habitations of Modernity: Essays in the Wake of Subaltern Studies*, 138–148. Chicago: University of Chicago Press.

Chakrabarty, Dipesh, and Amitav Ghosh. 2002. "A Correspondence on *Provincializing Europe*." *Radical History Review* 83 (spring): 146–172.

Chakravarty, Sumita. 2000. "Fragmenting the Nation: Images of Indian Terrorism in Indian Popular Cinema." In *Cinema and Nation,* ed. Mette Hjort and Scott Mackenzie, 222–237. New York: Routledge.

Chandra, Vikram. 1995. *Red Earth and Pouring Rain: A Novel*. Boston: Little, Brown.

———. 1997. *Love and Longing in Bombay*. Delhi: Viking Penguin.

———. 1998a. "Interview with Vikram Chandra" by Kevin Mahoney. *Genre* (summer): 1–3

———. 1998b. "The Writer as Loner." Interview by Aishwarya Mukherjee. *Indian Express,* 15 July, 2.

———. 2000. "The Cult of Authenticity." *Boston Review* 25, 1: 42–49. *bostonreview.mit.edu*.

Chatterjee, Lola. 1992. "Landmarks in Official Educational Policy." In *The Lie of the Land: English Literary Studies in India*, ed. Rajeswari Sunder Rajan, 300–308. Delhi: Oxford University Press.

Chatterjee, Partha. 1998a. "Beyond Nation? Or Within?" *Social Text 56* 16, 3: 57–69.

———, ed. 1998b. *Wages of Freedom: Fifty Years of the Indian Nation-State*. New Delhi: Oxford University Press.

Chatterjee, Upamanyu. 1989. *English August: An Indian Story*. Calcutta: Rupa.

———. 1993. *The Last Burden*. Delhi: Penguin.

———. 1996. "In Bits and Pieces." In *The Telegraph Autumn Collection*. October, 6–21.

———. 1997. "Rambling at Fifty." *India Today,* 18 August, 172.

———. 2000. *Mammaries of the Welfare State*. New Delhi: Viking Penguin.

Chaudhuri, Amit. 2001. Introduction to *The Picador Book of Modern Indian Literature*. London, Picador.

Cheah, Pheng. 1999. "Spectral Nationality: The Living On [*sur-vie*] of the Postcolonial Nation in Neocolonial Globalization." *Boundary 2* 26, 3: 225–252.

Chen, Kuan-Hsing. 2000. *Trajectories: Inter-Asia Cultural Studies*. New York: Routledge.

Clifford, James. 1994. "Diasporas." *Cultural Anthropology* 9, 1: 302–338.

Clute, John. 1997. "A Tale Decent Folks Can Buy." Review of *Calcutta Chromosome,* by Amitav Ghosh. *Science Fiction Weekly,* 20 October, 1–2. *www.scifi.com/sfw/issue* 56.

Cohen, Robin. 1997. *Global Diaspora: An Introduction*. Seattle: University of Washington Press.

Cowley, Jason. 1997a. "Where Is the British Novel?" *Statesman,* 16 October, 1.

———. 1997b. "Why We Chose Arundhati." *India Today,* 27 October, 28.

Cundy, Catherine. 1996. *Salman Rushdie*. Manchester: University of Manchester Press.

Dalvi, Pradeep. 1998. *Mee Nathuram Godse Boltoy*. Opening Mumbai, June.

Das, Arvind N. 1997. "Journey into Twilight." *Outlook Magazine* 18 (August): 1–3.

Das, Soumitra. 1997. "National Language Act: English and Indian Unity." *Statesman,* 5 August, 2.

Dasgupta, Swapan. 1997a. "Imaginary Homelands." *India Today,* 28 July, 5.

———. 1997b. "Some History Lessons." *India Today,* 30 June, 13.

Derrida, Jacques. 1994. *Specters of Marx: The State of Debt, the Work of Mourning, and the New International*. Trans. Peggy Kamuf. New York: Routledge.

———. 1996. *Archive Fever: A Freudian Impression*. Trans. Erin Prenowitz. Chicago: University of Chicago Press.

Desai, Anita. 1984. *In Custody*. New York: Harper and Row.

———. 1988. "Against the Current: A Conversation with Anita Desai." Interview by Corrine Jemas. *Massachusetts Review* 29, 3 (fall 1988): 531–540.

———. 1989. "Indian Fiction Today." Interview. *Daedalus* 118, 4 (fall): 207–213.

Desani, G. V. 1986. *All about Hattrer*. London,: Aldor Press, 1948. Reprint, London: McPherson's.

Deshpande, Shashi. 1995. "Language No Bar." *Times of India,* 28 April.

Dharwadker, Vinay, and Aparna Dharwadkar. 1996. "Language, Identity, and Nation in Postcolonial Indian Literature." In *English Postcoloniality: Literatures from around the World*, ed. Radhika Mohanram and Gita Rajan, 89–106. Westport, Conn.: Greenwood Press.

Dienst, Richard, and Henry Schwarz, eds. 1996. *Reading the Shape of the World: Toward an Internationalization of Cultural Studies*. Boulder, Colo.: Westview Press.

Dingwaney, Anuradha, and Carol Maier, eds. 1994. *Between Languages and Cultures: Translation and Cross-Cultural Texts*. Pittsburgh: University of Pittsburgh Press.

Dirlik, Arif. 1994. "The Postcolonial Aura: Third World Criticism in the Age of Global Capitalism." *Critical Inquiry* 20: 328–356.

———. 2000. "Formations of Globality and Radical Politics." In *Postmodernity's Histories: The Past as Legacy and Project*. New York: Rowman and Littlefield.

During, Simon. 1990. "Waiting for the Post: Some Relations between Modernity, Colonization, and Writing." In *Past the Last Post: Theorizing Postcolonialism and Postmodernism*, ed. Helen Tiffin and Ian Adam, 23–45. Calgary: University of Calgary Press.

———. 2000. "Postcolonialism and Globalization: Toward a Historicization of Their Inter-Relation." *Cultural Studies* 3, 4: 385–404.

Dutta, Madhusree, Flavia Agnes, and Needra Adarkar. 1996. *The Nation, the State, and Indian Identity*. New Delhi: South Asia Books.

Fenton, James. 1991. "Keeping up with Salman Rushdie." *New York Review,* 28 March, 26–31.

Fernandes, Leela. 1999. "Reading India's Bandit Queen: A Transnational Feminist Perspective on the Discrepancies of Representation." *Signs* 25, 1: 123–153.

Fleming, Jim, host. 1997. "To the Best of Our Knowledge." National Public Radio, 10 August.

Friedman, Thomas L. 1997. "The Globalutionaries." *New York Times,* 24 July.

Ganahal, Ranier. 2001. "Free Markets: Language, Commodification, and Art." *Public Culture* 13, 1: 23–38.

Gandhi, Leela. 1998. "Indo-Anglian Fiction: Writing India, Elite Aesthetics, and the Rise of the Stephanian Novel." *Australian Humanities Review* 4: 1–7. *www.lib.latrobe.edu.au*

Gaonkar, Dilip Parameshwar. 2002. "Toward New Imaginaries: An Introduction." *Public Culture* 14, 1: 1–20.

García Canclini, Nestor. 1995. *Hybrid Cultures: Strategies for Entering and Leaving Modernity*. Trans. Christopher L. Chiappari and Silvia L. Lopez. Minneapolis: University Minnesota Press.

———. 2001. *Consumers and Citizens: Globalization and Its Multicultural Contents*. Trans. George Yúdice. Minneapolis: University of Minnesota Press.

Gates, Henry Louis. 1996. "Planet Rap: Notes on the Globalization of Culture." In *Fieldwork: Sites in Literary and Cultural Study*, ed. Majorie Garber, Paul B. Franklin, and Rebecca L. Walkowitz, 55–66. New York: Routledge.

George, Rosemary Marangoly. 1996a. "At a Slight Angle to Reality: Reading Indian Diasporic Literature." *Melus* 21, 3: 179–193.

———. 1996b. *Politics of Home: Postcolonial Relocations and Twentieth Century Literature*. Cambridge: Cambridge University Press.

Ghosh, Amitav. 1988. *The Shadow Lines*. London: Bloomsbury.

———. 1992. *In an Antique Land*. New Delhi: Ravi Dayal.

———. 1994. "The Global Reservation." *Cultural Anthropology* 9, 3: 412–422.

———. 1995a. "The Ghosts of Mrs. Gandhi." *New Yorker,* 17 July, 35–43.

———. 1995b. "India's Untold War of Independence." *New Yorker,* 23 June, 105–121.

———. 1996. *The Calcutta Chromosome: A Novel of Fevers, Delirium, and Discovery*. Delhi: Ravi Dayal.

————. 1998a. *Dancing in Cambodia, At Large in Burma*. New Delhi: Ravi Dayal.

————. 1998b. "The March of the Novel through History: The Testimony of My Grand-father's Bookcase." *Kenyon Review* 20, 2: 13–24.

————. 1999. "Countdown." *New Yorker,* 26 October, 187–197.

————. 2001a. "Letter to the Administrators of the Commonwealth Prize." *www.amitavghosh.com.*

————. 2001b. *The Glass Palace: A Novel*. New York: Random House.

————. 2002a. "Diaspora in Indian Culture." In *Imam and the Indian,* 243–250. Delhi: Ravi Dayal.

————. 2002b. "Amitav Ghosh on the Nobel Prize for V. S. Naipaul." *Literary Review,* 22 November. *www.tehelka.com.*

————. 2002c. "The Fundamentalist Challenge." In *Imam and the Indian,* 268–288. Delhi: Ravi Dayal.

————. 2002d. "The Gujarat Carnage," *Outlook,* 4 May. *www.outlookindia.com.*

————. 2002e. *The Imam and the Indian*. Delhi: Ravi Dayal.

————. 2002f. Lecture on mourning and ethical mapping. University of California, Riverside, February.

————. 2002g. "Slave of Ms H.6." In *Imam and the Indian,* 169–241. Delhi: Ravi Dayal.

Ghosh, Bishnupriya. 1998. "The Postcolonial Bazaar: Thoughts on Postcolonial Pedagogy." *Postmodern Culture,* October. *www.iath.virginia.edu/pmc.*

————. 1999. "An Invitation to Postmodernity." In *Critical Essays on Salman Rushdie,* ed. M. Keith Booker, 129–153. London: G. K. Hall.

————. 2000. "An Affair to Remember: Scripted Performances in the Taslima Nasrin Affair." In *Going Global: Women in Transnational Frame,* ed. Amal Amireh and Lisa Majaj, 39–83. New York: Garland.

————. 2002. "Queering *Hindutva*: Unruly Bodies and Pleasures in Sadhavi Rithambara's Performances." In *Right Wing Women: From Conservatism to Extremism around the World,* ed. Paola Bacchetta and Margaret Power, 259–272. New York: Routledge.

Ghosh, Nandita. 2001. "Fixing Language, Fixing Nation." *Jouvert* 5, 3 (summer). *www.social.chass.ncsu.edu\jouvert.*

Ghosh, Sagarika. 1992. "'Rational' vs. 'National': Right-Wing Historians Usurp the Ishr." *Outlook,* 22 June, 18–20.

"Godse on Trial." 1998. *India Today,* 3 August, 22–28.

Gopal, Madan. 1996. "How AIR Killed Hindi." *Times of India,* 3 March.

Gordon, Avery. 1997. *Ghostly Matters: Haunting and the Sociological Imagination*. Minneapolis: University of Minnesota Press.

Guhathakurta, Tapati. 1992. *The Making of a New Indian Art*. Cambridge: Cambridge University Press.

————. 1998. "Instituting the Nation in Art." In *Wages of Freedom,* ed. Partha Chatterjee, 89–122. New Delhi: Oxford University Press.

Hansen, Kathryn G. 1998. "Malarial Imaginings." Review of *Calcutta Chromosome,* by Amitav Ghosh. *Kathmandu Post Review of Books* 3, 9 (30 August): 1–7

Hansen, Thomas Blom. 1996. "Globalisation and Nationalist Imaginations: *Hindutva's* Promise of Equality through Difference." *Economic and Political Weekly of India,* 9 March, 603–616.

————. 1999. *The Saffron Wave: Democracy and Nationalism in Modern India*. Princeton: Princeton University Press.

Hardt, Michael, and Antonio Negri. 2000. *Empire*. Cambridge: Harvard University Press.

Hiatt, Shobha. 2002. Review of *Red Earth and Pouring Rain,* by Vikram Chandra. *Indolink,* 5 December, 1–3. *www.indolink.com.*

Hubel, Teresa. 1996. *Whose India? The Independence Struggle in British Indian Fiction and History.* Durham, N.C.: Duke University Press.

Huggan, Graham. 1997. "Prizing 'Otherness': A Short History of the Booker." *Studies in the Novel* 29, 3: 412–433.

———. 2001. *The Postcolonial Exotic: Marketing the Margins.* New York: Routledge

"Indecent Exposure." 1997. *India Today,* 30 June, 65.

Indian Bureau of Education. [1929] 1965. *Selections from Education Records, Part I (1781–1839),* ed. H. Sharp. Calcutta: Superintendent Government Printing. Reprint, Delhi: National Archives of India.

Jacobs, Jane. 1996. *The Edge of Empire: Postcolonialism and the City.* New York: Routledge.

Jain, Ajit. 2001. "Rohinton Mistry's Book Makes It to Oprah Winfrey's Book Club." 3 December. *www.rediff.com.*

Jameson, Fredric. 1991. *Postmodernism, or, the Cultural Logic of Late Capitalism.* Durham, N.C.: Duke University Press.

———. 1998. "Globalization as a Philosophical Issue." In *Cultures of Globalization,* ed. Jameson and Masao Miyoshi. Durham, N.C.: Duke University Press.

Jameson, Fredric, and Masao Miyoshi, eds. 1998. *Cultures of Globalization.* Durham, N.C.: Duke Unversity Press.

Jeffery, Robin. 2000. *India's Newspaper Revolution: Capitalism, Politics, and the Indian Language Press, 1977–99.* New Delhi: Oxford University Press.

John, Binoo K. 1997. "The New Deity of Prose." *India Today* 27 (October): 23–26.

John, Mary. 1998. "Globalisation, Sexuality, and the Visual Field: Issues and Non-Issues for Cultural Critique." In *A Question of Silence: The Sexual Economies of Modern India,* ed. Mary John and Janaki Nair, 368–396. New Delhi: Kali for Women.

Johnson, Adrienne. 1997. "India Ink." *Los Angeles Times,* 19 August.

Joseph, May. 1999. *Nomadic Identities: The Performance of Citizenship.* Minneapolis: University of Minnesota Press.

Joshi, Priya. 2002. In Another Country: Colonialism, Culture, and the English Novel in India. New York: Columbia University Press.

Joshi, Ruchir. 2001. *The Last Jet-Engine Laugh.* New Delhi: HarperCollins.

Joshi, Svati, ed. 1991. *Rethinking English: Essays in Literature, Language, History.* New Delhi: Trianka.

Juneja, Monica. 1997. "Reclaiming the Public Sphere." *Economic and Political Weekly of India,* 25 January, 155–157.

Kachru, Braj. 1986. *The Alchemy of English: The Spread, Functions, and Models of Non-Native Englishes.* Oxford: Pergamon Institute.

Kala, Pablo. 2000. "In Spaces of Erasure: Globalisation, Resistance, and the Narmada River." *Economic and Political Weekly of India,* 15 June. *www.epw.com.*

Kapur, Geeta. 1993. "When Was Modernism in India?" *South Atlantic Quarterly* 92, 3: 473–514.

———. 1998. "Navigating the Void." In *Cultures of Globalization,* ed. Fredric Jameson and Masao Miyoshi, 191–217. Durham, N.C.: Duke University Press.

Kaviraj, Sudipto. 1995. "Religion, Politics, Modernity." In *Crisis and Change in Contemporary India,* ed. Upendra Baxi and Bhikhu Parekh, 295–316. Delhi: Sage.

Kesavan, Mukul. 1998. "An Area of Brightness." *The Week* online edition, *www.pugmarks.com/week.*

Khosla, Mukhesh. 2003. "Great Authors but Few Great Books." January. *www.the-south-asian.com.*

Kirpel, Viney, ed. 1997. *The Postmodern Indian English Novel.* New Delhi: Allied.

Kosambi, D. D. 1997. "Behind the White Khaddar." *Statesman,* 15 August, 2.

Krishnaswamy, Revathi. 1995. "Mythologies of Migrancy: Postcolonialism, Postmodernism, and the Politics of (Dis)Location." *Ariel* 26, 1: 125–146.

Kumar, Amitava. 1995. "Postcolonial Tour 93 (All Major U.S.) Cities." In *Order and Partialities: Theory, Pedagogy, and the Postcolonial,* ed. Jerry McGuire and Kostas Myrsiades, 229–260. Albany: SUNY Press.

———. 1996. "Jane Austen in Meerut, India." In *Between the Lines: South Asians and Postcoloniality,* ed. Deepika Bahri and Mary Vasudeva, 315–336. Philadelphia: Temple University Press.

———. 2002. "Elsewhere Histories." Review of *Real Time,* by Amit Chaudhuri. *Outlook,* 3 June. *www.outlookindia.com*

Lal, Sham. 1992. "Culture Wars." *Times of India,* 28 November, 10.

Lalvunga, K. C. 1996. "The Heritage We Received from Our Forefathers." In *Nationalism, Democracy, and Development: State and Politics in India,* ed. Madhusree Dutta, Flavia Agnes, and Needra Adarkar, 15–26. New Delhi: South Asia Books.

"Language." 1997. *India Today,* 18 August.

Lee, Benjamin, and Edward LiPuma. 2002. "Cultures of Circulation: The Imaginaries of Modernity." *Public Culture* 4, 1 (winter): 191–213.

Lim, Bliss Cua. 2001. "Spectral Times: The Ghost Film as Historical Allegory." *positions: east asia cultures critique* 9, 2: 287–329.

Lingis, Alphonso. 1994. *The Community of Those Who Have Nothing in Common.* Bloomington: Indiana University Press.

Lipscomb, David. 1991. "Caught in Strange Middle Ground: Contesting History in *Midnight's Children.*" *Diaspora* 1, 2: 163–189.

Lowe, Lisa, and David Lloyd, eds. 1997. *The Politics of Culture in the Shadow of Capital.* Durham, N.C.: Duke University Press.

Macaulay, Thomas Babington. [1835] 1965. "Macaulay Minute on Indian Education." 2 February. Reprint, Delhi: National Archives of India, 1965, 107–117.

Malkani, K. R. 1992. *How Others Look at RSS.* New Delhi: Deendaya Upadhyaya Research Institute.

Mallick, Heather. 2002. "Mistry Said No. We All Must Say No." *Globe and Mail,* 9 November.

Mankekar, Purnima. 1999. *Screening Culture, Viewing Politics: An Ethnography of Television, Womanhood, and Nation.* Durham, N.C.: Duke University Press.

Mann, Harveen Sachdev. 1995. "Being 'Borne Across': Translation and Salman Rushdie's *Satanic Verses.*" *Criticism* 37, 2: 281–308.

McGuire, Jerry, and Lalitha Pandit. 1995. Introduction to *Order and Partialities: Theory, Pedagogy, and the "Postcolonial,"* ed. Jerry McGuire and Kostas Myrsiades, 1–14. Albany: SUNY Press.

Mehta, Suketa. 1997. "From the Outside." *Business India,* 11–24 August, 39.

Mignolo, Walter. 2000. *Local Histories, Global Designs.* Princeton: Princeton University Press.

————. 2002. "The Many Faces of the Cosmo-Polis." In *Cosmopolitanism,* ed. Carol A. Breckenbridge, Sheldon Pollock, Homi K. Bhabha, and Dipesh Chakrabarty, 157–188. Durham, N.C.: Duke University Press.

Mishra, Vijay. 1996. "The Diasporic Imaginary: Theorizing the Indian Diaspora." *Textual Practice* 10, 3: 421–447.

Mishra, Vijay, and Bob Hodge. 1991. "What Is Postcolonialsim?" *Textual Practice* 5, 3: 399–414.

Miyoshi, Masao. 1993. "A Borderless World? From Colonialism to Transnationalism and the Decline of the Nation-State." *Critical Inquiry* 19, 4:726–751.

————. 1995. "Sites of Resistance in a Global Economy." *Boundary 2* 22, 1: 61–84

————. 1998. "Globalization, Culture, and the University." In *Cultures of Globalization,* ed. Fredric Jameson and Masao Miyoshi, 247–270. Durham, N.C.: Duke University Press.

Mohan, Peggy. 1995. "Market Forces and Language in Global India." *Economic and Political Weekly of India,* 22 April, 887–890.

Moraga, Cherríe. 1993. *The Last Generation: Prose and Poetry.* Boston: South End Press.

Mufti, Aamir R. 1999. "Reading the Rushdie Affair: 'Islam,' Cultural Politics, Form." In *Critical Essays on Salman Rushdie,* ed. M. Keith Booker, 51–77. London: G. K. Hall.

Mukherjee, Meenakshi. 1971. *The Twice-Born Fiction.* Delhi: Heinemann.

————. 1993. "The Anxiety of Indian Englishness." *Economic and Political Weekly of India,* 27 November, 2607–2611.

————. 2000. *The Perishable Empire: Essays on Indian Writing in English.* New Delhi: Oxford University Press.

————, ed. 1997. *Rushdie's Midnight's Children: A Book of Readings.* Delhi: Pencraft International.

Muralkindharan, Sukumar. 1997. "Fundamentalist Hues." *Frontline,* 15 November, 13.

Nagpal, Om. 1998. "Is He (Husain) an Artist or a Butcher?" *Vichar Mimansa,* September, 1.

Naipaul, V. S. 1990. *India: A Million Mutinies Now.* London: Heinemann.

————. 1997. "A Million Mutinies." *India Today,* 18 August, 36–39.

Nair, Rukmini Bhaya. 1997. "History as Gossip in *Midnight's Children.*" In *Rushdie's Midnight's Children: A Book of Readings,* ed. Meenakshi Mukherjee, 48–67. Delhi: Pencraft International.

Namboodri, Udayan. 1997. "The Language Cauldron." *India Today,* 30 June, 42.

Nancy, Jean-Luc. 1991. *The Inoperative Community.* Trans. Peter Connor. Minneapolis: University of Minnesota Press.

Nandy, Ashis. 1995a. "The Discreet Charms of Indian Terrorism." In *The Savage Freud and Other Essays on Possible and Retrievable Selves,* 1–31. Delhi: Oxford University Press.

————. 1995b. *The Savage Freud and Other Essays on Possible and Retrievable Selves.* Delhi: Oxford University Press.

Narayan, R. K. 1980. *The English Teacher.* London: Eyre and Spottiswoods, 1945. Reprint, Chicago: University of Chicago Press.

Nehru, Jawaharlal. 1997. "Tryst with Destiny." In *Mirrorwork: 50 Years of Indian Writing, 1947–1997,* ed. Salman Rushdie and Elizabeth J. West, 3–4. New York: Holt.

Niranjana, Tejaswini, P. Sudhir, and Vivek Dhareswar, eds. 1993. *Interrogating Modernity: Culture and Colonialism in India.* Calcutta: Seagull Press.

Nixon, Rob. 1992. *London Calling: V. S. Naipaul, Postcolonial Mandarin*. New York: Oxford University Press.

North, Michael. 2001. "Ken Saro-Wiwa's *Sozaboy*: The Politics of 'Rotten English'." *Public Culture* 13, 1: 97–112.

Ondaatje, Michael. 2000. *Anil's Ghost*. New York: Knopf.

Ong, Aihwa. 1999. *Flexible Citizenship: The Cultural Logics of Transnationality*. Durham, N.C.: Duke University Press.

Padikkal, Shivaram. 1993. "Inventing Modernity: The Emergence of the Modern Novel in India." In *Interrogating Modernity: Culture and Colonialism in India*, ed. Tejaswini Niranjana, P. Sudhir, and Vivek Dhareswar, eds. 220–241. Calcutta: Seagull Press.

Pandey, Gyanendra. 1990. *The Construction of Communalism in Colonial North India*. Delhi: Oxford University Press.

———. 1991. "In Defence of the Fragment." *Economic and Political Weekly of India*, March, 559–572.

———. 1994. "Modes of History-Writing: New Hindu Histories of Ayodhya." *Economic and Political Weekly of India*, 18 June, 1523–1528.

Parekh, Bhikhu. 1995. "The Rushdie Affair in the British Press." In *The Rights of Minority Cultures*, ed. Will Kymlicka, 303–320. New York: Oxford University Press.

Patwardhan, Anant. 2001. *Jang Aur Aman* [War and peace]. Documentary, produced by Sameer Rizwi, Mumbai. Distributed by Icarus Films, U.S.A.

Pollock, Sheldon. 1989. "Mimamsa and the Problem of History in Traditional India." *Journal of the American Oriental Society* 109, 4: 603–610.

———. 2002. "The Vernacular and the Cosmopolitan in History." In *Cosmopolitanism*, ed. Carol A. Breckenridge, Sheldon Pollock, Homi K. Bhabha, and Dipesh Chakrabarty, 15–53. Durham, N.C.: Duke University Press.

Povinelli, E. A. 2001. "Translation in a Global Market—Editor's Note." *Public Culture* 13, 1: ix–xi.

Radhakrishnan, R. 1996. *Diasporic Mediations: Between Home and Location*. Minneapolis: University of Minnesota Press.

Rahatekar, R. 1998. "Gandhi Viruddha Godse." *Mid-day*, 18 July, 6–7.

Rao, Raja. 1967. *Kanthapura*. London: Unwin and Allen, 1938. Reprint, New York: New Directions.

Rajagopal, Arvind. 1999. "Thinking through Emerging Logics: Brand Logics and the Cultural Forms of Political Society." *Social Text* 17, 3: 131–149.

———. 2001a. *Politics after Television*. New York: Cambridge University Press.

———. 2001b. "Thinking about the New Indian Middle Class: Gender, Advertising, and Politics in the Age of Globalisation." In *Signposts: Gender Issues in Post-Independent India*, ed. Sunder Rajan, 57–99. New Brunswick: Rutgers University Press.

Ramaswamy, Anindita. 2002. "Two Worlds of Indian Writing Meet, Hesitantly." *News India-Times*, 1 March. *www.newsindia-times.com*.

Reddy, Sheela. 2002. "Midnight's Orphans." *Outlook*, 25 February. *www.outlookindia.com*.

Rege, Josna. 1997. "Victim into Protagonist?" *Studies in the Novel* 29, 3 (fall): 188–211.

Renu, Phaniswarnath. 1986. "Smells of a Primeval Night." In *The Third Vow and Other Stories*, trans. Kathryn G. Hansen, 133–151. New Delhi: Chanakya Press.

"Report on Education." 1997. *The Pioneer*, 28 April, 4–5.

Robbins, Bruce. 1999. *Feeling Global: Internationalism in Distress*. New York: New York University Press.

Robbins, Bruce, and Pheng Cheah. 1998. *Cosmopolitics: Thinking and Feeling Beyond Nation*. Minneapolis, Minnesota University Press.

"Rohinton Mistry Cancels U. S. Book Tour Due to Racial Profiling." 2002. *Bookselling This Week,* 5 November. *www.bookweb.org.*

Roy, Ajit. 1995. "Civil Society and Nation State: In Context of Globalisation." *Economic and Political Weekly of India,* 12–15 August, 2005–2010.

Roy, Arundhati. 1997a. "A Conversation with Arundhati Roy and Salman Rushdie." PBS, Los Angeles, 14 August.

———. 1997b. *The God of Small Things*. New York: Random House.

———. 1997c. "India Ink." Interview with Adrienne Johnson. *Los Angeles Times,* 19 August.

———. 1998. *The End of the Imagination*. Kottayam: DC Books.

———. 1999. *The Cost of Living*. New York: Modern Library.

———. 2001. *Power Politics*. Cambridge, Mass.: South End Press.

———. 2002a. "Shall We Leave It to the Experts?" *Nation,* 18 February, 16–20

———. 2002b. "Under the Nuclear Shadow." *London Observer,* 2 June.

Roy, Parama. 1996. "Discovering India, Imagining *Thuggee.*" *Yale Journal of Criticism* 9, 1: 212–245.

———.1998. *Indian Traffic: Identities in Question in Colonial and Postcolonial India*. Berkeley: University of California Press.

———. 2002. "Figures of Famine." Cultural Analysis Colloquium, University of California, Santa Barbara.

Rudolph, Lloyd. 1992. "Media and Cultural Politics." *Economic and Political Weekly of India,* 11 July, 1489–1496.

Rushdie, Salman. 1981. *Midnight's Children: A Novel*. New York: Knopf.

———. 1984. "Outside the Whale." *Granta* 11, 125–138.

———. 1988. *The Satanic Verses*. London: Viking.

———. 1991a. "'Commonwealth Literature' Does Not Exist." In *Imaginary Homelands: Essays and Criticism, 1981–1991,* 61–70. London: Granta and Penguin.

———. 1991b. *Imaginary Homelands: Essays and Criticism, 1981–1991*. London: Granta and Penguin.

———. 1991c. "In Good Faith." In *Imaginary Homelands: Essays and Criticism, 1981–1991,* 393–414. London: Granta and Penguin.

———. 1994. *East, West Stories*. New York: Vintage Books.

———. 1995. *The Moor's Last Sigh*. New York: Pantheon Books.

———. 1997a. "Damme, This Is the Oriental Scene for You!" *New Yorker,* 23 and 30 June, 50–61.

———. 1997b. "Introduction," *Mirrorwork*. ix.

———. 1997c. Interview by Christopher Hitchens. *The Progressive* 61, 10 (October): 34–45.

———. 1997d. "The Fantasy That Is India." *India Today,* 18 August, 58–63.

———. 1997e. "There Is a Kind of Buzz around Indian Writing in English." Interview by Swapan Dasgupta. *India Today,* 14 July, 88–90.

———. 1999. *The Ground beneath Her Feet: A Novel*. New York: Holt.

———. 2000a. "A Dream of Glorious Return." *New Yorker,* 19–26 June, 94–108.

———. 2000b. "Fictions Are Lies That Tell the Truth: Salman Rushdie and Günter Grass: In Conversation." In *Conversations with Salman Rushdie,* ed. Michael Reder, 72–78. Jackson: University of Mississippi Press.

————. 2002a. "Arundhati Roy." In *Step across This Line: Collected Non-Fiction, 1992–2002,* 331–333. New York: Random House.

————. 2002b. "Damme, This Is the Oriental Scene for You!" In *Step across This Line: Collected Non-Fiction, 1992–2002,* 145–158. New York: Random House.

————. 2002c. "Gandhi, Now." In *Step across This Line: Collected Non-Fiction, 1992–2002,* 165–172. New York: Random House.

————. 2002d. "If You Make People Laugh." Interview by Amit Rai. *India Today,* 6 May, 16–18.

————. 2002e. "October 2001: Attacks on America." In *Step across the Line: Collected Non-Fiction, 1992–2002,* 336–338. New York: Random House.

————. 2002f. *Step across This Line: Collected Non-Fiction, 1992–2002.* New York: Random House.

Rushdie, Salman, and Elizabeth West. 1997a. Introduction to *Mirrorwork: 50 Years of Indian Writing, 1947–1997,* eds. Rushdie and West. New York: Holt.

————, eds. 1997b. *Mirrorwork: 50 Years of Indian Writing, 1947–1997.* New York: Holt.

Sainath, P. 1997. *Everybody Loves a Good Drought.* Delhi: Penguin.

Samuel, John. 1993. "Language and Nationality in North-East India." *Economic and Political Weekly of India,* 23 January, 91–92.

Sangari, Kumkum. 1993. "The Politics of the Possible." In *Interrogating Modernity: Culture and Colonialism in India,* ed. Tejaswini Niranjana, P. Sudhir, and Vivek Dhareswar, 242–272. Calcutta: Seagull Press.

————. 2002a. "Figures for the 'Unconscious': The Pressure on Description." In *The Politics of the Possible: Gender, History, Narrative, Colonial English,* 74–95. London: Anthem Press.

————. 2002b. *The Politics of the Possible: Gender, History, Narrative, Colonial English.* London: Anthem Press.

Sangvai, Sanjay. 1994. "On Nation and Other Mega-Projects." *Economic and Political Weekly of India,* 5 March, 537–540.

Saran, Mitali. 2002. "August in the Winter." *Outlook,* 11 December, 1–2. *www.outlookindia. com*

Sardar, Ziauddin. 1998. *Postmodernism and the Other: The New Imperialism of Western Culture.* London: Pluto Press.

Sardar, Ziauddin, and Meryl Wyn Davis. 1990. *The Distorted Imagination: Lessons from the Rushdie Affair.* London: Grey Seal.

Sarkar, Bhaskar. 1999. "Allegories of Dispersal." Ph.D. diss., University of Southern California.

Sarkar, Tanika, and Urvashi Butalia, eds. 1996. *Women and the Hindu Right: A Collection of Essays.* Delhi: Kali for Women.

Sassen, Saskia. 1998. *Globalization and Its Discontents: Selected Essays, 1984–1998.* New York: New Press.

Sen, Suchismita. 1995. "Memory, Language, and Society in Salman Rushdie's *Haroun.*" *Contemporary Literature* 36, 4: 654–675.

Seshadri-Crooks, Kalpana. 2000. Introduction to *The Pre-Occupation of Postcolonial Studies,* ed. Fawzia Afzal-Khan and Kalpana Seshadri-Crooks, 3–23. Durham, N.C.: Duke University Press.

Sethi, Rumina. 1999. *Myths of Nations.* Oxford: Clarendon Press.

Shapiro, Michael. 2000. "National Times and Other Times: Re-Thinking Citizenship." *Cultural Studies* 14, 1: 79–98.

Shapiro, Michael, and Hayward Alker, eds. 1996. *Challenging Boundaries: Global Flows, Territorial Identities*. Minneapolis: University of Minnesota Press.

Shiva, Vandana. 1997. *Biopiracy: The Plunder of Nature and Knowledge*. Boston: South End Press.

Shohat, Ella. 1992. "Notes on the Postcolonial." *Social Text* 31–32 (spring): 99–113.

Singh, Dhiraj. 2002. "Writerly Lives." *Outlook,* 18 February, 1–3. *www.outlookindia.com.*

Singh, Malavika. 1997. "Shame on Us." *Business India,* 11–24 August, 33.

Singhal, Arvind, and Everett M. Rogers. 1989. *India's Information Revolution*. New Delhi: Sage.

Spivak, Gayatri Chakravorty. 1985a. "The Rani of Sirmur: An Essay in Reading the Archive." *History and Theory: Studies in the Philosophy of History* 24, 3: 247–272.

———. 1985b. "Three Women's Texts and a Critique of Imperialism." In *'Race,' Writing, and Difference,* ed. Henry Louis Gates, 262–280. Chicago: University of Chicago Press.

———. 1988. *In Other Worlds: Essays in Cultural Politics*. New York: Routledge.

———. 1993a. *Outside in the Teaching Machine*. New York: Routledge.

———. 1993b. "The Politics of Translation." In *Outside in the Teaching Machine,* 179–200. New York: Routledge.

———. 1996a. "How to Teach a 'Culturally Different' Book." In *The Spivak Reader: Selected Works of Gayatri Chakravorty Spivak,* ed. Donna Landry and Gerald MacLean, 237–266. New York: Routledge.

———. 1996b. "Subaltern Talk: Interview with the Editors." In *The Spivak Reader: Selected Works of Gayatri Chakravorty Spivak,* ed. Donna Landry and Gerald MacLean, 287–308. New York: Routledge.

———. 1997. "Diasporas, Old and New: Women in the Transnational World." In *Class Issues: Pedagogy, Cultural Studies, and the Public Sphere,* ed. Amitava Kumar, 87–111. New York: New York University Press.

———. 2001. "Question on Translation: Adrift." *Public Culture* 13, 1: 13–22.

Sunder Rajan, Rajeswari. 1992. "Fixing English: Nation, Language, Subject." In *The Lie of the Land: English Literary Studies in India,* ed. Sunder Rajan, 7–28. Delhi: Oxford University Press.

———. 1993. Real and Imagined Women: Gender, Culture, and Post-Colonialism. London: Routledge.

———. ed. 2001. *Signposts: Gender Issues in Post-Independent India*. New Brunswick: Rutgers University Press.

Suri, Manil. 2001. *Death of Vishnu*. New York: HarperCollins.

Swami, Praveen. 1998. "Predatory Pursuit of Power." *Frontline,* 23 May, 1–3.

Tagore, Rabindranath. [1895] 1916. "The Hungry Stones." New York: Macmillan.

———. [1895] 1995. "The Hunger of Stones." In *Civil Lives,* trans. Amitav Ghosh, 2: 152–156. New Delhi: Ravi Dayal.

Updike, John. 1997. "Mother Tongue: Subduing the Language of the Colonizer." *New Yorker,* 23 and 30 June, 156–161.

Van der Veer, Peter. 1996. "Writing Violence." In *Contesting the Nation: Religion, Community, and the Politics of Democracy in India,* ed. David Ludden, 250–269. Philadelphia: University of Pennsylvania Press.

Venuti, Laurence. 2000. *The Translation Studies Reader.* London: Routledge.

Viswanathan, Gauri. 1989. *Masks of Conquest: Literary Study and British Rule in India.* New York: Columbia University Press.

———. 1992. "English in a Literate Society." In *The Lie of the Land: English Literary Studies in India,* ed. Rajeswari Sunder Rajan, 29–41. Delhi: Oxford University Press.

Wagner, Erica. 1997. "Arundhati Roy Gets Booker for First Novel." *Statesman,* 6 October, 1.

"What It Means to Be an Indian." 1997. *India Today* special issue, 18 August.

Wilber, Alex. 1997. "Passages to India." *Seattle Times,* 10 August.

Wilson, Rob, and Wimal Dissanayake. 1996. *Global-Local: Cultural Production and the Transnational Imaginary.* Durham, N.C.: Duke University Press.

Wood, James. 1997. "An Indelicate Balance: The Noisy Pluralism of Indian Fiction." *New Republic,* 29 December, 32–36.

———. 2001. "Tales from the Lost City." *Guardian,* 8 September, 5.

Young, Robert. 2001. *Postcolonialism: A Historical Introduction.* New York: Blackwell.

Yúdice, George. 1992. "Postmodernity and Transnational Capital in Latin America." In *On Edge: The Crisis of Contemporary Latin American Culture,* ed. George Yúdice, 1–28. Minneapolis: University of Minnesota Press.

———. 1996. "Cultural Studies and Civil Society." In *Reading the Shape of the World: Towards Internationalization of Cultural Studies,* ed. Richard Dienst and Henry Schwarz, 50–66. Oxford: Westview Press.

Zabus, Chantal. 1991. *The African Palimpsest: Indigenization of Language in the West African Europhone Novel.* Amsterdam: Rodophi.

Index

About the Author

With a doctorate from Northwestern University, Bishnupriya Ghosh currently teaches postcolonial literature and theory, gender/sexuality, and film studies at the Department of English, University of California, Davis. Besides publishing essays on South Asian cultural and gender studies, Ghosh has edited *Interventions: Feminist Dialogues on Third World Women's Literature and Film* (Garland, 1997). She is working on a second book, *Stray Embers: Tthe Global Afterlife of Four South Asian Female Icons.*